AUSTRALIA

By the Editors of Sunset Books and Sunset Magazine

LANE PUBLISHING CO. • MENLO PARK, CALIFORNIA

FOREWORD

More and more travelers are discovering that Australia possesses a stimulating variety of attractions beyond its well-known koalas and kangaroos and cities like Sydney and Melbourne. In this book, we have tried to depict the country's diversified appeals—from her famous beaches to her equally renowned outback, from the unique Australian plant and animal world to the invigorating lifestyle of her residents.

Here, in guide form, we have collected many details on where to go, what to see, and what to do. In some areas, hotels are named or prices quoted; tourist facilities and prices are constantly changing, and your travel agent can provide up-to-the-minute details. Additional information is available from the Australian Tourist Commission, or the state or territorial government tourist offices listed in each of the chapters.

The Australian Tourist Commission's headquarters are located at 414 St. Kilda Road, Melbourne, Victoria 3004, Australia. Overseas branch offices of the ATC are located in the following cities:

3550 Wilshire Blvd., Los Angeles, California 90010

1270 Avenue of the Americas, New York, N.Y. 10020

22 Old Bond Street, London W.1, England

55 Customs Street E., Auckland 1, New Zealand

D6 Frankfurt a. M. 1, Neue Mainzerstrasse 22, West Germany

Sankaido Building, 7th Floor, 9-13,1-Chome, Akasaka Minato-ku, Tokyo, Japan

Australia has an Embassy in Washington D.C. and Consulates-General in New York, San Francisco, and Los Angeles. In Australia, the United States Embassy is in Canberra, and U.S. Consulates are in Perth, Adelaide, Brisbane, Sydney, and Melbourne.

Many persons helped in assembling information and checking the manuscript of this book. We particularly wish to acknowledge the help and cooperation provided by the following: L. R. Watson of Canberra; R. Murdock of Sydney; Brian D. Johnston of Darwin; John Newland of Alice Springs; J. Wilson of Brisbane; Percy Pollnitz of Adelaide; L. Butler and V. A. Barling of Hobart; W. Moran of Melbourne; M. Semmens of Perth; Hazel and Anthony Berry of Melbourne; Judy Nason of Armidale, N.S.W.; the editors of *Pacific Travel News;* the photographic library of the Pacific Area Travel Association; the editorial staff of *Sunset* Magazine; the staff of the Australian Tourist Commission.

Supervising Editor: Frederic M. Rea, Publisher, Pacific Travel News

Research and Text: Lawrence A. Clancy, Frances A. Coleberd, Valerie McLenighan

Coordinating Editor: Cornelia Fogle

Editor, Sunset Books: David E. Clark
Fourth Printing **(Updated)** April 1977

Copyright © 1973, Lane Publishing Co., Menlo Park, California 94025. Third Edition. World rights reserved. No part of this publication may be reproduced by any mechanical, photographic, or electronic process, or in the form of a phonographic recording, nor may it be stored in a retrieval system, transmitted, or otherwise copied for public or private use without prior written permission from the publisher. Library of Congress No. 73-75760. ISBN Title No. 0-376-06060-3. Lithographed in the United States.

COVER PHOTOGRAPH, by Shostal Associates, shows a life-saving crew participating in one of Australia's famous Surf Carnivals.

CONTENTS

AUSTRALIA—an ancient continent, pulsing with change and growth   **4**

AUSTRALIA'S WONDERFUL WILDLIFE—the koala, the emu, the wattle   **20**

SPECTATOR OR PARTICIPANT—sports are a way of life   **26**

SYDNEY—effervescent first city of Australia   **32**

SYDNEY SIDE TRIPS—to beaches, mountains, rivers, history   **46**

CANBERRA—the nation's capital, city of grand design and artistic order   **56**

MELBOURNE—gracious and green, conservative and cultural   **64**

EXPLORING VICTORIA—mountains, rugged coasts, gold towns, the Murray   **74**

EXPLORING TASMANIA—Australia's lush, green island state   **84**

SOUTH AUSTRALIA—graced by Adelaide, the Murray River, wine country   **94**

WESTERN AUSTRALIA—booming Perth, surrounded by a vast frontierland   **104**

SUBTROPICAL BRISBANE—centerpiece for a beach-lined playground   **112**

THE GREAT BARRIER REEF—1,250-mile watery wonderland   **120**

THE NORTHERN TERRITORY—it centers on Darwin and Alice Springs   **130**

CALENDAR OF EVENTS—running the gamut of Australian life styles   **139**

SPECIAL FEATURES

Driving on the "wrong" side of the road 9	Australia's golden bonanza 78
Aborigines—Australia's link with the Stone Age 10	Summertime tour—to watch a parade of penguins 82
Ever see a jumbuck drinking at a billabong? 17	Tasmanian Aborigines—a vanished race 90
Touring Australian wine country 18	Opal fossicking at Coober Pedy 99
Every day is racing day down under 29	River trip on a paddlewheeler 102
The great Sydney Opera House 38	Little Sicily on the Indian Ocean 109
Summer in Sydney is surf carnival time 45	Game fishing in the waters of the reef 125
Visiting a sheep station: a day in Dubbo 51	Tagging along with the flying mailman 132
Moomba!...it means "have fun" 71	Mysterious paintings of the Aborigines 136
	The "Royals"—Aussie-type state fairs 142

SYDNEY SKYLINE (above) marks the city as one of the world's major metropolitan centers. In stark contrast is the bushland (right) where sheep graze over thousands of acres. Melbourne residents (far right) borrowing English formality, make an outdoor picnic a rather formal affair.

4 INTRODUCTION

AUSTRALIA—an ancient continent, pulsing with change and growth

In many respects, Australia is the world's strangest, most unusual land mass. This island continent spent its vigorous youth far back in the dim ages of geologic time, so isolated that unique plant and animal forms evolved—found nowhere else on earth—and so remote that modern man arrived only in recent time.

Early explorers missed the continent. Finally discovered in the 17th century, the island was characterized as "the barrenest spot upon the globe" and dismissed as being an improbable area for use or development by modern man. In the eyes of the explorers, perhaps this was understandable; Australia is fundamentally incompatible with European culture and lifestyles. The land is mostly hostile—hot, dry, desolate. Compared with the lush, rich lands of England and Europe, Australia reflected almost no potential for development.

But develop it did, and that evolvement is Australia's other fascination; for despite its slow start, the country pulses with change and growth. You can feel the freshness and sense the vigor and enthusiasm of its citizens now shaping this dynamic 20th century nation.

Comparable in size to the United States (excluding Alaska), Australia possesses a great diversity of attractions. Some travelers regard the country as a vast agricultural laboratory. Others find fascination in its newfound mineral wealth and the accompanying surge of industrial activity. Some visitors consider Australia the world's most active sports land.

A number of travelers know only the city of Sydney—a bustling, dynamic, and cosmopolitan way point on a trans-Pacific or around-the-world tour. For some travelers, the country's highlight is "the Reef"—that great mass of coral sweeping more than a thousand miles along the northeastern coast; others are entranced by the deserts and the bush country, the land of "Waltzing Matilda" fame.

Of course, Australia is all these and more.

Sydney and Melbourne rank with the major cities of the world in offering a comprehensive choice in accommodations, activities, and entertainment.

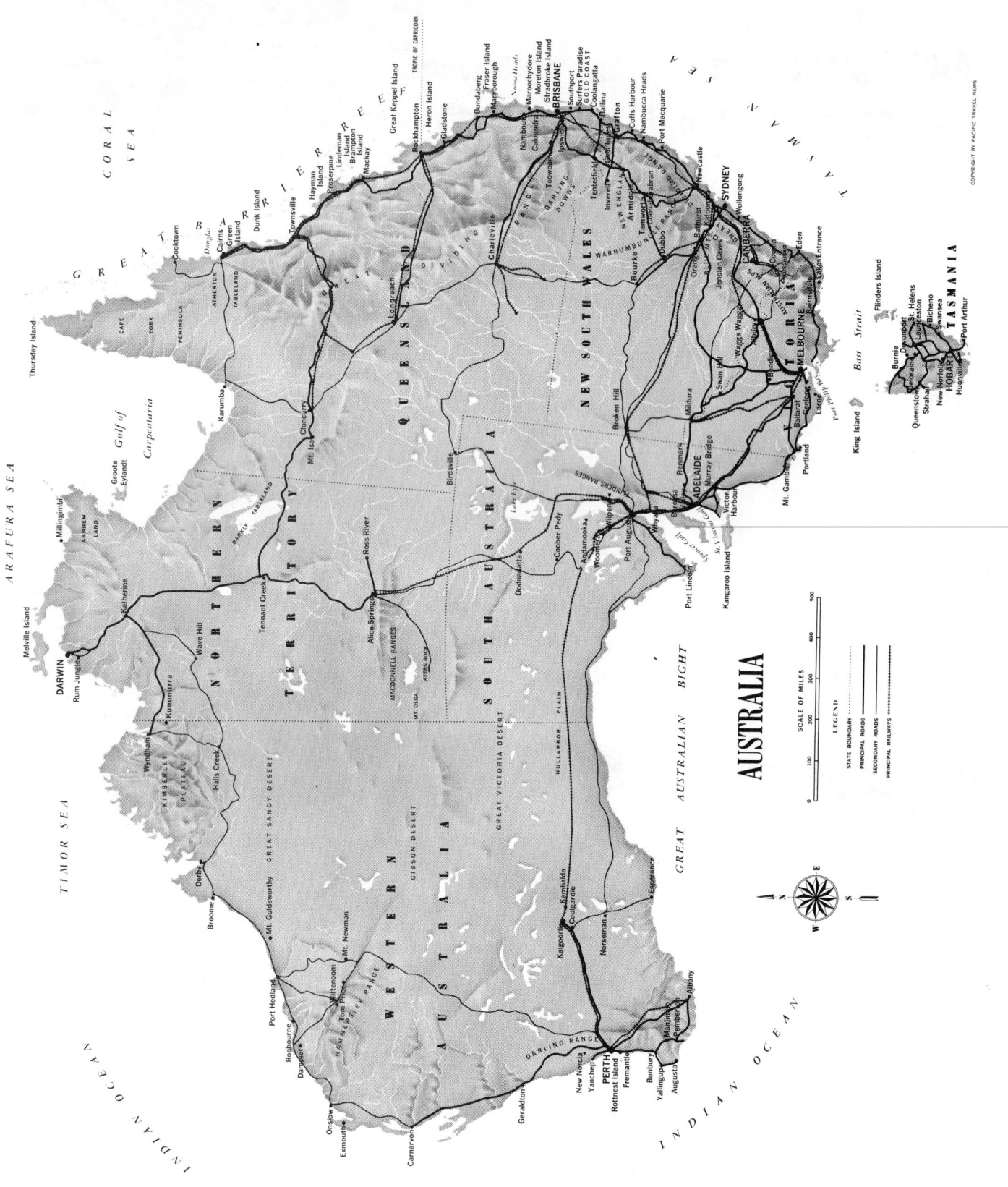

Thousands of miles of shoreline provide a seemingly limitless arena for water sports—swimming areas fringed by golden sand, the world's best surfing beaches, protected harbors for boating, and superb fishing waters.

Beyond the friendly coastal strip is one of the world's great frontierlands. Here sheep and cattle graze, vast irrigation projects have transformed nearly 3 million acres of arid land into rich farm and grazing lands, and the forbidding desert is yielding as yet uncounted wealth in minerals.

BRITISH INFLUENCE

Australia is part of the British Commonwealth—and the influence of England is evident in the formality pervading the Australian lifestyle. Spoken English recalls the polite and proper British pattern of speech—but with the addition of some of the most vigorous idiom in the English language (see page 17). The Australian drives on the left side of the road, cherishes his garden, eats as the English do (keeping his knife in his right hand and fork in his left), and dearly loves his afternoon tea.

Many newcomers—immigrants from Europe since World War II—have added zest and an international flavor to Australia's cities; more than a million new Australians have arrived since the war. British immigrants comprise more than half of the new arrivals, followed by Italians, Greeks, and Yugoslavs. Other nationalities contributing to the cosmopolitan melange are Spaniards, Scandinavians, Americans, Hungarians, South Americans, Czechoslovaks, Turks, Poles, Icelanders, and Arabs.

History

Australia, the oldest continent, was also the last great habitable land mass to be colonized by Europeans. As early as the second century A.D., geographers suspected the existence of a land they called *Terra Australis* somewhere in the far southeastern seas. By 1688 Portuguese, Dutch, and British navigators had carried out preliminary explorations of its northern and western coastlines; but the dour accounts of the early explorers were enough to convince even the greediest of empire-builders that Australia held no future, and interest in the continent lapsed for three-quarters of a century.

Credit for the "rediscovery" of Australia goes to the intrepid English explorer, Captain James Cook, who in 1770 took possession of the "whole eastern coast by the name of New Wales" and sent back glowing reports of the possibilities for colonization.

Since the American Revolution had caused England to lose a place to transport the overflow from its innumerable prisons, Britain sent a shipment of convicts under the command of Captain Arthur Phillip to establish a settlement in Australia. In a simple ceremony on January 26, 1788, Phillip unfurled the Union Jack at what is now Sydney, drank to the King's health, and set to work building the colony of New South Wales.

Crops failed, stock escaped, supply ships were delayed; but slowly, painfully, over the next six decades, the colonists succeeded in the most difficult pioneering effort in history. Explorers probed the continent's vast inner reaches, and pastoralists and botanists developed strains of sheep and wheat able to withstand the harsh conditions of the interior.

The real beginnings of nationhood came with the discovery of gold in 1851. A tide of immigration began, doubling the population in ten years and continuing strong to this day. New South Wales peacefully achieved responsible self-government in 1855, and by 1890 the rest of the colonies had followed suit. Federation came quickly—January 1, 1901, saw the birth of the Commonwealth of Australia.

With the exception of a brief uprising during the gold rush period, the nation's history has been one of unbroken domestic tranquility. Australian troops fought with distinction in two world wars and the conflicts in Korea and Vietnam. The city of Darwin was bombed by the Japanese in 1942, but no enemy troops have ever set foot on Australian soil.

Australia belongs to the United Nations and ANZUS and has taken an active interest in the economic welfare of Asian countries. Since World War II, rapid development of the continent's natural and industrial resources has provided most Australian citizens with a comfortable standard of living and political stability.

Government

Since 1901 Australia has been governed as a federal commonwealth, with both federal and state parliaments modeled on a thoughtful mixture of British, American, Canadian, and Swiss democracies. A prime minister heads the national government, and a premier leads each of its six states: New South Wales, Victoria, Queensland, South Australia, Western Australia, and Tasmania.

Governors in each of the states, along with a governor-general, represent the British Crown in Australia—a token acknowledgment of the two nations' common political and legal traditions.

The federal government, as the principal taxing authority, exercises even broader executive and legislative powers than the U.S. central government. An unusual feature of Australian politics is that enfranchised adults are required to vote under penalty of fine.

The two territories on mainland Australia are the large Northern Territory and the Australian Capital Territory (ACT), site of Canberra, the nation's capital

AUSTRALIANS' *love of sunshine and outdoors is reflected in people-dotted scene at Manly Beach near Sydney.*

city. Six more territories—ranging in size from tiny Christmas Island to Australia's huge holdings in the Antarctic—lie outside the continent.

Geography

Largely a dry and sparsely populated land, the Australian continent is dominated by a plateau rising from the narrow western coast and occupying about three-fourths of the entire country.

The highlands of the center, north, and northwest relieve the monotony of the heartland with fantastic, sandsculpted rock towers and canyons and a rich variety of ground colors. The Great Dividing Range, the continent's principal mountain chain, parallels the eastern coastline for almost 2,500 miles. Its well-watered slopes provide fertile grazing and farm land, and the coastal strip along its eastern flanks supports the majority of the nation's population.

Two-thirds of the country (including most of its major cities) lies within the South Temperate Zone; the northern third is semitropical to tropical.

Stretching languidly along the Queensland coast, the monumental Great Barrier Reef supports a greater variety of plant and animal life than any other marine habitat in the world.

The country's most important river is the Murray, rising in the Great Dividing Range and flowing about 1,600 miles—along the New South Wales-Victoria border, then through South Australia on its way to the Southern Ocean at Lake Alexandrina, south of Adelaide. Many of the continent's rivers run into the great desert lands of the center, at times turning vast salt flats into shallow lakes, more often diminishing along their downward course until they disappear into moonlike wastelands.

Climate

Seasons in Australia are the reverse of those in the Northern Hemisphere. Summer lasts from December through February; autumn from March through May; winter from June through August; and spring from September through November.

In Sydney and Melbourne, summers are warm to hot for the most part, and winters are mild to cool. Sunshine can be expected the year round, with an annual rainfall averaging about 31 inches. As you travel farther inland, the climate becomes hotter and drier. In the arid interior, temperatures average 95°.

Along the southeastern coast and in the south, the temperature runs about 41° in the winter and 69° in summer. The hot and humid northern coastal areas average 80° in winter and 91° in summer.

If the Sydney-Canberra-Melbourne circuit is your Australian target, the best months to visit are from October through May. In the northern part of the continent, the dry season—from early April through the end of October—is most comfortable for visitors.

HOW TO GET THERE

Sydney lies 7,560 miles from San Francisco and 5,150 miles from Honolulu. When it is 10 A.M. Monday in Sydney, it is 4 P.M. Sunday in San Francisco—an actual time difference of 18 hours.

More than 30 shipping companies and 22 international airlines operate regular services to Australia from all parts of the world.

By air

Sydney and Melbourne rank as the major Australian air terminals—although international flights also make Darwin, Perth, Brisbane, and Cairns important airports of entry. Flight time from the west coast of the United States to Sydney is about 15½ hours.

Direct and connecting flights link Sydney with major U.S. cities. Airlines providing service from the United States to Australia are Qantas, Pan American, Air New Zealand, and Union de Transports Aeriens (UTA). CP Air (Canadian Pacific) and Qantas fly direct to Sydney from Vancouver, British Columbia, with a stop in Honolulu.

Stopover possibilities include Honolulu, Fiji, American Samoa, Tahiti, Noumea, or New Zealand. You can travel to Australia by one route and return via another (or travel one way by ship, the other by air). If you want to stop over in Fiji, Tahiti, or some of the other South Pacific islands on your way to or from Australia, ask your travel agent how you can make these stops at no additional cost. He can also provide current information on special excursions, package tours, and family and group rates.

By sea

Most cruise ships visiting Australia stop in Sydney, some visit Brisbane and Melbourne. Hobart, in Tasmania, has been added to some recent cruise itineraries. Travelers coming from Europe or from Asian ports often disembark at Fremantle, near Perth, in Western Australia.

Cruises departing from U.S. west coast ports that include Australia are offered by Pacific Far East Line, P & O Line, Princess Cruises, Royal Viking Lines, and Sitmar Cruises. The one-way trip from the west coast to Sydney takes 16 to 19 days, depending on the stops en route.

Ask your travel agent about air-sea packages combining a transpacific flight with a cruise that stops in Australian ports. He can also give you information on passenger-freighter services.

DRIVING ON THE "WRONG" SIDE OF THE ROAD

In Australia you drive on the left side of the road—which, at first, can be a rather unsettling experience, taking some concentration. And if you're a pedestrian, you look to your right instead of left before you step off the "kerb" to cross a street.

Hand signals are no longer required. Turn indicators are compulsory on all vehicles.

Speed limits are generally lower in Australia than in the United States. In built-up areas, the speed limit is usually 35 m.p.h. Outside these areas, the maximum speed is 60 m.p.h. in New South Wales, Victoria, South Australia, and Queensland; 65 m.p.h. in Western Australia and Tasmania. In the Australian Capital Territory, no maximum speed has been designated.

Drivers must always give the right-of-way to *any* car approaching from the right, regardless of traffic circumstances.

Street signs are similar to those in the United States and, in any case, are easy to decipher.

If you take your automobile with you to Australia, you must have the words "Left-hand Drive" (in three-inch letters on a white background) placed in a conspicuous place at the rear of your vehicle before you can drive it. (In Queensland, Western Australia, and the Australian Capital Territory, the wording must read "Caution Left-hand Drive").

Many motorists are hesitant about driving on the left side of the road. If this is your first experience, ask the attendant at the car hire agency in Australia to give you a lesson and check you out before you start off on your own.

HIGHWAY SIGNS help visitors make proper turns from driving lanes on the left side of the road.

ABORIGINES... AUSTRALIA'S LINK WITH THE STONE AGE

Australia's original inhabitants—the Aborigines—are known by anthropologists as "Australoids." They are primitive, dark-skinned people who, for the most part, have lived at a Stone Age level through the ages.

If you visit the Australian outback, the Aborigines you are most likely to see are those who have left their tribes to work in mission settlements and mines or on cattle stations as stockmen. Many have left the outback to become artists, athletes, soldiers, or urban wage earners.

By special arrangement you can visit one of the extensive Aboriginal reservations (protected areas in central Australia and along the northern coast). An easy one to reach is Amoonguna Aboriginal Settlement, 8 miles southeast of Alice Springs; you must obtain permission from the Welfare Department, Hartley Street, Alice Springs. For information on other trips, contact the Northern Territory Tourist Bureau, Box 1155, Darwin, or Todd Street, Alice Springs.

ABORIGINE is decorated with intricate skin painting for a corroboree *in Central Australia.*

In spite of extreme heat during the day and biting night time cold, some of these nomads wander naked in the desertland of Central Australia in search of water, game, and edible vegetation. Because of the vast expanses of the reservations, visitors seldom see these nomadic hunters.

Scrub brush or bark lean-tos provide the Aborigines' only shelter. Sticks are rubbed together to produce fire. Women carry babies and *tucker* (food) in *dilly-bags*, woven from tough grass or roots. Implements of stone, bone, shell, and wood are used to cut bark, chop trees, shape objects, grind, and pound.

Since most of the hunting is at close range, the wood spear is the Aborigine's most essential weapon; he throws it by hand or by his *woomera* (spear thrower), which gives him more thrust. This throwing stick and his boomerang, the Aborigine's own invention, are useful in the pursuit of kangaroos, wallabies, emus, lizards, or birds—all of which are food. Dogs, the Aborigines' only domesticated animal, help the men with the hunting, while women and children collect ants, worms, bugs, and edible roots.

As a people the Aborigines are very graceful and have great dignity. Their remarkable keenness of observation has made them useful as trackers, and they have often found people lost in wild bush or desert.

Because the Aborigines have no written language, they resort to art and storytelling to pass on their lore, laws, and myths from generation to generation. Myths explain the origin of the world and their own physical environment in terms of battles and animal-spirit people (see page 136).

For festive *corroborees* and religious rituals, the Aborigine paints his body with ocher and clay in intricate geometric designs. The corroboree is a ceremonial dance performed as a comment on the daily life of the Aborigine, his legends, and folklore.

Many of the Aborigines are expert craftsmen; their unique arts and crafts—carved and painted bark, boomerangs, spears, ritual objects, and dillybags—are available in shops in Alice Springs, Darwin, and most of the capital cities.

A number of steamship lines provide service to Australia from Europe, from New Zealand, and from ports in Asia and Africa.

ACCOMMODATIONS AND FOOD

Accommodations in Australia vary as widely as the landscape itself, ranging from modern, high-rise hotels offering first-class facilities to comfortable motels, serviced apartments, resort cabins, youth hostels, trailer parks (the Australians call them caravan parks), and campgrounds.

In general, travelers can expect a more limited choice of lodgings outside the major urban and resort centers. Outback facilities cannot always offer such features as air-conditioning and private bathrooms; but they often compensate with good home cooking, a family atmosphere, and valuable information about local attractions and road conditions.

Hotels and motels

The wide choice of hotels and motels in major Australian cities is tailored to satisfy every taste and budget. Your travel agent has up-to-the-minute information on rates and reservations and can help you find suitable accommodations.

Establishments labeled "private hotel" or "guest house" do not serve liquor; regular hotels serve drinks in bars, restaurants, lounges, and guests' rooms. Hotel rates may or may not include meals; many establishments offer rooms with cooking facilities. Make reservations several months in advance, if possible, to secure the best rooms in major tourist centers.

Built mainly in recent years, Australian "motels," "motor lodges," and "motor inns" enjoy a high reputation. You can choose from small, four or five-unit "family" motels in the smaller towns to luxurious, high-rise establishments in the capital cities. Most motel rooms provide refrigerators and facilities for preparing coffee and tea. Rates often include breakfast. Many motels feature family units for up to six people, with special rates for children. The Australian Tourist Commission can provide information on the country's officially recognized motels, and on other regional accommodations as well.

Australians enjoy traveling themselves, so you'll find accommodations a little tight during the Australian school holidays. Though varying from state to state, the holidays are generally as follows: summer holidays—a week or two before Christmas through the end of January; May holidays—one or two weeks in mid-May; August holidays—two or three weeks beginning mid-August (in Queensland) to late August (in New South Wales) and ending early to mid-September; Easter, usually a few days before and after Easter. If you are planning your trip during any of these periods, confirmed reservations are essential, particularly in vacation areas.

Youth hostels

Affiliated with the International Youth Hostel Federation, the more than 70 youth hostels in Australia vary in size and facilities. Though it is impossible to stay in youth hostels all the way across the continent, short trips can be made with hostel linkups all the way. Besides the YMCA and YWCA, a number of church groups sponsor youth hostels. For hosteling information, write to the Australian Youth Hostels Association, Sussex Street, Sydney, N.S.W.

Culinary specialties

In your pursuit of good food and spirits in Australia, you'll make numerous savory discoveries. Here are a few suggestions to get you started in your gastronomic explorations.

Seafood. Early in your visit, stop at an oyster bar. The famous Sydney rock oysters rank among the tas-

VARIED MENU at the Bistro Restaurant in Sydney reflects international tastes; many new foods have been brought in by immigrants from Europe and the Mid-East.

tiest, juiciest, and best in the world. A plate of these plump morsels, glistening in their shells atop a bed of ice, served only with lemon and a piquant sauce, will delight the most selective gourmet.

Oysters are only the beginning of a good Australian meal. If you relish fish, follow up with barramundi (a Queensland fish), snapper steaks, John Dory (a Sydney favorite), scallops served fresh, Queensland mud crab, or crayfish.

Meat dishes. If you prefer steak, Australian menu offerings range from steak and eggs at a roadside cafe to carpetbag steak (stuffed with oysters) to a Chateaubriand at an elegant restaurant.

For a typical Australian dinner, try lamb chops or roast leg of lamb with mint sauce and trimmings. An Australian staple is the meat pie—meat and gravy in a flakey crust—that makes an inexpensive, nourishing meal. They're sold throughout the country.

One unusual soup—witchetty grub—is part of the fare served aboard the *Gem*, a vintage paddle steamer moored at the Swan Hill Pioneer Settlement in northern Victoria. When cooked with a variety of spices, witchetty grubs (fat creamy larvae considered a delicacy by the Aborigines, both roasted and raw) make a thick salty soup resembling cream of chicken.

Fresh fruits. "Home grown" fruits and melons add zest to local menus: mangoes, pineapples, custard apples, Queensland pawpaws (papaya), cantaloupes, and bananas from the tropical northern plantations, and crisp apples from Tasmania.

INTRODUCTION 11

The Queensland pawpaw is second only to the mango in popularity. As sweet as its Hawaiian counterpart, it is much larger, almost the size of a coconut. Though grown commercially, many handsome pawpaw trees, with their dark green, palm-shaped leaves, will be found in residential gardens.

The custard apple resembles an artichoke in color and shape, but it has a ridged skin instead of leaves. The delicious pulp—the color of vanilla ice cream and the consistency of thick custard—is scooped out with a spoon. This soft fruit is not widely grown, since it is difficult to transport custard apples to market before they spoil. Look for the fruit in the Brisbane area and in northern New South Wales.

Beverages—from beer to billy tea

The country produces first-rate wines—particularly red wines: dry reds from the Barossa Valley and from the vineyards east of Adelaide and Coonawarra, clarets from southeastern Australia. Dry white wines come from Eden Valley in South Australia, and fruity full-bodied white wines from the Hunter River Valley (see pages 18 and 19).

Australian beer is unsurpassed, and Australians consume it with gusto. Most of the beer is heavier (7 to 8 per cent alcoholic content) than American and British beers. Scotch and gin are plentiful, but not rye or bourbon.

Throughout Australia, hotels can serve liquor to guests at any time; but serving hours for bars, restaurants, and nightclubs vary from state to state. In New South Wales and Victoria, bars and cocktail lounges stay open from 10 A.M. until 10 P.M. Nightclubs and restaurants may serve beer and wine until midnight. Bars are for men only, lounges for men and women.

Australians drink tea quite as avidly as the English, and they have concocted one brew you won't find in England—billy tea. If you go on a bush picnic or a cookout, try some billy tea with your grilled steak or chops; it is made by first boiling creek water in a covered tin can over a campfire kindled with aromatic gum leaves, and then adding tea.

You can also quench your thirst with fruit squashes, colas, and other soft drinks. Coffee, too, is popular.

TRAVEL POSSIBILITIES

Australia's internal transportation services vary as widely as those in the United States.

New South Wales and Victoria are packed with adventuresome trips that you can make in a taxi, rental car, or comfortable armchair coach. When you go further afield, distances are great and towns are far apart; take an air-conditioned express train or bus or a domestic plane flight.

To get to Darwin from Sydney or Melbourne, make plane, bus, or ship reservations; no trains go that far north. For travelers wanting to explore the island's coastline, passenger ships depart from Fremantle in Western Australia and circle the continent with stops in major ports.

You can also take a cruise in a yacht, motorboat, or ferry to view coral gardens and sea life; plow along dirt roads, tracks, and sandhills in a Land Rover; see farmlands from a paddlewheel steamer; or take to the air in a small plane to view the North Queensland mountain jungle country.

Rent-a-car services

A fine system of highways links most major Australian cities and outstanding tourist attractions. However, be prepared to drive on the left side of the road and on two-lane thoroughfares in many areas.

Avis, Bewglass Empire, Budget, Hertz, and Kays head the list of car rental agencies with offices throughout Australia. Special economy arrangements are available, including reduced rates for long rentals and "fly one way, drive the other" combination packages. You buy your own gas; prices are about the same as in America. Drivers must be at least 25 years of age. Overseas licenses are valid, but International Driving Permits are preferred.

Be sure to check insurance coverage when you rent a car; Australian law holds the driver responsible for all consequences of his driving, and foreign insurance policies are not valid. Fastening your seat belt is compulsory in Australia; failure to do so may result in a stiff fine.

Camper-van and trailer hire

This mode of sightseeing enjoys considerable popularity among both Australians and overseas visitors. In

MODERN COACHES provide air-conditioned comfort for travel throughout Australia. Service is frequent, the fares reasonable, and the network of schedules excellent.

MT. OLGA, hunching 1,800 feet above spinifex plains in central Australia, is largest dome-shaped monolith in the Olgas range.

all Australian states, you can rent modern trailers (caravans) or self-contained, luxury camper-vans accommodating up to five persons. For full details, contact the Government Tourist Bureau in the state or states of your choice.

Bus services

Whether you want to sightsee your way through Australia or travel between major cities, numerous bus companies exist to serve you. The main bus services—Sinclair-Northern, Greyhound, Australian Trailways, and Ansett-Pioneer—operate an intercapital network, with coaches featuring air-conditioning and toilet facilities, fully adjustable seats, picture windows, individual reading lights, and public address systems.

Bus companies recently introduced low-cost unlimited travel passes; usable throughout the company's network, they also entitle the holder to sightseeing discounts in the cities the buses serve. Tour packages vary in length from 8 to 30 days.

Rail travel

Three of Australia's trains have been ranked among the best in the world: the Indian-Pacific, operating between Sydney and Perth; the Trans-Australia Express, linking Adelaide and Perth; and the Southern Aurora, connecting Sydney and Melbourne. These plus a network of other rail lines provide more than 27,000 miles of rail travel opportunities in Australia.

The principal lines follow the east and south coasts, linking Cairns and Sydney, Sydney and Melbourne, Melbourne and Adelaide. From Adelaide other main rail lines cross the continent to Perth on the southwest coast and travel into the interior to Alice Springs. The Tasmanian route connects Devonport and Hobart.

You can buy an Australpass, an all-lines passenger ticket allowing unlimited first-class travel for a specified amount of time—14 days (with a seven-day extension available), 21 days, and one, two, and three months.

Information on the Australpass and other aspects of Australian rail travel may be obtained by writing the Secretary, Australian Railways Conferences, 325 Collins Street, Melbourne, Victoria.

Domestic air services

Two major domestic airlines—Trans-Australia Airlines (TAA) and Ansett Airlines—provide daily service to all important Australian urban centers. First-class passengers enjoy full-course meals; tourist class features light refreshments.

Ansett Airlines offers helicopter service between downtown Melbourne and the city's international airport at Tullamarine. Helicopters also fly among several of the island resorts and mainland departure points along the Great Barrier Reef.

Regional and interstate lines—such as Airlines of NSW, East-West Airlines, and MacRobertson Miller Airline Services—operate feeder services; and other small companies conduct air tours and operate charter planes for individuals or groups. In Australia, the small plane offers the only way of seeing some of the relatively inaccessible tourist attractions.

Boat trips

Travel by boat can be one of the highlights of an Australian holiday. The state capital cities lie along the coast, and in all of them ships can berth within a few miles of the business district. Ships operating between states and nearby islands follow regular schedules; you have a choice of passenger-cargo steamers for long coastal and inter-island runs or launches, cruisers, excursion boats, and ferries for shorter trips. Two passenger-car ferries schedule regular trips from Melbourne and Sydney to Tasmania.

Dozens of fully equipped big-game fishing boats, available for charter, dock at Cairns, Port Lincoln and Kangaroo Island (South Australia), and Tasmanian harbors. In most of the major coastal cities, you can charter yachts or boats for light fishing or cruising.

River cruises take you up Australia's great waterways, on day trips or extended cruises.

ENTRY FORMALITIES

The United States Department of State recommends that you register at your nearest American consulate upon arrival in any foreign country. The U.S. Consulate Services in Australia can help you in case of a personal emergency or if you want to contact local organizations.

The U.S. Embassy is located at Yarralumla in Canberra, the diplomatic center of Australia. U.S. consulates are located in Sydney (37–49 Pitt Street), Melbourne (24 Albert Road, South Melbourne), Brisbane (359 Queen Street), Perth (171 St. George Terrace), and Adelaide (32 Grenfell Street).

Passports and visas

Your travel agent has the necessary forms and knowledge of regulations to help you with passports, renewals, and visas. Australian consulates supply free visas to United States citizens.

Official representatives of the Australian government in the United States include the Australian Embassy, 1601 Massachusetts Avenue, Washington, D.C. 20036; and Australian Consulates-General in the following cities: 636 Fifth Avenue, New York, N.Y. 10020; 111 East Wacker Drive, Chicago, Ill. 60601; Qantas House, 360 Post Street, San Francisco, Calif. 94109; 3550 Wilshire Boulevard, Los Angeles, Calif. 90010; Penthouse Suite, 1000 Bishop Street, Honolulu, Hawaii 96863.

Inoculations

If, prior to reaching Australia, you have visited a country where cases of smallpox still occur, you will be required to have evidence of smallpox vaccination. The World Health Organization has a list of such countries.

Persons arriving from areas in which cholera or yellow fever persist must submit proof of vaccination against these diseases.

Customs regulations

Most personal effects are admitted duty free. Each visitor 18 years of age and over may import a litre (approximately a quart) of alcoholic liquor duty free, as well as 200 cigarettes or 250 grams (approximately a half-pound) of tobacco or cigars.

Sporting equipment and camping gear are admitted without duty, but the importation of firearms and ammunition is restricted, subject to approval by state police authorities. Reasonable limits are placed on the importation of radios, tape recorders, tape players, dictating machines, and record players.

Customs officers prohibit entry of certain items —dangerous weapons (spring-bladed knives, daggers, and the like), pornographic materials, addictive drugs (narcotics, amphetamines, barbiturates), and goods subject to quarantine (animals, plants, germ cultures). Books and films may be subject to censorship.

Strict controls are maintained, also, on the importation of animals and plants and on the transport of plants between the various Australian states.

Money

Australia adopted a decimal currency system in 1966. As in the United States, $1 equals 100 cents. The new Australian notes come in denominations of $1, $2, $5, $10, and $20; the new coins are minted in denominations of 1 cent, 2 cents, 5 cents, 10 cents, 20 cents, and 50 cents. Pounds, shillings, and pennies— Australia's former currency — are still legal tender, but you will probably find only the 2 shilling (20 cents), 1 shilling (10 cents), and 6 penny (5 cents) coins in active circulation.

Exchange rates have been affected by the floating U.S. dollar and by recent devaluations in Australia. You may find slight variations each day, but you won't be far off if you figure the two currencies to be just about on a par. You can bring any amount of currency into the country, but you can't take out more than the amount you brought in.

SHOPPING

"We live on the sheep's back," say Australians, and no country produces finer wool. Lambswool travel rugs—or throws—head the list of especially good buys, followed by blankets, sweaters, wool skirts, suits, and slacks. High quality and bargain prices go together; a good wool blanket usually costs about half what you'd pay in the United States. Australian stores stock a wide selection of woolen textiles—Botany flannels, worsteds, cashmeres, and tweeds. In Sydney you'll find significant savings on good men's suits, ready-made with English-style tailoring.

Australia's fabulous black opals—uncut or set in rings, pendants, bracelets, earrings—constitute a shopper's prize. Bowls and ashtrays carved from native woods—mulga, karra, or Jarrah (one of the hardest of woods)—combine beauty with utility. Kangaroo skin is used for soft and pliable leather goods; including wallets, purses, cases, and shoes. Most Australian leather goods—from shoes and handbags to gloves and belts—cost less than in the United States.

Souvenirs copy the country's odd and fascinating animals; toy kangaroos and koalas sell from about A$5 up. Real and imitation boomerangs, spears, waddies, and shields line the shelves of almost every Australian gift shop—mementos of early inhabitants.

Take a good look at the "primitive" artwork you'll find for sale; discerning critics rank certain Aboriginal watercolorists among the world's finest.

Most of Australia's stores are open from 9 A.M. to 5:30 P.M. weekdays and from 9 A.M. to noon Saturday.

Gourmets, take note

You can buy unusual and intriguing foods and wines to take home. Canned Tasmanian quail, crayfish tails, and kangaroo tail soup can add a taste of Australia to your meal long after you've left the continent.

Most wineries in Australia welcome visitors to their cellars to look around and sample wines; you might purchase a bottle for a picnic.

Tax-free stores

Outgoing travelers who accept merchandise delivery aboard their ship or plane prior to departure can enjoy sales tax and import duty benefits by purchasing from tax-free stores located at Castlereagh Street, Sydney; Collins Street, Melbourne; Kingsford Smith Airport, Sydney; and Tullamarine Airport, Melbourne. But the tax benefit doesn't apply to some items—opals, emeralds, costume jewelry, woolens, suit lengths, leather goods, toy koalas and kangaroos, Aboriginal artifacts, weapons, and carved wooden articles.

Remember that U.S. Customs allows you to bring home U.S. $100 worth of purchases duty free. Save your sales receipts so that you can declare your purchases upon your arrival home.

PRACTICAL INFORMATION

Before you leave—or during your visit—the Australian Tourist Commission will provide information on any and all aspects of travel in Australia.

You can write to the head office at 414 St. Kilda Road, Melbourne, Victoria, or contact any of the following offices in the United States: 3550 Wilshire Boulevard, Los Angeles, Calif. 90010; 1270 Avenue of the Americas, New York, N.Y. 10020. In Sydney, the ATC office is located at ADC House, 95 York Street, Sydney 2000. Additional ATC branch offices will be found in London, England; Frankfurt, Germany; Auckland, New Zealand; and Tokyo, Japan (see Foreword, page 2).

Time zones

When it's noon in Perth, it's 1:30 P.M. in Darwin and Adelaide and 2 P.M. from Cairns down to Hobart. Australia's three time zones are Eastern Standard Time, 10 hours ahead of Greenwich Mean Time; Central Australian Standard Time, 9½ hours ahead; and Western Standard Time, 8 hours ahead. Most Australian states set their clocks ahead in summer; but the introduction of daylight saving time is well publicized and should be no more confusing than at home.

Health conditions

Australia claims to be one of the world's healthiest countries. Modern, well-equipped city hospitals pro-

TRAVELERS arriving at Sydney's International Air Terminal find a full range of facilities available and a helpful information center to assist visitors.

INTRODUCTION 15

WIGGED LAWYERS waiting to cross the street in Sydney (left) are a reminder of the country's ties with England. Street cars (above) remain a part of Melbourne's transportation system.

vide competent medical service—though space is often at a premium. The Royal Flying Doctor Service speeds emergency medical aid to travelers in the outback. A two-way radio system links the service to every sheep and cattle station, as well as to the Land Rovers and tourist coaches used on most long overland tours.

Australian drug stores, called chemist shops, carry most well-known European and American pharmaceuticals.

What to wear

Except for business and certain evening functions, casual, informal clothing is the rule. Australians reserve their formal attire for opening nights and diplomatic functions. Women usually wear long dresses to dinners at hotels or restaurants and to private parties in the big cities. Sydneyites dress a little more casually than their somewhat more conservative countrymen in Melbourne.

Pantsuits are acceptable street wear for women, but shorts are usually reserved for the beach. Race meetings, real fashion shows for the sporting set, call for smart daytime attire. Hats seem to be coming back into fashion and are particularly in evidence at the race meetings. Many elderly Australian women wear gloves and hats whenever they come into town.

Remember that the seasons are reversed in the Southern Hemisphere. If your visit comes between October and May, be sure to include some lightweight, tropical clothes. A lightweight sweater for air-conditioned rooms is a useful wardrobe addition, and don't forget your swimsuit and sunglasses.

In winter you will need warm clothing; bring a lined raincoat, warm topcoat, boots or galoshes, wool shirts and sweaters, warm slacks. Though the temperature rarely descends to freezing, the cold penetrates.

Electrical appliances

Electric current in Australia is 240 volts A.C. If you are bringing an electric razor, hairdryer, or other appliance, you may need a transformer. Some of the newer hotels provide them; your travel agent can tell you whether yours does or not.

To tip or not to tip

General practice in Australia calls for light tipping; the following suggestions should guide you:

Baggage porters. Most porters charge a set fee per bag. Airport porters are not supposed to be tipped, but they usually are—about A20 cents per bag.

Hotels. Tipping practices are not rigidly defined and generally depend upon appreciation for services rendered: doormen (commissionaires), A20 cents, de-

16 INTRODUCTION

pending on service; porters and bellboys, A20 or A25 cents per bag for normal luggage; dining room and cocktail waiters, 10 per cent at first-class hotels, usually on presentation of each bill.

At resort hotels where the traveler has the same table waiter throughout his stay, the tip is presented at the last meal. No extra tipping is necessary for dry cleaning or laundry delivery by valet to the room.

Restaurants. Ten per cent of the bill at first-class restaurants.

Taxis. Normally the balance of the change (i.e., 50 cents for a 42-cent fare) for good, quick service.

Guides, tour conductors. Normally not tipped.

On trains. Porters have a set scale of charges; for dining car waiters, 10 per cent is sufficient.

Beauty and barber shops. Six to 10 per cent of the bill will suffice for most services.

Miscellaneous. Washroom and cloakroom attendants, A5 to 10 cents.

EVER SEE A JUMBUCK DRINKING AT A BILLABONG?

The rollicking dialect and salty slang of the Australians reflect a nimble-witted humor unique to Australia. This dialect, plus a lilting tune, has made "Waltzing Matilda" the national folk song of Australia. Lyrics for the song were written about 75 years ago by A. B. "Banjo" Paterson. While visiting a cattle ranch near Winton in central Queensland, he put words to a catchy tune his hostess was playing.

A statue of Paterson stands beneath a coolabah (a type of eucalyptus) in Winton today, but elsewhere—virtually everywhere—his memorial is the song itself:

"Once a jolly swagman camped by a billabong,
Under the shade of a coolabah tree,
And he sang as he watched and waited till his billy boiled,
You'll come a waltzing Matilda with me.

Waltzing Matilda, waltzing Matilda,
You'll come a-waltzing Matilda with me,
And he sang as he watched and waited till his billy boiled,
You'll come a-waltzing Matilda with me.

Down came a jumbuck to drink at the billabong
Up jumped the swagman and grabbed him with glee,
And he sang as he shoved that jumbuck in his tucker bag,
You'll come a-waltzing Matilda with me."

The next verse tells how the swagman (tramp), while waltzing matilda (carrying one's bundle or swag on the back), got caught by the squatter (large land owner) for stealing his jumbuck (sheep). The swagman committed suicide by jumping into a billabong (a water hole in a dried-up bed of a river) before he got caught by the troopers "one, two, three."

Billy is a large smoke-blackened tin can used to boil water over a campfire for tea; *tucker* is food you tuck in your *tucker-bag* or *dilly-bag*.

The hobo on the road carrying his bundle goes a-waltzing matilda, but the Aborigine goes *walkabout* when he abandons his *wurley*, a flimsy shelter of bark and branches. Other terms commonly used for the Aborigine's hut are *gunyah*, *goondie*, and *humpy*.

Corroboree and *didgeridoo*, also Aboriginal words, have entered the familiar Australian speech. *Corro* means to jump and leap; *boree* means to shout and yell. That's what the Aborigine does to the droning rhythm of his *didgeridoo*, a musical instrument, at a festival or ceremonial emulating a kangaroo or emu hunt, or celebrating war or peace.

Other vigorous Aussie terms you might hear that have little meaning to the outsider include *dinkum* (real, honest, true), *fair go* (give me a chance), *back chat* (impudence), *rat bag* (an eccentric person), *a bit of a dill* (a silly one), *wowser* (a straight-laced person, spoil sport), *hit your kick* (open your wallet), *grizzle* (to complain), *good guts* (inside information), *yabber* (talk), *wog* (flu or slight illness), *give it a burl* (try it), *boss cocky* (farm owner or top man), *plonk* (cheap wine), *possie* (a place, position), *fossicking* (rummaging for shells or rocks), *drink with the flies* (to drink alone), *no-hoper* (a fool), *winge* (to complain), *trouble and strife* (a nagging wife), *crook* (sick), *jackaroo* (a young ranch hand), *digger* (soldier), *hooroo* (goodbye), *chook* (chicken).

The Aussie's sports heritage produces such terms as *tee-up* (set up an appointment) and *lob-in* (drop in to see someone). *Have a yarn* means to talk to someone.

It's important, especially in making telephone calls, to recognize that the most outstanding difference in the language is the pronunciation of the letter "A". It takes a long sound, either as in I (or eye) or somewhere between A and I. Thus, "Good day, mate" is pronounced "Goo'die, mite". More obvious in pronunciation is the disappearance of the letter "R" in the middle or last syllable of a word. Thus Melbourne is pronounced Mel'bun.

Of all Aussie slang adjectives, *bloody* is the most commonplace. You hear it everywhere except in polite English households—where the youngsters, particularly, bloody well better not use it.

But in Australia, whether you arrive by ship or plane, it's a bloody cold day if somewhere along the line you fail to hear the friendly Aussie greeting: "Goo'die mite; 'owyer goin'? Can I shout yer a beer and bickies?" (buy you a beer and snacks).

TOURING AUSTRALIAN WINE COUNTRY

Wine country touring in Coonawarra or the Barossa Valley of Australia can be every bit as interesting, educational, and fun as it is in the Cote d'Or of France or the Napa Valley of California.

Australia's wines are diverse. The wineries making them range from small to large, family-owned to cooperatives, historic châteaux to modern functional structures. And the wine people are friendly—they enjoy sharing their story and their product.

Most of Australia's large wine firms have wineries in several of the wine-producing states, so they can offer a full range of wines, including both red and white table varieties, appetizer and dessert wines. Brandies also play a big role in the Australian wine industry; about 50 per cent of the wine ultimately becomes brandy.

Some Australian wine labeling borrows from its European namesakes: Claret, Burgundy, Chablis. Some are varietals, named for the grape: Cabernet Sauvignon, Hermitage, Pinot Noir, Shiraz. Some have blended names reflecting a blend of grapes, such as Cabernet-Shiraz and Pinotage. Some labeling is a result of whim, as in the case of wine from Semillon grapes being labeled Semillon, White Burgundy, or Riesling. (Rhine Riesling contains Riesling grapes.)

You'll find most of the wine-producing vineyards concentrated in three states—South Australia, New South Wales, and Victoria—though smaller wine producing areas are located in Western Australia, Queensland, and Tasmania.

Full information on vineyards and wineries in Australia is available from the Australian Wine Bureau, Hosking Place, Sydney, New South Wales.

Barossa Valley and South Australia

The country's largest wine production occurs in South Australia, where many of the wineries operate on the outskirts of Adelaide. Several can even be reached by public transportation from the downtown area. As in most Australian wine districts, all types of wines are produced in the state, but the focus is on white table wines, sparkling wines, and ports. A few winery names to look for: Penfold's, Stonyfell, and Woodley.

The Wine Industry of South Australia issues a comprehensive list of wineries and their visiting hours. A reliable guide for visitors, it is available through the South Australia Government Tourist Bureau, 18 King William Street, Adelaide. Rental cars are available in Adelaide and in the Barossa Valley at Tanunda.

The Barossa Valley. About 30 miles north of Adelaide you'll find the origin of some of Australia's finest wines—Rhine Riesling, Cabernet, Cabernet-Shiraz, and Hermitage. Nearly 30 wineries thrive in this valley, named after the Barossa district of Andalusia, Spain; the region was settled by German immigrants in the early 1840s. Numerous small wineries vie with the more widely known names of Seppelt, Kaiser-

SEPPELT'S WINERY in the Barossa Valley (left) was established in the 1840's. March and April are colorful months in the wine country during harvesting of season's crop (above).

18 INTRODUCTION

Stuhl, Yalumba, Hamilton, Gramp's Orlando, Penfold's, and Hardy's.

Not only does the Barossa Valley have celebrated wines but also it holds a celebrated vintage festival every odd numbered year in March or April. For more on the area, see page 100.

The Clare District. North of Adelaide some 83 miles is a smaller district of considerable charm; it encompasses the towns of Clare and Watervale, where light whites, robust reds, and sherries are produced. The town of Clare (named after County Clare, Ireland) is a peaceful little agricultural center gaining charm from old buildings that remain from the area's settlement in the early 1800s.

Southern Vales District. Due south of Adelaide about 20 miles, there's a 15 to 20 mile stretch of vineyards and wineries known as the Southern Vales district. Wines from this area are Rhine Riesling or Cabernet-Shiraz, Claret, or Burgundy. The welcome is big, too—about 15 wineries have regular visiting hours daily except Sunday.

Langhorne Creek. Another 20 miles further south, Langhorne Creek produces some very reputable, full-bodied, dry red wines and ports.

Coonawarra. The Coonawarra district, 270 miles southeast of Adelaide, has a long-standing reputation for excellent red wines. Now white varieties are being tried, as well. The area remains unspoiled, the climate is cool, the soil is volcanic, and the wineries—including Mildara, Wynn's, Lindeman's, Penfold's, Hungerford Hill, Owen Redman, and Brand's—take great pride in the wines they produce. Most of them have weekday visiting hours.

Murray River. The development of irrigation along the Murray River northeast of Adelaide opened this great river valley to productive vineyards between 1915 and 1930. Extensive vineyards around the towns of Barinera, Berri, Loxton, and Renmark provide the grapes for a number of winery cooperatives, as well as for small, independent wineries. Some are open for inspection; check locally for visiting hours.

Dessert and appetizer wines were the early specialties of this area, but table wines of sound quality and reasonable price are increasing in volume.

New South Wales wine districts

Wine growing areas dot the map of New South Wales from the coastal lowlands north of Sydney to the fertile valleys of the Murray and Murrimbidgee rivers.

Hunter River Valley. It takes only three hours by car to drive the hundred miles north from Sydney to the Hunter River Valley, noted for its large concentration of wineries and thousands of acres of vineyards.

The largest wineries in the area are located near Cessnock and Pokolbin, about 20 miles west of Newcastle. Australia's oldest wine producing area, the Hunter River Valley combines coal mining with its vineyards. As a result, Cessnock resembles a busy mining center more than a picturesque wine town. But the cellars and winery buildings around Pokolbin have the traditional look about them.

Table wines are the thing here, dominated by the red grape Shiraz and the white Semillon. Names familiar in other parts of Australia—McWilliams, Penfold's, Lindeman's—welcome visitors, as do most of the smaller wineries.

Riverina District. Sixty per cent of the wines of New South Wales come from the Riverina district, about 400 miles southwest of Sydney and 200 miles northeast of Melbourne. The vineyards here thrive on a warm climate and an irrigation system watering some 200,000 acres through a canal system fed by the Murrumbidgee River.

The district's principal town is Griffith, with a population of about 10,000, situated on the main irrigation canal. It's a handsome town, designed by the American architect Walter Burley Griffin, who also designed Canberra.

McWilliams has three wineries here, and Wynn's and Penfold's are the other big names in the area. These contrast with a number of smaller wineries owned by Italian families. The area is known for its table and fortified wines.

Victoria's historic districts

The state of Victoria was once Australia's major wine producer. Then, at the close of the 19th century, the plant louse *phylloxera* (that earlier had played havoc with French and California vineyards) found its way to Victoria. The infestation was contained before it spread further in Australia, but Victoria never regained its crown.

Rutherglen, about 173 miles northeast of Melbourne, has staged one of the state's strongest recoveries. Wine followed gold in the Rutherglen district, with the first plantings taking place in 1851. Almost wiped out in 1899 by the vine disease, it was among the first areas to plant resistant strains.

Today the Shiraz grape does particularly well, and each winery treats it a bit differently. Often it comes up in the class of Cabernets.

This region also produces some delicate white wines, sherry, and dessert wines that have a good reputation. All Saints winery is worth a visit for its historical interest as well as the wines. Rutherglen is the site of a wine festival each March.

Great Western District. Another important Victorian wine area is near the town of Ararat, 126 miles northwest of Melbourne along the foothills of the Grampians. The first vines were planted here by French immigrants in 1863; today, most of the vineyards are owned by the big Seppelt winery. Known primarily for its champagne, the area also produces some fine dry red wines. Tours of Seppelt's cellars and winery, located about 10 miles west of Ararat, can be arranged on the spot.

BOTANIC GARDENS are an integral part of most Australian cities; picnickers enjoy Melbourne gardens (top). Thousands of lorikeets visit the Currumbin sanctuary on the Gold Coast (right) at feeding time. Baby koala rides on mother's back (far right) during its first year.

20 ANIMALS, BIRDS, PLANTS

AUSTRALIA'S WONDERFUL WILDLIFE—
the koala, the emu, the wattle

In Australia the laughing jackass (kookaburra) is a bird; the kangaroo paw is a flower; red soldiers are militant ants; and koala bears aren't bears—they're marsupials.

The kangaroo (animal, that is) dances in the rain, and the spindly-legged brolgas (companion birds) do a fine quadrille on the plain. The ostrichlike emu is a bird; it can swim like a fish and race like a horse, but it can't fly.

Plants eat insects. And if you hear a buzz saw in the bush, don't expect the call of "Timber"—it may be a lyrebird, prince of the mockingbirds, atop his dancing mound, strutting for his mate and sounding like whatever bird or sound he pleases.

The natural world of Australia—the plants, animals, and land forms—is one fascinating part of travel on this island continent. You can see "living fossils" like Tasmania's Antarctic beech tree, an echo of the country's link to a larger land mass; or Queensland's lungfish, which breathes air directly at the surface of a pool when the water becomes stagnant. And all whimsical travelers, whose experience with koalas may be limited to the stuffed toy variety, can see—and perhaps hold—the real thing.

Here are some of Australia's plants and animals that you may be meeting for the first time:

Marsupials have pouches

Marsupials are animals whose newborn drink milk inside their mothers' pouches for four or five months before facing the world. Not satisfied with this protective treatment, two kinds—the koala and the opossum—climb on their mothers' backs and continue the free ride in the open for a few more months.

Koala. The little native koala—Aboriginal word for "no drink"—has won all of the popularity contests as the most lovable Australian marsupial. He is cuddly—snuggling close or crawling up your arm—except when he gets frightened or when you tease him. He has wooly gray, yellowish-white fur, white paws, in-

ANIMALS, BIRDS, PLANTS   21

flated balloon cheeks, and a nose that looks like a leather button. When he wants to be heard, he makes a crying sound like a small baby. He is choosy about his food, selecting only the oilier types of gum leaves for both food and drink.

Kangaroo. The largest and best known marsupial, the kangaroo is considered the national animal and has a place of honor—along with the emu—on the Australian coat of arms.

All kangaroos descended from tree-dwelling animals, and a climbing variety still exists in northern Queensland. Great red and gray kangaroos, the wallaroos, and the wallabies are all in the kangaroo family; the main difference is size. All live on grassy plains or in lightly timbered country. They range from seven-foot red bucks to the rabbit-sized musky rat-kangaroos.

A baby kangaroo is called a "joey." When born, he's about one inch long, blind, and furless. By natural instinct he makes his way through his mother's fur into her pouch; the pouch seals itself, and joey stays there until he can hop out to nibble grass and plants. He continues to use the pouch as an emergency shelter; when he gets scared, he dashes headlong into it, often leaving his long hind legs dangling outside.

The great red "roo" or "boomer" kangaroos are the bucks. Youthful ones are gray, and they redden as they develop, though the does remain gray. These large kangaroos have huge hind legs, small forelegs, and a stout, elongated tail that they use as a shooting stick or prop when grazing or standing. Reds and grays live together as a family around a favorite siesta clearing known as "the nest," but they often hop far afield searching for food and water. The leader of the herd is known as the "old man." When a young buck matures and wants to be leader, he has to fight the "old man" or take off on his own.

Female kangaroos are gentle and make good pets. The "old man," however, can be dangerous when a buck challenges his command or tries to steal a wife from his harem. Sometimes his powerful claws kill with a single stroke. He disciplines his wives and children harshly. When there is danger, however, he is the last to desert the nest. He keeps a sentinel on watch for dingos (native dogs) and hunters at all times. The sentinel alerts the family with loud thumps on the ground with his great hind feet, then joins the others as they bound to safety in great leaps—more than 20 feet—at speeds up to 30 miles an hour.

Mammals that lay eggs

Monotremes are the lowest order of mammals—unique animals laying eggs that hatch into mammals. Once hatched, the young are suckled. The combination of laying eggs and nursing the young dumbfounded English and French scientists who studied the first monotremes brought back from Australia in the early 1800s. Australia possesses the only two monotreme survivors: the platypus and the echidna.

Platypus. Of the two, the platypus seems more indecisive. The adult platypus is less than two feet long. In front he has a duckbill, giving him a nose-in-an-old-shoe appearance. In back he has a large, flat, furry tail which he uses like a rudder when swimming. His coat also is fur, but his feet are webbed. He has a trick, too: the webbing is retractable; underneath he has paws with sharp claws like those of a cat.

He can burrow, swim, and dive, and the male carries a poisonous spur, about a half-inch long, on the inside of each short hind leg.

For a home, the platypus uses two burrows; one serves as general living quarters, and the other is a nesting chamber 10 to 60 feet long. The female excavates the elaborate breeding burrow and then lays and hatches two or three eggs, about ¾ inch in diameter, which are attached to each other and look like snake eggs, with tough leathery shells.

Echidna. Though he is really a spiny anteater, the echidna resembles a porcupine in size and appearance. He is the only remaining kinfolk of the platypus. Like his cousin, the spiny anteater is an egg-laying mammal of prehistoric vintage. The female has one unique talent; she grows a pouch when she has the urge to lay an egg.

Although the echidna comes in several varieties, the best known are a short-legged variety living on the Australian mainland, and two long-beaked, densely furred species living in New Guinea. The slender

FEEDING TIME at Sydney's Taronga Zoo. Kangaroo nibbles a tidbit offered by a young visitor. Kangaroos, koalas, and emus are the star attractions.

22 ANIMALS, BIRDS, PLANTS

LYREBIRD displays his handsome plumage at Sherbrooke Forest near Melbourne, one of the best places to see this prince of the mocking birds.

THOUSANDS OF TERNS take flight, startled by visitors strolling leisurely along the sandy beach on Michaelmas Cay, off Cairns in North Queensland.

pointed beaks of the latter—about the size of a pencil—curve downward like upholstery needles and are twice as long as their heads. All echidnae are burrowers—they're masters at disappearing into the sand.

For bird watchers

Australia's birds vary in size from the tiny weebil to the stately emu. Most of them can fly, but some can't. Australia has some birds—for example, the handsome black swan, with scarlet beak and feet—that are found nowhere else. Others—like the brightly plumed parrot family of lorikeets, cockatoos, ringnecks, rosellas, and budgerigars—make the country their headquarters.

Some of Australia's birds are known for their unusual habits. Mallee fowls build incubators of organic matter for their eggs, ingeniously keeping them at a temperature of 92°F for several months by scraping the covering soil off the mounds every morning and replacing it at night. Bower birds build elaborate structures as settings for their mating dances, decorating them with shells, feathers, cigarette wrappers, and glittering objects. They have even been known to steal car keys and teaspoons.

Emu. Appearing with the kangaroo on the Australian coat of arms, the emu is considered the most outstanding of the country's birds. Powerfully built, he grows to almost six feet in height and is second in size in the bird kingdom only to the ostrich, which he resembles.

The body of the emu is covered with drooping, grayish-brown feathers. His wings are rudimentary, and he long ago lost the power of flight.

Emus graze in flocks on the plains and in wooded country. When alarmed, they run at tremendous speed or will strike out viciously at an enemy with their feet. They swim well, even though their feet are not webbed.

Lyrebird. This Australian native lives in the mountain forests of the east coast between Melbourne and Brisbane. He can project his own rich melodious voice up to a quarter of a mile or convincingly mimic birdcalls ranging from a kookaburra's raucous laugh to a thornbill's treble. A handsome bird, he has a brown body and long, curved tail feathers that look like silver filaments, except for the broad outer feathers; these are black at the curved ends, patterned with crescents of brown and silver.

The lyrebird's most outstanding feature is his dance. To attract a mate—or maybe just for fun—the male pirouettes gracefully atop a specially built bush mound about three feet in diameter. (One busy bird can have as many as ten of these.) In the dramatic final stage of the dance, the bird flips his outspread tail over himself so he is completely covered by silvery-white feathers. His brown body shows through only faintly, as though shielded by a fancy fan.

ANIMALS, BIRDS, PLANTS

GUM TREE FORESTS (upper left) shade mountains of Victoria and Tasmania. Wildflowers surround visitors (top) to Murchison area of Western Australia. Green kangaroo paws (left) are only one of Western Australia's 6,000 wildflower varieties. Even rocky Mount Buffalo (above) in the Victorian Alps provides a foothold for flowers.

24 ANIMALS, BIRDS, PLANTS

Kookaburra. The country's most popular bird is known primarily for his call, a rollicking laugh. Attempts to describe this insulting sound have given him the nickname "laughing jackass" and alluded to his call as the "laughter of demons." The regularity of the call at dawn and sunset has earned the bird the additional title of "bushman's clock."

The largest of the kingfishers, the kookaburra is a native of Australia, and he appears throughout the country. The male is colorful, with bright blue rump and a white patch over one eye. You will probably hear him before you see him, however, for the call of the laughing jackass resounds everywhere, even in cities and suburbs.

The flowering "bush"

The term "Australian bush" applies to rain forests, tropical jungle, rolling hills covered with scrub, forests of gums or conifers, and even grasslands. And much of the bush boasts a profusion of colorful blossoms and pervading fragrance. After a rain in the desert, the air is cloyingly sweet. Sailors say they can smell the sharp, medicinal scent of the gum trees (eucalyptus) far out to sea.

Emblem plants. Two of Australia's native plants have gained national fame: the acacia, found in some variety over most of the continent, appears on the country's coat-of-arms; and the red-flowered waratah is the emblem of New South Wales.

In the early days, colonists used acacia branches to make "wattle and daub" huts, resulting in the name "wattle" becoming attached to the acacia. More than 600 species are found in Australian gardens, parks, street plantings, and as part of the "bush." The waratah, with a bloom averaging four inches in diameter, is found in four species, all native to Australia.

Gum trees. The eucalyptus, as Australian as the kangaroo, is only one of numerous trees adding their fragrance to the country's 13,000 native plants and flowers. More than 700 different species have been identified, and many have colorful pungent blossoms—scarlet, coral, and white. Separated by ocean from the rest of the world since prehistoric times, the gums now are among the most transplanted trees in the world. They were first planted in California for windbreaks more than a hundred years ago, and now more than 150 varieties grow in California and Arizona; you'll also find them in parks and gardens in 72 other countries.

In the mountains of eastern Victoria and in parts of Tasmania, you can see dense forests of giant gums, some standing more than 300 feet tall. Smaller varieties are found in the drier woodlands; these trees, having an open structure and small leaves, attain heights of only 15 to 20 feet. Vinelike, crawling varieties exist along the fringes of the country's deserts.

A profusion of wildflowers

Many of Australia's native plants are found nowhere else in the world. Among these are plants that bloom profusely: Sturt desert pea stretching like a red carpet across vast tracts of inland desert; dainty white snow daisies brightening the slopes of the Australian Alps; and more than 600 varieties of orchids lending their beauty to the steamy rain forests of the north.

Western Australia alone grows more than 6,000 species of wildflowers and flowering shrubs and trees, many found nowhere else. For eons, this southwestern corner of Australia was virtually a floral island, isolated from the rest of the continent and other land masses by the Indian Ocean on the west and south and by the desert areas to the east and north.

Among the most colorful of Western Australia's plants are the kangaroo paw, the Geraldton wax flower with either white or deep rose flowers, the *Banksia coccinea* with its scarlet conelike flowers, and pine grevillea with its big spikes of deep orange flowers crowning plants growing to 20 feet in height.

The Aussie's Christmas tree is not a conifer, but a mistletoelike parasite *(Nuytsia floribunda)* that blooms at Christmastime with masses of orange balloonlike blossoms.

For strange shapes, nothing can equal the blackboy; from a distance it looks like an Aborigine in a grass skirt raising his spear. Related to the lily, it grows about 5 feet tall, and the "spear" can add another 6 feet to its height. The bush blossoms along its spear, which bears hundreds of tiny flowers.

Two native plants are carnivorous: the pitcher plant and the rainbow plant. They're designed to attract insects, the pitcher plant with a pitcherlike flower full of sweet nectar, and the rainbow plant with rainbow-colored, threadlike leaves.

Where the wildlife is

You won't find kangaroos hopping about on Sydney's Circular Quay, but you will find them—and Australia's other unique inbred marsupials and the equally rare monotremes—in areas providing natural habitats for the animals.

Australia has made an outstanding effort to protect its natural environment and wildlife by establishing more than 200 sanctuaries and National Parks. By visiting some of these reserves, you can observe many of the country's 400 kinds of native animals, over 1,200 species of birds (half of these unique to Australia), a plant life including more than 7,600 wildflower varieties, and geological forms cut to extraordinary shapes by natural forces.

Check with the government tourist bureau in each capital city you visit for lists and descriptions of the sanctuaries in their area.

SURFING (above) is a popular sport along Australia's ocean beaches. Football rooters of all ages (right) turn out to cheer their teams. Picking the winner from a racing form (far right) requires serious study.

26 SPORTS...A WAY OF LIFE

SPECTATOR OR PARTICIPANT—
sports are a way of life

To Australians, sports are more than a mere pastime or form of recreation—they are a way of life. A zest for living only partially explains their sports-mindedness. Their fanatical loyalty and competitive spirit develop from rigorous physical training at school, a continuing drive to beat the other fellow, and the double advantage of a favorable climate and a high living standard.

SPECTATOR SPORTS

You can learn a great deal about the character of the Aussie if your travels include a sports event—either one of the big exhibitions attracting huge crowds or a smaller, more intimate affair where you stand a better chance of meeting and talking with the locals.

If you're tennis-minded, you may wish to plan your visit to coincide with a Davis Cup Challenge Round. Dates for this and other big matches are available from the Australian Tourist Commission. Usually you'll see the best play and the top pros in action from November through March.

Golf enthusiasts can attend major tournaments during October and November. The Australian Spring Circuit has five major events held over a 5-week period, attracting some of the world's finest golfers.

But the major spectator sports in Australia are horse racing, Australian rules football, and cricket.

Horse racing

Most pervasive of the spectator sports is horse racing. The sport of kings has millions of followers who wager bets at race gatherings held throughout the year—from small country meetings (see page 29) to colorful major events like the Melbourne Cup, the AJC Derby, and the Caulfield Cup. Visitors from around the world travel to Australia just to attend these turf highlights.

The biggest horse race—in number of spectators and impact on Australians—is the Melbourne Cup,

BOOKMAKERS' UMBRELLAS (above) stand out from packed crowd at Melbourne racecourse. Young cricket player (right) shows intense concentration on ball; sport is popular with all ages.

known as the world's greatest two-mile handicap (see page 73). Other major racing events during the year include the AJC (Australia Jockey Club) Derby held at Randwick Racecourse, Sydney, in October; Melbourne's Caulfield Cup (second only to the Melbourne Cup) in October; the Brisbane Cup in June and Doomben Cup in July, both held in Brisbane; the Grand National Hurdle and Grand National Steeplechase at Flemington Racecourse, Melbourne, on successive Saturdays in July; and the Australian Steeplechase at Caulfield Racecourse, Melbourne, in August. These big meets are always sell-outs, requiring advance arrangements; your travel agent can usually make them for you.

You place your bets at windows operated by the Totalisator Agency Board, the state-controlled betting organization which uses the pari-mutuel machine, an Australian invention (the Aussies also were the first to introduce the photofinish camera). You'll also find TAB "shops"—betting agencies—in most cities throughout the country, enabling you to bet on the big races whether or not you can attend.

Harness racing—called "trots"—has developed rapidly in popularity since the introduction of night racing meets and legalized betting. Major tracks are at Harold Park in Sydney, Melbourne's showgrounds, Gloucester Park in Perth, and Elwick in Hobart. Harness races are run year round.

Football mania

Each year Australians are gripped with a seasonal passion second to none when it comes to numbers of avid, highly partisan followers. Visitors from the United States are taken by surprise with the national excitement over Australian Rules football. Although there's soccer (association football) as played in many parts of the world, and both Union (amateur) and League (professional) rugby, few football games have the emotional appeal for Australians that "Rules" does. It is said to have greater support per person than any other field sport in the world—and it's played only in Australia.

Australian Rules football is played on a huge oval-shaped field—120 yards wide and 190 yards long—using an oval shaped ball. Each end zone has four goal posts and each team 18 players.

At club matches in Melbourne, the heartland of the game, more than 100,000 spectators jam the stadium to watch a series of matches every Saturday from April to September. The grand finals, held in September, attract even greater crowds. This final event is booked months in advance, but overseas visitors can obtain tickets through special arrangements with the Victorian Football League in Melbourne.

Bowling on the green

Every Saturday, and often on weekdays as well, you can watch white clad members of lawn bowling teams rolling their black balls down immaculately kept greens toward a white "kitty" or "jack," the target.

And the bowling greens seem to be everywhere, from small town to capital city. As a visitor, you are welcome to watch; and if you're interested, it's relatively easy to get an invitation to participate. The sport's major event, the Australian Gold Coast Winter Bowls Carnival, is held in July along the Gold Coast, attracting more than 1,000 entries.

28 SPORTS...A WAY OF LIFE

Ball, bats, and wickets

Cricket, the English game, has an avid following in Australia during the summer season. It was first played in Sydney in 1803; by 1877 the Australians felt qualified to hold their first Test Match with England. Their first victory on English soil came in 1882; since then, they have bested the English at their own game—73 matches to 67 with 43 draws.

International Test Matches—Australia versus England or another cricket-playing country—are held in capital cities every second year from December to February. All states except Tasmania play each other twice a season (at home and away) for the Sheffield Shield, a symbol of Australia's cricket supremacy.

If you don't understand the game—with its opposing teams of eleven players spread over an open field —you'll probably find at least one avid local spectator willing to explain the rules to you.

FOR THE ACTIVE SPORTSMAN

With more than 80 sports enthusiastically played Down Under, there's something for everyone—so you shouldn't miss the opportunity of enjoying your favorite sport while on Australian soil. In most cases, you'll meet Australians on a personal basis. Many games are followed by get-togethers, often with an invitation to someone's home.

Racquets and lawn courts

Australia has produced so many of the world's top tennis players that it qualifies as a giant of the tennis world. Beautifully maintained lawn courts, playable the year round, are almost standard throughout the country, presenting a tempting lure to tennis-oriented travelers. Most resort hotels have courts (with racquets available), and in the big cities you can usually obtain guest privileges at a nearby tennis club. If you are a club member at home, you can almost always get honorary privileges.

Know your handicap

Australia's golf courses challenge every type of golfer, from the tournament hardened professional to the casual amateur. You can choose your style, playing a quiet round on a public course, enjoying a more social game as the guest of a country club member, or perhaps making a circuit of the course at a major resort.

As Australia's big cities enlarged, the greenbelt of golf courses remained where placed 40 to 60 years

---

EVERY DAY IS RACING DAY DOWN UNDER

On a given day, you can bet your bottom bob that somewhere in Australia a horse race is being run. The races range from bush or picnic meetings held outside the urban area—where the racing is semi-amateur and the atmosphere friendly and informal—to the big meetings at courses such as Caulfield in Melbourne, Randwick in Sydney, and Eagle Farm in Brisbane—where stakes are high and fashions vie with the horses for attention.

Though the big meets attract the major attention, the little ones—the bush or picnic meetings—provide an even better way to get to know the Aussie on his home ground. Some of these bush meets have race tracks and stands; others are simply a course marked out with stakes, and the spectators bring canvas chairs or stand through the entire race. Often the picnic is almost as important as the races—with hearty spreads for frontier appetites.

Bush horseracing has no season. Races are held through the year, followed with great enthusiasm from remote outposts like Oonadatta in South Australia, where the land is flat and dry, to cattle stations such as Tolga, surrounded by tropical rain forests 30 miles southwest of Cairns in Queensland.

Deep in the dry and lonely outback of northwestern Queensland, you'll find "raceday" at the Mount Isa racecourse whenever horses' hooves kick up clouds of red dust and head for the first turn. Horses and jockeys are cheered around the track by tanned miners dressed in wide-brimmed hats, blue singlets, and shorts.

At a place called Hanging Rock in Woodend, 50 miles northwest of Melbourne, picnics and horse racing occupy the locals on New Year's Day, mixed with good cheer and revelry. At the Oakbank Race Track in the Mount Lofty Ranges, 15 miles from Adelaide, picnic meetings are held year round.

NEIGHBORS gather for informal racing at picnic meeting on Talbingo Station, New South Wales.

ago; so today many of the top golf courses are only a 30-minute ride from the city center. Each Australian course has its own special character, from Sydney's "sand-dune country" to Melbourne's tea-tree "jungles" and outback towns with oiled-sand courses.

Clubs can be hired on all public courses, and the greens fee is modest. If you are a member of a club, ask your club's secretary-manager for a letter of introduction to the Australian club and have him include your handicap.

Fishing—from rainbows to marlin

Fishing in Australia varies from dangling a line tied to a willow stick in an outback rivulet to sophisticated, deep-sea fishing expeditions resembling a waterborne safari.

Ocean fishing. The incredible variety of fish in the seas surrounding Australia attracts fishermen from around the world. The best season is between November and May, though sharks are caught the year round. Fishermen claim the prime area is along Australia's eastern and southeastern coast—particularly Queensland, New South Wales, Southern Australia, and Tasmania.

Australian anglers recommend the following waters as the best ocean fishing areas: the seas off North Queensland for tropical quarry such as marlin, sailfish, grouper, red emperor, sweetlip, bream, coral cod, and Spanish mackerel; off the coast of southern Queensland; the waters of southern New South Wales—around Sydney and the Bermagui-Eden area; and off Tasmania's rugged southeastern coast. In South Australia, most favored waters are Streaky Bay, where the world's largest shark, 2,664 pounds, was landed; the mouth of Spencer Gulf near Port Lincoln; and the prolific waters of Backstairs Passage, between Kangaroo Island and the mainland, especially for kingfish and yellowtail.

Numerous game fishing charter boats and water safaris are available. In north Queensland, for example, big game fishermen can charter launches in Cairns, Mackay, and from Emu Park and Yeppoon near Rockhampton. Charter and tariff information is available from the Australian Tourist Commission and from the N.S.W. Government Tourist Bureau. (For more information on big game fishing in the Barrier Reef waters, see page 125.)

Tuna tournaments. Tuna sport fishing is so good around the island of Tasmania and off the South Australia coast that annual tuna tournaments are held at both places—off Eaglehawk Neck in Tasmania in March or April and at Port Lincoln, South Australia, in January. Individuals and teams from all over the country participate. Their main target is the bluefin tuna; the current festival record is a 245-pounder, caught on a 50-pound line. Other great sporting fish from these waters include broadbill swordfish, albacore, and the yellow tail kingfish.

Inquiries regarding big game fishing in Tasmania are welcomed by the secretary of the Tasmanian Game Fishing Association (contacted through the Tasmanian Government Tourist Bureau in Hobart). You can arrange for boats, gear, accommodations, and transportation to and from the boat harbor of your choice. Information on South Australia may be obtained from the South Australian Tourist Bureau, 18 William Street, Adelaide.

Streams and lakes. The Australian Alps, lying between New South Wales and Victoria, offer many mountain streams and lakes teeming with good-sized brown and rainbow trout. Recent power and road developments have opened up some fine back country waters.

Among the best of these spots is massive Lake Eucumbene, formed by the big Snowy Mountain hydroelectric scheme southwest of Canberra. Catches average six to ten pounds. Thousands of fingerling trout are released each year into this huge reservoir by the New South Wales Fisheries Department.

Some of Tasmania's good fishing streams and lakes are rarely visited by fishermen, and the quality and size of trout are very high. Catches range from five-pounders caught in rivers to seven and eight-pounders from lakes. Brown trout up to 15 pounds have been taken from Lake Crescent. Best Tasmanian haunts are the northwest coastal rivers, the highlands, the Huon Valley area in the south, and the upper reaches of the Derwent River.

In most states the fishing season is from September through April. In Tasmania the season lasts from November to April on lakes, and from September through April for inland streams and estuaries.

Hunting safaris

Sportsmen from all over the world are familiar with the hunting grounds in the Northern Territory. Water buffalo and crocodiles are the primary targets here, but other game includes rabbits, pigs, foxes, goats, dingoes, and several additional animals (some of which are considered pests).

Several hunting centers cater to the tourist, supplying guides, transportation, equipment, and assistance in obtaining hunting permits. Three such centers are Ansett's Karumba Lodge, on the Gulf of Carpentaria; and Muirella Park and Nourlangie Camp, in Arnhem Land about 120 miles east of Darwin. Several operators in the Northern Territory have all-inclusive hunting safaris (see page 135).

Skiing—increasingly popular

Improving alpine accommodations, world class ski jumps, chair lifts, and other ski slope amenities are signs that skiing has established its popularity in Australia. Extensive snowfields are skiable from June through October.

Several thousand beds are available for skiers in clubs, lodges, and alpine hotels. Slopes are reached by chairlifts, T-bars, poma-lifts, and rope tows.

Most popular resorts can be found about 300 miles southwest of Sydney in the Perisher Valley and Thredbo (boasting an Olympic-standard ski jump). In Victoria, Falls Creek and Mounts Buller, Hotham, and Buffalo offer good skiing on gently rounded mountain slopes. Tasmania has Ben Lomond and Mount Field, both fast gaining in popularity.

Resorts in these areas are well serviced by ski rental shops, restaurants, and ski schools with European instructors. Bookings can be made through the government tourist bureaus in New South Wales, Victoria and Tasmania.

THE SURF WORLD

Australia has beaches to suit everyone—from wading children to daring surfers to the retired person seeking sun and relaxation at the shore. The coastline provides more than 3,000 miles of ocean play land, stretching from the southeast corner of the continent to the interminable sands north of Cairns and the uncrowded miles of beach along the western coast. In and around Sydney alone, you'll find more than 30 readily accessible beaches. Some of these beaches are sites for Australia's famous surf carnivals (see page 45).

Hot dogging the waves

By the hundreds of thousands, Australians take to the sea on surfboards. Body surfing became popular in the early 1900s, but it wasn't until 1915 that Hawaii's Duke Kahanamoku introduced board riding at Freshwater Beach, Sydney. The first boards were 16-foot hollow models ridden straight in, at the same speed as the wave. By the 1960s, short and lightweight plastic-foam surfboards made the beach scene, and trick riding was born.

Surfers may be reluctant to tell you their favorite beaches (preferring to keep down the traffic), but the eastern coast has many beaches from Melbourne to north of Brisbane offering excellent waves for surfing. For detailed information, contact the Australian Surfers Association, Clarendon Street, South Melbourne, Victoria.

Skin and scuba diving

Stretching 1,250 miles north and south along the Queensland coast, Australia's Great Barrier Reef provides a paradise for skin divers and underwater photographers. Bright sunlight shafts down 30 feet or more into the coral-studded depths, providing an almost ethereal descent for divers. Hundreds of varieties of tropical fish, the varied marine life on the bottom, and the fascinating coral grottoes provide an enthralling setting.

Heron Island and Green Island, the major coral island resorts in the reef area, are the two main areas for skin divers and photographers. Divers prefer them for the marine life, ease of accessibility, and availability of equipment and service. Spearfishing is prohibited in most of these waters, so the fish have multiplied and are quite tame. Big Boomie, only 200 yards from the boat basin on Heron, is a regular haunt for schools of barracuda, kingfish, cod, and numerous varieties of tropical fish.

Trans-Australian Airlines' travel service will arrange itineraries for individual divers and groups on request—to Heron, Green, or any of the myriad of other islands in the Whitsunday Passage. Leading sporting goods stores in the coastal cities offer a full range of skin diving equipment, including rubber suits, masks, flippers, goggles, scuba gear, and spears for underwater diving, but you should bring your own regulator. Additional information is available from the Australian Underwater Federation, New Lampton, New South Wales.

SKIN DIVING is year-round sport in the shallow, clear water surrounding Heron Island. At low tide, you can walk onto some of the exposed coral beds.

SYDNEY'S CHANGING SKYLINE (above) is surrounded by parks, suburbs, rivers, and coastline. Row of Victorian houses (right) lines South Dowling Street near Taylor Square. Sydney family (far right) strolls at sunset along one of the beaches near the city.

32 SYDNEY

SYDNEY—effervescent first city of Australia

Sydney looks eastward to the Pacific, absorbing some of the fun-loving freedom of that huge ocean, coming to life each day with the continent's earliest glimpses of the morning sun.

With its population nearing three million (almost a fourth of all Australians), Sydney is the major city of Australia. Spreading over some 670 square miles, its boundaries are not precisely defined. An undulating coastline marks city limits on the east. Numerous rivers, their mouths broadening into estuaries, meander into the Sydney area from north, west, and south.

CITY WITH A ZEST FOR LIVING

This waterworld—Sydney's priceless heritage—gives the city a pronounced maritime character, an immense vitality, and a lasting beauty. Ships enter the deep-water harbor in an almost endless procession to dock not far from the downtown area. Magnificent beaches stretch for miles north and south along the coast (34 within the city limits). And the residents are outdoor people who really relate to the waters around them: surfers, swimmers, yachtsmen, fishermen, water-skiers, sun bathers.

Sydney sprawls; suburb after suburb merges and pushes into the bush. It grows vertically, too, as year after year new office monoliths rise in the heart of the city. Its streets seem to be arranged according to a pixilated pattern: wandering, curving, going off at unexpected angles.

Like many of the world's major cities, Sydney combines beauty and ugliness, sometimes juxtaposed. The conflict of architectural styles is sometimes jarring, yet interesting; strangely, the new structures—such as the Opera House—often add an interesting, fresh dimension to familiar landmarks like Harbour Bridge. When you see Sydney from a high rooftop in full sun—and it *is* a sunny city—or in the incredible glitter of night lights, it can have an unexpected loveliness.

But the feel of Sydney is pure Australian—vital,

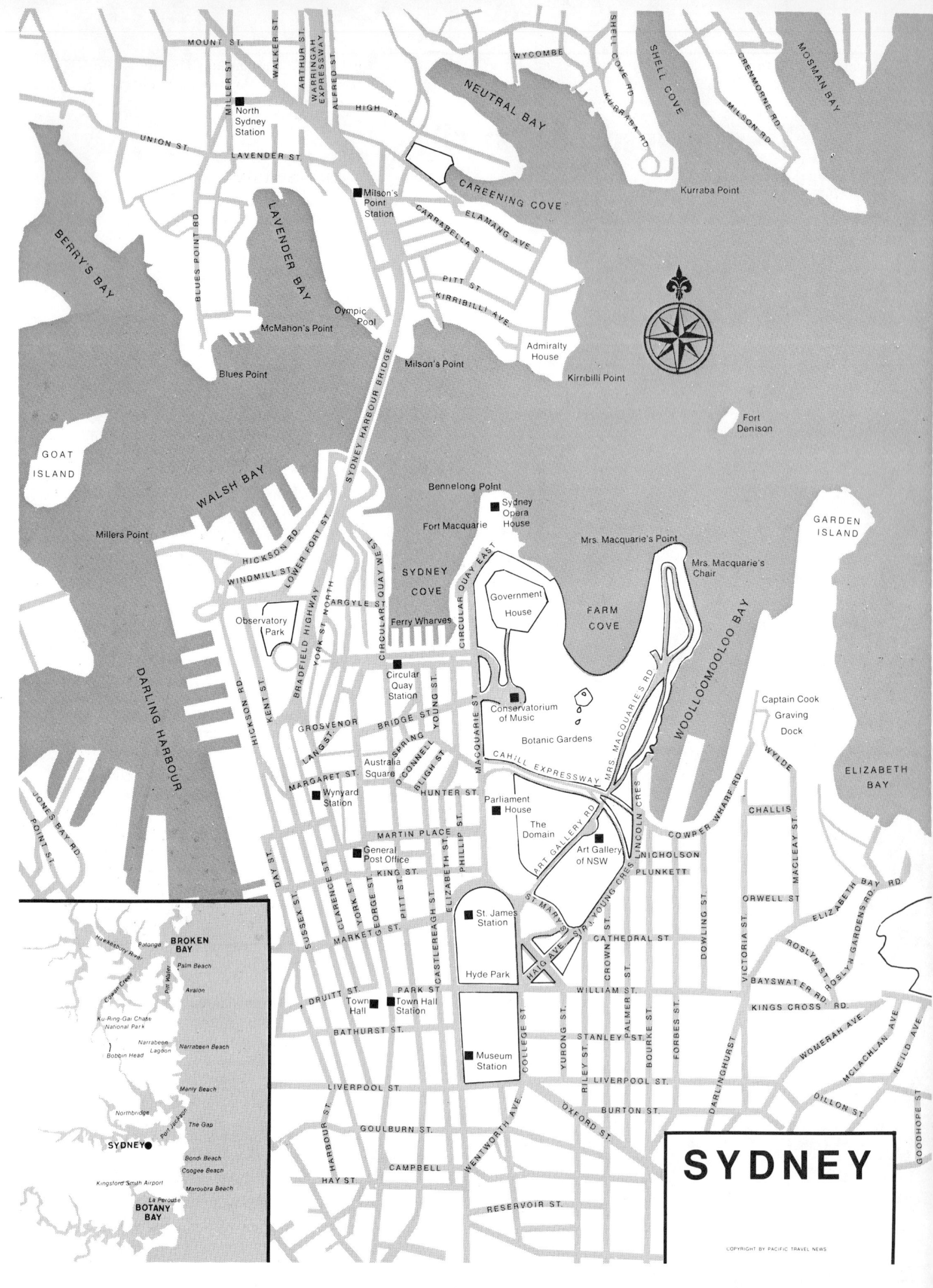

breezy, brash, busy, getting-on-with-it, a zest for enjoying life. In this respect Sydney epitomizes the feeling many travelers have about Australia as a whole—that it is more rewarding as a place to feel and experience than merely to see.

Getting your bearings

The heart of Sydney is Circular Quay (pronounced *key*), where you will certainly find yourself at one time or another. Here much of the city's transport begins and ends. Ferries and hydrofoils depart for cross-harbor destinations, and the two symbols of Sydney—the Opera House and Harbour Bridge—loom large. Within minutes you can walk to the two best view spots—the 50-story A.M.P. Building and the 48-story Australia Square Tower (Sydney's two tallest buildings)—where you can survey the entire city in a painless orientation course. Your view is even more pleasurable if enjoyed from the vantage point of a table in the revolving Summit Restaurant on the Tower's 47th floor.

Two government tourist organizations provide assistance for visitors. The New South Wales Government Travel Centre has a free accommodation-reservation and advisory service; the Centre is located at 16 Spring Street. The Australian Tourist Commission, 2nd Floor, ADC York, 95 York Street, is also a source of helpful information for travelers.

A comfortable climate

Sydney enjoys a pleasant climate that encourages outdoor activities. Summer daytime temperatures average 78°, but occasionally soar over 100°. Sydney residents, however, have two escape areas should the weather get too warm for comfort: the beaches that are a stone's throw from urban areas and the Blue Mountains forming Sydney's backdrop.

Winters are relatively mild, with most daytime temperatures in the 50s and 60s. Snow is unknown, but early-morning temperatures in the outer districts occasionally drop to near-freezing. Sydney's annual rainfall averages 47 inches, spread throughout the year. Australian weather talk: "It may fine up."

The main hotels and motels

Sydney's major tourist hotels are the Menzies Sydney, the Chevron, the Wentworth, the Boulevard, and the Hilton—in addition to many motor hotels, inns, lodges, and motels that abound in the city.

Of this group, some of the best are the Town House, the Carlton-Rex, the Gazebo, the Commodore Chateau, the Crest, the Hyatt Kingsgate, six different TraveLodges, and a variety of motor-inn types run by local chain operators: Commodore, Koala, Noah's, and Zebra. More hotel and motel accommodations spring up nearly every year—so it's best to check with your travel agent to find one fitting your needs and pocketbook.

Getting around the city

Taxis are inexpensive—35 cents at flag fall and 42 cents a mile. A lighted sign on the cab roof indicates a taxi available for hire. Tipping is not necessary. Rental cars are readily available, but this means driving on the left side of the road (see page 9).

The inner city subway loops beneath the downtown area, making a circle from Central Railway Station and stopping at Town Hall, Wynard, Circular Quay, St. James, Museum stations, and then back to Central Railway Station. City buses, some of them double deckers, run just about everywhere. The Public Transport Commission of New South Wales offers economical unlimited travel tickets and a variety of low-cost packages for sightseeing in the Sydney area.

Dining and night life

If you check the local guide books when you get to Sydney, you'll find 70 to 80 restaurants listed—a small selection of the more than 3,000 restaurants in metropolitan Sydney representing the cuisines of the world. Night spots also abound—particularly in the Kings Cross area, which swings into the wee hours of the morning. You'll find Sydney a lively city after dark.

Heading the list of recommended local foods would have to be Sydney rock oysters; a little smaller than our Blue Points, they are mild, succulent, delicious, and plentiful enough that a dozen on the half-shell looks like a bargain. Other seafoods you should try include the local crayfish, prawns, snapper, and John Dory—a flat, flounderlike fish with delicate flavor, one of Sydney's favorites.

Sydney meat pie, a soft, flaky pastry pie enclosing a mixture of meat and gravy, is a favorite local staple. You'll find it moderately priced in restaurants, coffee shops, sidewalk shops, and little beach-side food stands. A companion item will probably be fish and chips.

Australian beef, lamb, and mutton can be excellent in the hands of the right restaurateur. Tropical fruits from the north come in a wide variety: bananas, mangoes, passion fruit, papaya, and custard apples.

Restaurants. Among the better, well-established restaurants are these:
• Chelsea, in Kings Cross near the El Alamein fountain landmark. Elegant, possibly Sydney's most expensive restaurant; excellent wine list.
• Coachmen, on Bourke Street in the suburb of Redfern. An old convict-built house restored to the

atmosphere of 1826; open log fires in the winter.
- French Tavern, on Hamilton Street. In an old cellar with open kitchen; fine French cooking.
- Argyle Tavern, in the historic Rocks area. Housed in an old maritime bond store, with early 19th-century atmosphere; the specialty is colonial-style steak and kidney pie.
- Victor's Tavern, 3 Kimber Street, a narrow lane near the produce market. Victor is an ebullient Italian who runs a small, pleasant restaurant: brick walls, no tablecloths, set menu with reasonable prices, good wine.
- Caprice, on Rose Bay overlooking the harbor. One of the city's prestige restaurants, it sits out over the water and has a dance floor and band.
- Fisherman's Lodge, on the harbor at Watson's Bay. Housed in Dunbar House, a two-story, colonnaded Georgian building, this restaurant has a balcony-terrace for outdoor eating and harbor-watching activities. Mud-crab, crayfish, oysters, and other seafood are excellent.
- Mischa's Place, at Balmoral Beach. Housed in a former beach cabana. Good food and a superb view through huge picture windows out across Middle Harbour and The Heads.
- Flanagan's Afloat, a floating restaurant on a permanently-moored ferry at Rose Bay. Good views, good sea food.
- L'Aubbergade, on Cleveland Street in Redfern area. Many local diners recommend this little French bistro with its simple fare, checkered tablecloths, and motherly proprietress.

DINING CHOICES in Sydney vary from Gallic surroundings and cuisine at French Tavern (upper left) to informal atmosphere in traditional setting at Old Spaghetti Factory (lower left). At Harbour Restaurant (above), outdoor tables offer patrons superb view of Sydney Harbour.

36 SYDNEY

- Prunier's Chiswich Gardens, on Ocean Avenue, Woollahra. Quiet tavern-on-the-green, the green being a small park in one of Sydney's finer residential areas (with a number of foreign consulates just around the corner); soft background music.
- Beppi's, corner of Yurong and Stanley, in the eastern suburbs. Highly regarded Italian cuisine.

Many new restaurants open every year. Three recent additions that have a sense of permanence are the Endeavour, Darcy's, and the Woolloomooloo Wool Shed, the latter being a facsimile of an old shed decorated with bales of wool as background for hearty Australian fare.

You'll also find excellent restaurants in some of the hotels—among them the Garden Court at the Wentworth, the Spanish Room at the Menzies, and the Pavilion Room Restaurant at the Gazebo.

Sydney after dark. At night Sydney presents a grand mixture of night clubs, bars, discothèques, strip-shows, rock and jazz spots, and all-night coffee shops. Center of the action is Kings Cross, a densely-populated square mile of noise, neon lights, and colorful exuberance. Restaurants and little cafes abound —Chinese, Italian, French, Japanese, Indonesian. So do people from every part of the world.

The city has a dozen permanent theaters and a host of amateur groups plus several theatre restaurants, where you enjoy a meal along with the entertainment. You take part in the act—singing with the singers and hissing the villains—at the Bull-Bush in the Kings Cross area and the Music Hall at Neutral Bay. Agencies handling theater ticket booking for Sydney's legitimate theater are listed in the telephone directory. Some agencies deliver tickets for an added fee.

And, of course, there's music: the Sydney Symphony, opera, chamber groups, ballet. Check the Sydney papers for current offerings.

Shopping in Sydney

Most of the big shops and department stores are concentrated in a six-block area bounded by Elizabeth, Park, George, and King streets. Shopping hours are 8:30 A.M. to 5:30 P.M.; stores close at 9 P.M. Thursdays and noon on Saturdays.

The largest stores are David Jones (in three locations—on Elizabeth, Market, and George streets); Farmer's, at Pitt and Market streets; Walton's, on George Street; and Mark Foy's near Museum station. Numerous little boutiques are located on King and Castlereagh streets. Don't overlook the smaller shops in the arcades: Angel, Australia Square Shopping Circle, Boulevarde, Carlton, Centrepoint, Her Majesty's, Hunter, Imperial, Menzies, Piccadilly, Royal, Strand, and Wesley. The most elite shopping district is at suburban Double Bay, a short distance by taxi from downtown Sydney.

Before you begin shopping, a good place to visit is the Australian Design Centre at 213 Miller Street. Similar to the Design Centre in London, the Sydney collection displays the best in Australian design.

Opals are one of the best buys, especially the glinting, deep black stones from Lightning Ridge in New South Wales. Good stores to shop for opals are Alan J. Davis; The House of Prouds; Percy Marks Pty., Ltd.; the Opal Skymine, in the Australia Square Tower; and Staffords. You can buy the stones unset or in rings, pins, and pendants.

Aboriginal wood carvings will be found at the Bush Church Aid Society, 135 Bathurst Street.

For antiques—currently much in demand—try Stanley Lipscombe (18th century and Regency furniture, early glass and silver); Clara Johnson (Victoriana of all kinds); Grafton Galleries (Regency and Victorian pieces); and Newman Antiques (small gifts, especially Oriental pieces and antique jewelry).

You can find anything from caps to coats made from kangaroo skin, but conservation movements are making such articles more difficult to import to the United States. Several species of kangaroo are now on the endangered species list. A new U.S. Department of Agriculture ruling prohibits importing any products made from such species into the United States for commercial purposes. Currently, Australia has put an embargo on kangaroos and kangaroo products.

Outside Sydney, some of the sheep stations have local products for sale to visitors. You can, for instance, buy a 6 by 8-foot Merino wool blanket for A$50 (the price includes packing and shipping to your home) or try out a boomerang before purchasing it.

SIGHTSEEING IN SYDNEY

In some respects Sydney resembles British colonial cities the world over. It has its Hyde Park, a spacious parkland within the limits of the inner city; a wonderfully sited Royal Botanic Gardens, spreading around a knoll, topped by Government House, sloping down to the harbor shores; and The Domain, a large, wooded piece of land owned by the State. And it has its Queen's Square, Town Hall, and Parliament House.

But many of Sydney's points of interest are uniquely Australian, place names and public monuments that could not be anywhere but Australia—such as Woolloomooloo Bay and Kirribilli Point and Mrs. Macquarie's Chair, a resting place hewn out of the sandstone overlooking the harbor.

In this young and vigorous city, the old is not so very old, but nonetheless it has interest. Yesterday's landmarks confer a sense of history, the very foundation of any city.

Many of Sydney's points of interest can be seen on a walking tour of the downtown district. Scheduled sightseeing tours and cruises cover most of the following places; some additions—bushland trips, Sydney's

THE GREAT SYDNEY OPERA HOUSE

The Sydney Opera House, the city's most striking architectural feature, may well be the most talked about building in the world. Between its inception in 1956 and its completion in 1973, the building has been the subject of endless arguments and discussions. It even became the subject of a book (*The Other Taj Mahal* by John Yeomans).

It all started when the New South Wales government decided to build an opera house on Bennelong Point—a 4½-acre headland jutting into Sydney Harbour. A commanding site, it is bounded with water on three sides and the Royal Botanic Gardens on the fourth. The government asked architects from all over the world to submit designs for a building on that site. From the 223 entries submitted, one by a Danish architect, Joern Utzon, was selected by a distinguished panel of judges. Utzon did not submit a final set of plans with his entry. His was a schematic presentation of sketches—a dramatic concept—with the engineering and detailing to come later.

Utzon's sketches showed a building unlike any other in the world, its soaring roof structure disguised to resemble a cluster of billowing sails. What more fitting design for an opera house that would overlook a harbor usually alive with boats?

And so the detailing began, and construction got underway. From inception to completion, the building took 17 years. Costs, originally estimated at $10 million, rose through the years to over $125 million.

Many Sydneysiders, more inclined toward active outdoor sports than indoor cultural activities, took a dim view of the Opera House over these years of construction. In fact, many weren't sure they even wanted an opera house, but they were certain that $100 million dollars was a ridiculous amount for any building.

WHITE-WINGED Sydney Opera House, opened in 1973, juts out into the waters of Sydney Harbour.

Architect Utzon left before the building was half finished, adding further complications.

But finished it is—a vast complex housing some 90 rooms under its soaring roof: a concert hall seating 2,700 persons, an opera hall accommodating 1,530, a theater for 600, and smaller halls for music recitals and receptions. The Opera House was officially opened by Queen Elizabeth II on October 20, 1973, with the presentation of Beethoven's Choral Symphony No. 9. Since then it has been open to the public seven days a week, becoming one of Sydney's main attractions.

Now that the Opera House is finished (and since it is generally considered one of the most exciting new buildings in the world), Sydneysiders are almost unanimously proud of it—despite its price, architectural problems, and 17 years of endless arguments.

---

famed Royal Randwick racetrack, interesting residential areas. Listings of these tours are available through the New South Wales Government Travel Centre, 16 Spring Street, which keeps up-to-date on all the tours offered by Sydney sightseeing companies.

Harbor sights

A good place to get your bearings and to begin your acquaintance with downtown Sydney is the harbor district, with its landmarks and viewpoints.

A.M.P. Building, on the Circular Quay, has an observation deck on the top floor. It's open daily, offering a close-up view of Sydney Cove and the ferry boat wharves, plus a wide view of Sydney Harbour.

Sydney Harbour Bridge, second largest single-span bridge in the world. It's worth walking across; the views are great and you can get a train back from Milsons Point station to the city center. Sydneysiders call this bridge "the coathanger."

Opera House (see above).

Fort Denison, on a rocky islet in Sydney Harbour, was used as a prison for incorrigible convicts. A supply ship called at the fort once a week, and the prison's meager food rations earned it the sobriquet of "Pinchgut." Open daily, the fort is such a popular sightseeing place on weekends that Saturday visits must be arranged six months in advance (Room M26, Public Relations, Mezzanine Floor, Maritime Services Building, Circular Quay).

Along Macquarie Street

Several century-old buildings along Macquarie Street combine history with interesting architecture.

Royal College of Physicians and Surgeons, 145 Macquarie Street, presents an elegant reminder of this section's former residential character. Built about 1848, it was originally a two-story building; two more floors were added later, and they blend in well.

The Old Mint, on Macquarie Street, is one of the surviving wings of the Old Rum Hospital—so named because the three colonists who built it (between 1811 and 1816) did so in exchange for a virtual monopoly on the colony's rum trade. The structure's simple design and side verandas are typical of buildings constructed in the British colonies during this era. From 1855 to 1926 the building was part of the Royal Mint.

Parliament House, on Macquarie Street, is open daily except Saturdays, Sundays, and holidays. Part of this building—the central portion—was also built as part of the Rum Hospital. First occupied by the State Legislature in 1829, Parliament House has an interesting interior.

Richmond Villa, behind Parliament House, facing The Domain, is headquarters for the N.S.W. Parliamentary Country Party. This lovely Victorian Gothic house was built in 1849.

Parks and gardens

Sydney's three major parks—the Royal Botanic Gardens, The Domain, and Hyde Park—mark the eastern border of the downtown shopping district.

The Royal Botanic Gardens, sweeping down to the curve of Farm Cove, have been precious to Sydney since the 1780s when they provided growing space for vegetables for the Governor's table and the residents of the young colony.

Renowned for their beauty and layout, the gardens cover 67 acres, with more than 400 varieties of plants, shrubs, and trees collected from around the world. Lawn areas are interspersed with oblong flower beds, dotted with fountains, sculptures, greenhouses, a great variety of palm trees, and walkways shaded by fig trees.

Topping a knoll overlooking the harbor is Government House, home of the governor of N.S.W.

On the Macquarie Street roundabout is the Conservatorium of Music, a castlelike building built in 1819 to house the Government House stables. It now serves as the center of musical instruction in N.S.W.

The Domain is an open park bisected by Art Gallery Road. "Sydneyites" exercise the privilege of public domain during their lunch hour—playing football in the winter and cricket in the summer on the park's broad, open expanses of lawn.

In the 1800s public speakers used the park as a place to express religious thoughts ranging from strict Calvinism to freedom of personal religion. Today, there are still speakers—some thanking the stars that

SOAPBOX ORATORS have an outdoor forum in The Domain. Sydneyites also use the park for lunch, as a place to stroll, and for lively games of football.

they are atheists, others expressing the political philosophies of today.

Art Gallery of New South Wales is located on Art Gallery Road, in the center of The Domain. Its permanent collection includes many paintings by Australians. The gallery is open Monday through Saturday, and Sunday afternoons; it has a licensed restaurant.

Hyde Park, a half-mile-long island of green extending from the city's cluster of government buildings on the north to Sydney's main shopping center, is graced with tree-lined walks and flower gardens—but not a single "keep off the grass" sign.

Archibald Fountain at the northern end is the hub of the park, which also contains the Anzac Memorial, a statue of Captain Cook, and an assortment of other fountains, statues, and memorials. After lunch you may catch a band concert or choral performance. On special occasions art shows are held along the walks.

Several other buildings of interest are located in the Hyde Park district:

St. James' Church, at King Street and Queen's Square, faces the northern end of the park. Designed by talented convict-architect Francis Greenway and built in 1819, the church is a fine example of Georgian architecture, noted for its copper-sheathed spire and its pleasing proportions.

Hyde Park Barracks, now the Law Courts, stand on the opposite side of Queen's Square, on the corner

SYDNEY 39

of King and Castlereagh streets. Also designed in 1819 by Greenway, the completed barracks so pleased the governor of New South Wales that he pardoned the prisoner.

Australian Museum, at the corner of College and William streets, faces the park's eastern side. The museum features Australian natural history and includes an extensive Aborigine section. You can visit Tuesday through Saturday, and Sunday and Monday afternoons; a restaurant is located in the museum building (closed Sundays).

Town Hall, seat of Sydney's city government, is three blocks west of Hyde Park. Located on the corner of George and Park streets, the building was begun in 1866 and is one of Sydney's Victorian buildings most likely to be preserved. It includes a large concert and assembly hall and one of the world's finest pipe organs. Until the advent of the Opera House, it was the city's main concert hall. The building is open Monday through Friday.

The city's business center

Sydney's downtown commercial district is centered in the blocks northwest of Hyde Park.

Martin Place Plaza, between Pitt and George streets, is an attractive area for strolling where traffic is prohibited. Bright with flower stalls and pink granite paving, the pleasant walkway provides access to Sydney's main stores and specialty shops.

The Cenotaph, on Martin Place, memorializes those who died in two world wars. Every Thursday at 12:30 P.M., the smartly uniformed Eastern Command Band escorts the Guard to the Cenotaph, after which Guard and Band go to the Anzac Memorial in Hyde Park for a similar ceremony.

The General Post Office, also on Martin Place, is a monumental example of Renaissance-inspired architecture. A massive bulk of building, it was designed by James Barnet (who is depicted in one of the sculptured panels on the Pitt Street side).

Australia Square Tower, between George and Pitt streets, is the continent's second tallest building. Atop the cylindrically shaped structure, 600 feet in the sky, you can enjoy the superlative view from an observation deck and a revolving restaurant. A stop here early in your visit will help you to better visualize Sydney's city plan. And on the fifth floor: Opal Skymine, a simulated opal mine, plus display and sales rooms where you can watch gem cutters and polishers work on stones that took millions of years to develop.

Stock Exchange, 20 O'Connell Street, in the shadow of the Australia Square Tower, is a busy place on weekdays during trading hours—10 A.M. to 3:30 P.M. You can watch trading from the public gallery.

The Rocks

The Rocks is an historic area of old buildings located on a rocky promontory west of Sydney Cove, culminating in Dawes Point. The east side of The Rocks is being developed by the East Rocks Redevelopment Authority, and buildings are being restored.

Take a bus from George Street, get off at Argyle Street, and walk along it to the Argyle Arts Centre, an enjoyable stop for browsing.

The Observatory on Flagstaff Hill was established in 1858. It is open 2 to 4 P.M. on Wednesdays.

Argyle Place, a delightful corner of old Sydney, lies below Observatory Park. To get there on foot, start from the National Trust Centre on Bradfield Highway and walk to Observatory Park. Then take the path to the left, down the Agar Steps. Turn right into Kent Street, and soon you will come to Argyle Place.

Through Argyle Cut, the Argyle Arts Centre in the old bond store offers an intriguing spot to linger; you can shop as well as watch craftsmen at work on silverware, copperware, leather goods, pottery, stained glass, and art enamels. For dinner you might try the Argyle Tavern on Argyle Street (see page 36).

Church of the Holy Trinity, built in 1840 on Argyle Place, was the first Garrison Church of the Colony, where the members of the Queen's regiment worshipped. Its interior is especially graceful.

Lower Fort Street, in the western section of the Rocks area, marks the site of several gracious old Georgian buildings. Numbers 59 and 61 are particularly elegant, and so is Bligh House (number 43), built in 1833. Of an entirely different order is the Hero of Waterloo Hotel, a prestigious name for an ordinary pub, albeit an old one.

Geological and Mining Museum, 28 George Street North, contains one of the best displays of geological specimens in the Southern Hemisphere; you'll see mineral ores, rocks, fossils, and gemstones. Hours are 9:30 A.M. to 5 P.M. Monday through Friday, 11 A.M. to 4 P.M. on Saturday, and 2 to 5 P.M. Sunday.

Other interesting destinations

Beyond the central district, you'll find other destinations worth a visit. Unless you are a dedicated walker, you should seek out these spots by bus or taxi.

Paddington (called "Paddo" by the locals), a small section southeast of Sydney, contains handsomely restored old Victorian residences, along with restaurants, cafes, pubs, taverns, antique shops, book stores, studios, and an art colony of sorts.

Narrow terrace buildings, sharing common walls, are painted pastel colors. Most have balconies. Walk along some of these streets: Jersey Road (off Oxford

IRON GRILLWORK laces balconies of handsome Victorian buildings that line many Paddington streets (left). Limber koala (above) eyes visitors at Taronga Zoological Park.

Street), Underwood Street, Elizabeth Street, Queen Road, Union, Stafford, and Healey streets, Five Ways, Goodhope, Gurner, and Cambridge streets. Look into these galleries: Barry Stern, on Glenmore Road; Bonython, on Victoria Street; and Gallery A, on Gipps Street. When you're ready for lunch, stop in at the Hungry Horse restaurant, located in an old Paddington house on the corner of Windsor and Elizabeth streets.

You'll also find the immense Victoria Barracks on Oxford Street interesting: built in 1840 on a 35-acre site, they are still used by the military. The only time you can get inside is on Tuesdays at 11 A.M. for a changing of the guard ceremony.

Paddy's Market operates in the Producers' Market Building at Hay and Lackey streets and has all the typical stands of the old Paddy's: food, clothing, flowers, bric-a-brac, confectionery, art, jewelry, and leather goods. It's open only on Saturdays between 7 A.M. and 5:30 P.M.

The Flemington Markets, accessible by car from Marlborough Road or Potts Street, Flemington (or by walking from the Flemington Railway Station), has 1,172 stands offering fruit, vegetables, and goods of every description. It's open every Friday from 11 A.M. to 5:30 P.M.

Museum of Applied Arts and Sciences, on Harris Street between Mary Ann and Thomas streets in the Ultimo district, is open Monday through Saturday, and Sunday afternoons. The industrial museum contains exhibits of ceramics, glassware, and metalwork, and displays relating to shipping, aviation, and engineering.

The University of Sydney, on Parramatta Road. The main building was designed in 1859 by Edmund Blacket, Sydney's foremost exponent of Gothic Revival architecture. (Other works by Blacket include St. Andrew's Cathedral, adjacent to Town Hall; St. Philip's, on Church Hill; St. Mark's, on Darling Point.)

Taronga Zoological Park is located on a promontory on the northern shore of the main harbor, across the water from Sydney's business center. Take the ferry from Number 5 Jetty at Circular Quay to the base of the zoo area, climb aboard a bus going to the highest part of the zoo, then stroll downhill among the kangaroos, koalas, emus, platypuses, and other exotic creatures.

Historic buildings

Four additional structures in suburban Sydney rate special mention for their interesting architecture and historic significance.

Darlinghurst Court, on Taylor Square in Darlinghurst, is an impressive colonnaded building, an example of Greek Revival architecture. The central portion was designed by Mortimer Lewis in 1837.

The Old Gaol, now part of East Sydney Technical College on Forbes Street, is open daily during the school term. Enclosed inside a massive wall, a collection of austere buildings radiates from a round house, once a chapel. Begun in 1835, the jail buildings show Georgian influence.

Elizabeth Bay House, on Onslow Avenue, Elizabeth Bay, is one of the city's most graceful mansions. A Regency house, it was designed by John Verge and

SYDNEY 41

built in 1832. Currently the house is divided into 16 private residences.

Vaucluse House, on Wentworth Avenue, Vaucluse, was once the home of William Charles Wentworth, chief architect of the N.S.W. Constitution. The house is open daily.

Sightseeing by boat

To enjoy the sweep of Sydney and better appreciate its marine setting, you should take a ride on one of the ferryboats leaving from Circular Quay. The city's ferries sail at frequent intervals daily until 11 P.M. Some of their routes are as scenic for sightseeing as they are efficient for commuting.

During weekday commute hours, the ferries are a favorite haunt of local girl-watchers, who claim their young women sport the most abbreviated outfits found anywhere. In the afternoon, legions of schoolboys wearing short flannel pants and caps with sewn-on insignia head for playing fields and home. On weekends, families and outing groups board the ferries for regularly scheduled public excursions.

To sustain you on a harbor outing, visit one of the shops on the Circular Quay selling Sydney meat pies. You can also select an apple, pear, or other fresh fruit, cored, crushed, and served in a glass.

Short ferry trips. Three ferry lines leave from Number 6 Jetty. The shortest ride goes to Kirribilli and gives you a panorama of city skyline, Opera House, Harbour Bridge, and Luna Park—all on a round trip taking only 20 minutes.

Another ferry stops at Lavender Bay, across the harbor from Circular Quay, and then goes to McMahon's Point and Luna Park, a waterside amusement area with all the familiar attractions, including a merry-go-round, dodgems, and a ghost train. Families with young children make this outing on weekend afternoons. The amusement park is open evenings, and the nighttime view of Sydney is spectacular.

A third ferry leaves Number 6 Jetty for Rose Bay (runs only Monday through Friday).

From Number 5 Jetty, ferries leave for Taronga Zoological Park and Hunter's Hill. At the zoo you can see such Australian natives as the koala, kangaroo, and emu, along with performing seals and dolphins and a host of other creatures (see page 41).

The ferry to Hunter's Hill takes you under the Sydney Harbour Bridge (an impressive view) and makes stops at Darling Street Wharf, Balmain, Long Nose Point Wharf, Parramatta Wharf, and Valentia Street at Hunter's Hill.

From Number 4 Jetty one ferry goes to Kirribilli and on to Neutral Bay. Another crosses the harbor to Cremorne Point, with stops at Musgrave Street and Mosman, returning by way of Old Cremorne. On this trip you have spectacular views of the Opera House, the bridge, and the eastern suburbs of Kings Cross, Double Bay, and Watson's Bay. Cremorne Point is a residential area, but along the shore a natural green belt provides a parklike setting with splendid viewpoints; take along a picnic lunch and make it a delightful day's excursion.

The longest regular ferryboat run is the trip from Number 3 Jetty to Manly, covering 7 miles in 35 minutes. You can also get to Manly by hydrofoil from Number 2 Jetty; it takes only 14 minutes.

Harbor cruises. A 2½-hour Sydney Harbour scenic cruise leaves Circular Quay on Wednesdays, Saturdays, Sundays, and public holidays at 2:30 P.M. You sail along the southern shores of Port Jackson, then cross between Sydney Heads—the headlands at the entrance to the port—before cruising up Middle Harbour and returning to Circular Quay by way of the north shores of the main harbor; a commentator points out places of interest along the route. Another scenic cruise, operating on Sundays and holidays, covers Upper Harbour, Lane Cove and the estuary of the Parramatta River in 2 hours.

Other cruise possibilities: a 2½-hour excursion aboard the 112-foot *Captain Cook*, departing from Number 6 Jetty at Circular Quay and passing many of the places mentioned above. It makes a daily run plus a daily 1½-hour luncheon cruise. There are sev-

WEEKEND BATHERS (left) have plenty of room on Palm Beach, north of Sydney. Ferries cruise from Bobbin Head (below) to Palm Beach along the rugged coast or up the Hawkesbury River. Teenager's damp hair and big grin (bottom) indicate he thinks the water's great.

eral other vessels that also offer luncheon cruises.

Perhaps the sportiest of harbor cruises are those aboard the *Bacchus D*, a 50-foot ocean sailing vessel available for charter out of Doyle's Marina on Rose Bay. Designed by Alan Payne, who designed Australia's *Gretel* for the America's Cup races, the boat is seaworthy and fast—with five Sydney-Hobart races to her credit. On a cruise you can swim, sun on the deck, enjoy a barbecue lunch on an island, and partake of drinks from an open bar. The boat can also be chartered for an evening cocktail cruise.

Other vessels, ranging in size from 30-passenger yachts to 140-passenger vessels, are available for day or evening charter by large groups.

SYDNEY'S GOLDEN BEACHES

Sydneysiders claim they have more golden beaches than any of the Pacific islands, and it's true. Within Sydney's city limits are 34 magnificent beaches, most within easy reach of downtown. Many of Sydney's citizens can be found on them most any summer weekend or holiday.

Getting to the beach is easy: for about A$5 you can take the fast hydrofoil trip to Manly Beach, travel by taxi to Dee Why or Freshwater beaches north of Sydney, or go to one of the southern beaches—Bondi,

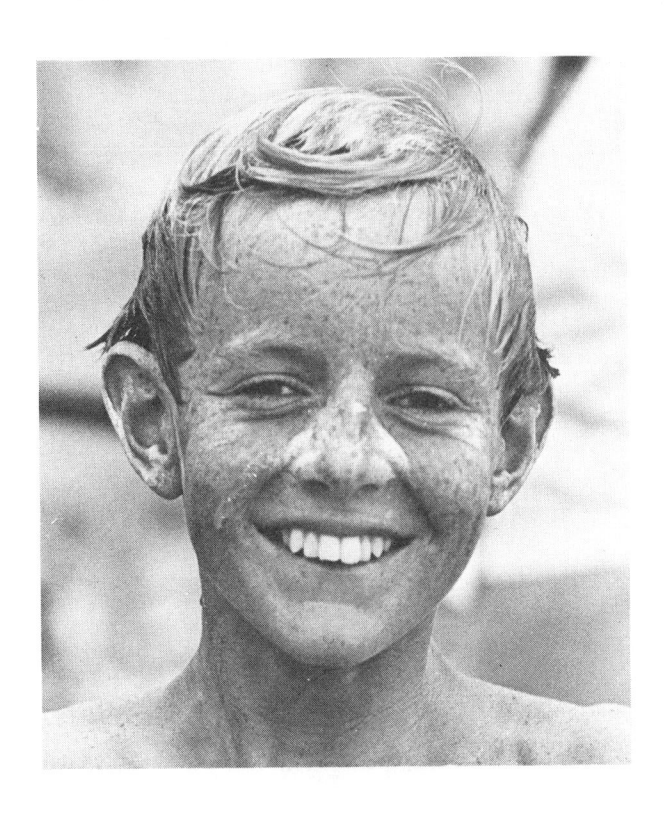

SYDNEY 43

ROYAL RANDWICK, one of six racetracks in Sydney, holds "meetings" twice weekly throughout spring, fall. At many Australian tracks, racing continues year-round.

Coogee, Maroubra (for A$3) or Cronulla (for A$8). Local buses also provide frequent service from downtown points to the beach world.

Inside the harbor

Within Sydney Harbour, a string of beaches stretches along the southern shore from Rushcutter's Bay east to Watson's Bay: Seven Shillings at Double Bay, Rose Bay, Milk Beach at Nielsen Park, and two good ones at Watson's Bay—Gibson's and Kutti. One of the best seafood places near the shore is Doyles Seafood Restaurant on the Rose Bay Pier (not licensed to sell liquor, but you can bring your own wine or beer).

Along the harbor's northern shores, the well-known beaches are Balmoral, Edwards, Chinaman's, Clontarf, and the magnificent beaches in the Manly area. Chinaman's Beach, edged by gum trees and bush, is one of the few relatively uncrowded beaches. Clontarf Beach, with barbecue facilities and an ample supply of wood, is popular for family picnics.

Ocean beaches, north and south

Most of Manly's resort section lies along the quarter-mile strip of land fronting the open ocean on one side and the harbor on the other. Connecting the two beach areas is the Corso, a wide avenue with an island of trees in the main shopping center. If you want to see some of the Aboriginal rock carvings in the Manly area, ask the Town Clerk for directions.

In addition to Manly's four ocean beaches and six harbor beaches, this sports-oriented village has bowling clubs, tennis courts, golf courses, squash centers, a rifle club, several sailing clubs, a women's croquet club, ocean and harbor swimming pools, ten-pin bowling, and fishing. Beyond Manly, the beach world stretches another 25 miles north to Palm Beach. One of the beaches is the surfers' favorite, Collaroy.

Along the coast below Sydney, beaches stretch for about 20 miles, beginning with the famous Bondi and including popular Bronte, Clovelly, Coogee, Maroubra, Malabar, Cronulla, Marley, and Wattamolla, the latter two in Royal National Park.

A word about sharks

Sharks are an overstated danger in Australian waters, but most of the beaches have been equipped with nets to keep the sharks offshore. The harbor, naturally, is not shark-proof—so it isn't wise to dive off a boat into harbor waters. On most beaches, bells have been installed to warn when a shark has been spotted by the aerial shark patrol. Obviously, when the bell rings, you get out of the water.

One other menace in Sydney's waters is the Portuguese man-o'war, appearing in armada strength in the ocean, estuary waters, and beaches throughout the area every summer. Their sting is poisonous—itchy and painful, but easily remedied.

Other sports

In Sydney you can sample the full variety of Australian sports, whether you watch or participate:

Golf. For the golfer, public courses are available, and some championship private club courses open their doors to visitors, among them, the New South Wales Golf Club and The Lakes Golf Club. Guests are admitted with home club membership cards or a letter from the club secretary.

Tennis. Some public courts and many private tennis clubs are available to tennis players. You can contact the two tennis associations—New South Wales Lawn Tennis Association and the New South Wales Hardcourt Tennis Association—for information on places to play and for dates of matches scheduled during your visit.

Boating and fishing. You can charter boats for sightseeing, cruising, or fishing. A number of good boatsheds can be found on the Harbour, Cowan Creek, Hawkesbury and George's rivers, and at Port Hacking. For details on cruising on the Hawkesbury, see page 50. Sports stores can provide tackle.

Horseback riding. From sunrise to sunset, horseback riders exercise in Centennial Park. Horses (and instruction, if desired) are available at a number of riding stables listed in the telephone directory.

For spectator sports:

In this sports-minded country, you also have a wide choice of spectator sports:

Racing. Sydney boasts six race tracks, with Randwick being the principal one (only A$1.40 for the cab ride from the heart of town). Randwick's big meets are held in the spring and fall, but meets are scheduled throughout the year at Canterbury, Rosehill, and Warwick Farm, which are farther from the city center. Trotting meetings and dog racing are scheduled at night under the lights at Harold Park, a race course just a mile from the city.

Swim meets. North Sydney Olympic Pool is a likely place to catch championship swim meets.

Cricket. On Saturday mornings beginning at 11 A.M. during the cricket season (September to March), you can watch cricket at Sydney Cricket Ground. Check the newspapers for cricket international test matches.

Football. Four codes of football (Australian national code, two rugby codes, and soccer) are played during the winter months (April to September), and are well worth watching. The Sydney newspapers have match details in the sports pages.

Sailboat races. Sailboats crowd Sydney Harbour most spring and summer weekends and turn out in full force for the annual Sydney Anniversary Day Regatta and for the start of the big Sydney-Hobart Yacht Race. You can watch the harbor races from a ferry following the boats. Every Saturday when races are held, the spectators' ferry leaves at 2:55 P.M., either from Circular Quay or High Street Wharf, Neutral Bay.

SUMMER IN SYDNEY IS SURF CARNIVAL TIME

The scene is unique to Australia: several groups of bronzed lifeguards in distinctive swim suits and headgear, marching with military precision along the beach. At the head of each column, a member carries the club pennant. They come to a stop and stand at parade rest. Then the action begins; the lifeguards launch surf boats into almost insurmountable waves, stage demonstration rescues of swimmers in distress, and compete in swimming and boat races.

It's a surf carnival, and the participants are volunteer members of surf lifesaving clubs. You'll find one or more such carnivals on the beaches of Sydney almost every weekend from December to March, and less frequently during the summer on other beaches in New South Wales, Queensland, Victoria, and South and Western Australia.

The first surf lifesaving club was originated at Bondi Beach in Sydney in 1907 (with the motto, "Vigilance and Service") to help save swimmers who tired in the rough surf or were caught in the undertow or riptide. Today, their numbers have increased to 160 affiliated clubs with more than 25,000 members. And their record of rescues is amazing—more than 7,000 yearly.

Surf rescues are carried out by three methods: by belt and reel, by boat, and by surfboard. Belt and reel rescue squads are seven-man teams. One member, wearing a belt and trailing a light line attached to a large reel on shore, swims out to a swimmer in trouble. While he holds up the swimmer, the reel men bring them both back to the beach. In a surf carnival, competing teams are judged on precision and speed and on their skill at artificial respiration.

Surf boat squads are five-man teams (four rowers and a helmsman). Boats are used when the surf is too rough for a lifeguard or when the swimmer is too far offshore. The five life-jacketed members launch their boats into the crashing surf, row through the breakers (see cover), and out to the swimmer in distress. The most thrilling event for spectators at a surf carnival occurs when these surf boat teams row out through the breakers, round a buoy, and race back to the beach.

SURF CARNIVALS, held on weekends throughout the summer, begin with the March Past.

SYDNEY 45

CAMPING SITE at Minnie Waters (above) overlooks north coast of New South Wales. Surveyor General Inn (right) in Berrima is Australia's oldest licensed inn. Katoomba Falls (far right) cascade over cliff in Blue Mountains.

SYDNEY SIDE TRIPS—to beaches, mountains, rivers, history

For most visitors to Australia, Sydney is the base for excursions to other regions of the country. Some travelers even use Sydney as a center for day trips to Canberra or Melbourne, though both cities deserve more time.

In the immediate Sydney area, however, many enjoyable side trips await you: the beach world, rural farm areas, relics of early settlements, mountains and river excursions, coastal trips, fishing and surfing.

WEST TO THE BLUE MOUNTAINS

A favorite holiday destination is the Blue Mountains, a segment of the Great Dividing Range beginning about 40 miles west of downtown Sydney. Accessible by automobile, tour bus, or electric train, this popular resort area enjoys abundant facilities for enjoying the outdoors. You can golf, swim, play tennis, go horseback riding, rock climbing, or hiking—or you can just relax and enjoy the scenery. Though not mountains of snow-capped grandeur (the highest parts are at 3,500 foot elevation), the Blue Mountains do provide accessible holiday destinations near Sydney.

The Katoomba resort area

A fast electric railway connects Katoomba and Leura with Sydney, and the two towns have become attractive to city commuters as well as to vacationers.

From Katoomba, center of the resort area, you can visit Echo Point Lookout, with its superb view of 2,000-foot-deep Jamieson Valley canyon and the massive weathered sandstone formation called the Three Sisters. Also at Echo Point is the Giants' Stairway; cut from rock, it descends nearly vertical cliffs for a thousand feet. Lookouts and rest spots along the way allow you to make the return climb in easy stages.

Other spectacular features of the Blue Mountains are Katoomba and Leura falls; Cliff Drive, taking in

SIDE TRIPS OUT OF SYDNEY 47

EXPERIMENT FARM COTTAGE (above) is one of Parramatta's historic buildings; colonial in design, the house contains an exhibit of early Australian farming tools. Extensive limestone formations (right) of Jenolan Caves highlight a popular day trip from Sydney.

a number of views and special features; and the Zig Zag Railway. The latter, a steam railway, winds down from the mountains near Lithgow.

For aerial views, the Skyway spans the valley—a distance of 1,500 feet—from a station on a spur opposite Echo Point. From your cable car you travel a thousand feet above the valley's bushland, with views of cascading waterfalls and vertical cliff faces.

Jenolan Caves

Scenic highlight of the Blue Mountains is Jenolan Caves, 48 miles southwest of Katoomba. Famous for their stalagmites, stalactites, pillars, canopies, and other formations, these limestone caves are the most spectacular and extensive formations of their type in Australia. The caves were first discovered in 1838, when a stockman tracked a bushranger (outlaw) to his hideout.

Only eight of the caves have been developed with lighting, pathways, and stairs for easy exploration. The caves are open daily with nine tours scheduled, the earliest at 10:00 A.M., the latest at 8:00 P.M. Photography is restricted to the 11:00 A.M. and 4:00 P.M. trips each day.

Part of the attraction of the Jenolan Caves is their location: in a 6,000-acre wildlife sanctuary where wallabies and possums scramble about. Along the well-graded trails outside the caverns, many birds can be spotted—among them bright-plumaged rosella parrots, satin bowerbirds, Blue Mountain parakeets, kookaburras, and cockatoos. In summer the reserve gains added color as masses of wildflowers bloom.

One-day trips to the caves are popular; however, if you wish to extend your visit, you can stay overnight at Jenolan Caves House, a comfortable hotel operated by the New South Wales Department of Tourism.

Trains leave Sydney's Central Station daily, except Tuesdays and Thursdays, for the 2½-hour trip across the Blue Mountains to Mount Victoria, where passengers board a coach. On the five-mile descent to Jenolan, you pass willow-lined Blue Lake and a natural tunnel named the Grand Arch. You have time to explore the caves and the wildlife sanctuary before returning to Sydney along the same route.

Three historic towns

If you drive to the Blue Mountains, you can add an interesting bonus to your trip by including a trio of historic old towns: Parramatta, about 15 miles west of downtown Sydney, and the sister towns of Windsor and Richmond, 13 and 18 miles northwest of Par-

48 SIDE TRIPS OUT OF SYDNEY

ramatta. Among Australia's earliest settlements, they contain historic buildings dating back to the late 18th and early 19th centuries. Most of the buildings are open to visitors.

Parramatta, at the time it was settled in 1788, was Australia's second permanent settlement, and it was considered by thriving young Sydney to be way out in the country. In the intervening years, it became a fashionable residential area; but in recent years, industry has crept in, and the town has lost its perimeters to the sprawl of metropolitan Sydney.

Parramatta's historic sites include three 18th century buildings. Old Government House (1799), now completely restored, was the country residence of Australia's early governors; its portico is generally thought to have been designed by convict-architect Francis Greenway.

Elizabeth Farm House (1793), Australia's oldest surviving dwelling, was built by John Macarthur, a pioneer of the wool industry.

Experiment Farm Cottage (1798) marks the site of Sydney's first wheat farm, with a museum of early farming tools; colonial in design, it has a particularly attractive doorway graced by an elliptical fanlight.

Other interesting buildings are Roseneath Cottage (1837), built by Janet Templeton, one of the first to import the Saxon-merino sheep, backbone of Australia's present-day wool industry; St. John's Church, built in 1815, with twin towers similar to the tower of a church in Kent, England; Lancer Barracks, used as a men's barracks in the early 19th century and now a military museum; and Harnbledon Cottage, built in 1805, surrounded by oaks and pines and a huge cork tree, the latter planted to celebrate the victory at Waterloo.

Windsor is famous for the buildings that convict-architect Greenway designed: Windsor's Georgian-style St. Matthew's Anglican Church (1820) and the Court House (1822). Faithfully restored in 1965, the church is considered by some to be the most beautiful building in the country, and its cemetery has headstones dating back to 1810. The Court House, also carefully restored, is constructed of sandstock bricks, its design preserved, its detail a fine example of early-day craftsmanship.

Other interesting Windsor buildings include the following: Toll House (1814 or 1816), used for the collection of tolls on the Fitzroy Bridge until 1887, now restored and fitted with period furnishings; Hawkesbury Museum, on Thompson Square, housing early 19th century furnishings and farm equipment in a well preserved colonial brick building, built on the site of an old general store; Tebbutt's Observatory (1863), built for the 19th century astronomer, John Tebbutt, discoverer of the Tebbutt Comet; and Doctor's Terrace (1830), the town post office in the 1850s.

Richmond's historic buildings include Hobartville (1828), another Greenway-designed residence; its "bushranger-proof" doors and barred cellars say something about pioneer security measures. Other buildings include Toxana House (1860), now a historical museum; St. Peter's Anglican Church (1837-1841), with a graveyard where many of the area's pioneers rest; and Woolpack Inn (1830s), which provided lodging for early-day travelers.

Gold rush region

Farther west you enter the region known as Australia's "Golden West," first populated more than 100 years ago by pioneers and bushrangers and the scene of the country's early gold rush.

A good loop trip in the area begins at Bathurst, 130 miles west of Sydney and links Carcoar, Orange, Ophir, Millthorpe, Wellington, Gulgong, Hill End, and Sofala.

Bathurst, Australia's oldest inland city (1815), is a sedate settlement of red brick and blue granite; it has preserved many mining relics and historic buildings. Carcoar's principal architectural gem is its charming old railway station. Elsewhere along the route, you will find local historical museums, a working gold dredge (near Wellington), old churches and hotels, quaint pubs, and a rural countryside of alfalfa and wheat fields, pasture land, grazing sheep and cattle.

TO THE NORTH

Visitors to Sydney can make the city their departure point for short side trips north along the coast or for exploring inland regions of New South Wales.

HISTORIC St. Matthew's Anglican Church in Windsor was designed by convict-architect Francis Greenway. The Georgian-style church was built in 1820.

SHOPPING FOR A PICNIC is easy. From roadside stands north of Sydney you can select cooked prawns and Sydney rock oysters fresh from Australian waters.

AT BOBBIN HEAD boat harbor, charter boats can be rented for leisurely cruising and exploring on the Hawkesbury River and adjacent waterways. One-day excursions are also available.

The Hawkesbury River

The wide and winding Hawkesbury River empties into Broken Bay 20 miles north of Sydney, after coursing more than 170 miles through the Australian bushlands from the northwest.

Dense brush covers the precipitous cliffs edging the river along much of its lower reaches; the cliffs are broken occasionally by the indentation of valleys or the cascade of small waterfalls. Palms, ferns, and gum trees grow along its banks. Waterfowl follow its course, and the raucous laughter of the kookaburra (bird) can be heard from the woods along the way. In the Broken Bay estuary, towering headlands rise above the river waters.

When Sydney was young, the river's course cut through rich alluvial lands in a major wheat-growing area. The river became the region's principal waterway. Produce was transported downriver, then across Broken Bay, and south along the coast to Sydney. For many years—beginning in the late 19th century—paddlewheel steamers plied the river on regular runs.

Today, fruit orchards, market gardens, and farms cover the lands bordering the river, while the Hawkesbury itself is popular for water-oriented recreation. Residents and visitors can explore the river by boat.

One day tours. Several short excursions allow Sydney visitors to experience the Hawkesbury's special pleasures.

One tour travels by coach from Sydney to Palm Beach, where passengers board a launch for a 1½-hour cruise up the river's lower reaches.

Another tour heads westward by coach, through historic Parramatta (second oldest settlement on the Australian continent), then north via the Koala Sanctuary at Pennant Hills. It loops to the north through Berowra Waters and then to the southeast, traversing part of the Ku-ring-gai Chase National Park to Bobbin Head. Here passengers board a launch for a 25-mile cruise down Cowan Creek into the lower Hawkesbury and out through Broken Bay to Palm Beach; they return to Sydney by coach, via Narrabeen Lakes.

Leisurely cruising. If you have several days to cruise on the Hawkesbury, you can rent a boat and explore on your own. You set your own course, fishing for your dinner, collecting oysters off the rocks in the river's lower reaches, or stopping at some of the historic old river towns.

At Ebenezer you can visit the Presbyterian Church, completed in 1809, the oldest church in use by an Australian congregation. A short distance upriver from Ebenezer, Windsor is one of Australia's oldest settlements (see page 49). Some 20 historic buildings, now restored, have been assembled at Wilberforce in the Australiana Folk Village. Also on display is a working ferry, raised from the river, and a model of the first train to run from Sydney to the Hawkesbury Valley.

Cruisers can be rented at Halvorsen Boats at Bob-

50 SIDE TRIPS OUT OF SYDNEY

bin Head, where you'll find a selection of 25 to 36-foot cruisers available at rates ranging from A$235 to A$460 per week, depending on the size and season (highest over the Christmas/New Year holidays). Boats sleep 4 to 9 persons, have hot and cold running water, gas stoves, ice boxes, flush toilets, and showers. No boating license is needed.

You'll find plenty of overnight anchorages and small refueling/restocking stops along the way.

Reservations should be made ahead during the peak period (from the Christmas holidays through April or May).

Ku-ring-gai Chase National Park

Fifteen miles north of Sydney, Ku-ring-gai Chase National Park is a vast bushland reserve, largely comprised of sandstone plateaus, rich in native plants and wildlife. You'll probably see koalas here, and if you

---

VISITING A SHEEP STATION: A DAY IN DUBBO

If you're willing to make an early start—well before sun-up—you can sample Australia's famous "outback" in a day trip from Sydney by plane.

Here's a typical junket: you arrive at Sydney's Kingsford Smith Airport before 6 A.M. Once airborne, you get a brief but memorable overview of the harbor, and an hour later you land at Dubbo, about 250 miles northwest of Sydney. Met by your tour guide, you are driven to the downtown Amaroo Hotel for a ranch-size breakfast. Then you're off for a tour of Dubbo (an Aboriginal word meaning red earth). You examine the artifacts in the town museum, stroll through Victoria Park and the Civic Centre, learn the history of the other town buildings.

Beyond Dubbo you head out into the vast open reaches, past gum trees, wheat fields, the red earth. This is the Macquarie Valley, a rich farming area. You stop to watch a sheep and lamb auction—all pandemonium, with auctioneer, hundreds of animals, scores of bidders and spectators.

Next you turn off on a country road that leads to a homestead—and in September and October, its front yard will be bursting with a glorious profusion of roses, delphiniums, and gloxinia. You go in to visit your "family," a household on the Dubbo list volunteering to meet visiting travelers. It's time for morning tea, served with scones and other fresh-baked delicacies, and you can't leave until you've been shown around the station—wheat fields, lush fields of alfalfa, and a great flock of sheep that the dogs muster efficiently.

By lunchtime you're out in the bush, sitting in the shade of gray gum trees, listening to the sizzle of steaks being barbecued over an open fire. For background music someone plays "Waltzing Matilda" on a record player, or an Aborigine sounds a tune with a eucalyptus leaf held between his lips.

Then more sightseeing: to another sheep station to watch the station crew shearing sheep, grading and packing the wool; a visit to Dubbo's zoo to see and feed the kangaroos, to look at the emus and a dozen different kinds of reptiles.

At the end of the afternoon, it's time to visit Dubbo's club—one of many similar ones throughout Australia—where members (and almost everyone in town belongs) may drink, gamble at slot machines, swim in the Olympic-sized pool, or attend any number of functions held throughout the year.

Then it's back to the Amaroo Hotel for another meal large enough for a ranch-hand. By 8 P.M. your Sydney-bound plane lifts off the ground. It's a long day and a busy one, and it leaves you with the feeling that you have had a quick look at part of the real Australia.

A similar tour goes to Cowra, a 55-minute flight from Sydney. This day trip also includes a visit to a sheep station and other features like those at Dubbo but leaves Sydney at a more civilized 10 A.M., returning at 9:45 P.M.

Coach tours leave Sydney to visit sheep properties near the towns of Mittagong, Bowral, and Moss Vale, all southwest of Sydney.

SHEEP RANCH activity and a steak barbecue highlight a day in the "outback."

SIDE TRIPS OUT OF SYDNEY 51

visit the Chase between July and November, abundant wildflowers will be in bloom. Most tours to the park stop at the Wildflower and Wildlife Reserve.

Like other Australian National Parks, Ku-ring-gai Chase is less developed than national parks in the United States. Park facilities include open fireplaces and barbecue areas; for a camping permit, apply to the Superintendent (telephone 919-4036). In the Chase you can go swimming, fishing, bush walking (hiking), and boating. Boats may be rented at Bobbin Head, Brooklyn, and Terrey Hills. On the plateaus, you'll see Aboriginal carvings on the larger outcroppings.

To reach the park from Sydney, take the Pacific Highway (Route 1) northwest to Turramurra and turn right onto Bobbin Head Road. A longer route leads to the eastern part of the park, following the coastal route out of Sydney, along Military, Manly, and Sydney roads, then Pittwater Road merges into McCarrs Creek Road near the park's eastern boundary.

Old Sydney Town

About 45 miles north of Sydney (and easily combined with a visit to Ku-Ring-Gai Chase) is Old Sydney Town, a re-creation of Sydney Cove as it appeared in the time of Governor Bligh at the beginning of the 19th century.

Built on a hilly, lightly wooded site, the 250-acre park slopes down to a large body of water. Building is continuous, giving you a chance to see the evolution of the township as it existed around 1810. The unpaved roads and paths are dotted with tents, tiny convict-gang huts, a bonded store, and houses of the free settlers and emancipists.

Stone has been used to recreate the Government Windmill and St. Phillip's Church. The original church was begun in 1798, consecrated in 1810, and demolished in 1856. The new windmill and church have been built using the same materials and the same methods of construction used originally.

In the body of water that fronts the township, the brig *Perseverance* is tied up beside Hospital Wharf and the *Lady Nelson* lies in the dockyard being outfitted.

All of the personnel of Old Sydney Town wear the costume of the period. Craftsmen may be seen at work—blacksmiths, coopers, wheelwrights, candle makers and tinsmiths. You get around on foot or hop aboard horse drawn vehicles or bullock drays that circulate around town. Open daily from 10 A.M. to 5 P.M.

New England and the North Coast

The coastal belt from Sydney north is bounded on the east by beaches, rocky cliffs, and shallow marshlands and on the west by a narrow shelf of land rising rather abruptly into the Great Dividing Range, a series of ranges and plateaus stretching north and south for more than 400 miles, with numerous peaks more than 5,000 feet high.

Fast, clear streams with cascades and waterfalls crease the slopes, wind down through heavy forests, and indent the coastline. From the range's higher altitudes, you can look over vast rain forests, broad rivers, and cultivated valleys.

Train ride to Newcastle. The industrial city of Newcastle, a hundred miles north of Sydney, might not qualify as a destination except for the train ride to get there. Leaving Sydney's Central Railway Station, your route traverses the lovely lands of the Hawkesbury River and cuts through Brisbane Water National Park with its great sandstone cliffs (and in November-December, the brilliant flowering of waratah and Christmas bells).

You have time for lunch, followed by a two-hour tour of the huge steel-making complex of the Broken Hill Proprietary Company. The return train to Sydney pulls out of the Newcastle station at 4:45 P.M.

Lake Macquarie. About 90 miles north of Sydney is a pleasant seaboard lake with more than a hundred miles of shoreline. Popular for swimming, waterskiing, surfing on the ocean, and fishing in both lake and ocean, it is well-equipped for visitors with good motels, a guest house, camp grounds, and a caravan park. A golf course, tennis courts, and lawn bowling greens complete the recreational facilities.

Guided boat trips around the lake leave the main jetty in Belmont and make stops at various points around the lake, including the Wangi-Wangi wildlife area.

Hunter Valley. At Newcastle the Hunter River empties into the Pacific. Winding west and north from that point, the river stretches nearly 300 miles into the Great Dividing Range. For much of the way, it flows through narrow valleys with precipitous walls; but in its lower reaches it broadens out onto a rich alluvial plain. Hiking and trout fishing are the attractions in the upper reaches.

The road from Newcastle, the New England Highway, follows the river as far as Singleton. Along this route, you drive past dairy farms, vegetable and fruit farms, sheep and cattle lands. Off the road near Pokolbin and Cessnock are vineyards producing some of Australia's finest table wines; the wineries are open to visitors daily. This area is also one of the richest coal producing centers in Australia (which obviously led to the naming of Newcastle).

The North Coast. A chain of quiet resorts with fine beaches and good fishing dots the coast north of Newcastle. At Port Macquarie, 267 miles north of Sydney, seascapes and beaches are the principal attractions. You can drive or walk along Pacific Drive, with its cliffs, headlands, and pocket beaches. Sea Acres, a 77-acre sanctuary for flora and fauna located between Pacific Drive and Shelly Beach, has been preserved as one of the few surviving corners of true primeval rain forest on the New South Wales coast.

Banana plantations surround Coff's Harbour, a holiday center for fishing, skin diving, and spear fishing. Seven miles northwest is Bruxner Park Flora Reserve, a tropical jungle of vines, ferns, and orchids (blooming in September); bird watching is good here, too. Kangaroos, emus, and other Australian animals and birds may be seen at Kumbaingeri Wildlife Sanctuary, 10 miles north of Coff's Harbour.

New England. The northern stretches of the Great Dividing Range become a great tableland, a 9,000 square mile plateau known as New England. These highlands mix rich farmlands with cattle and sheep holdings, all of it centered on Armidale, 352 miles north of Sydney. A town of 20,000, Armidale is the location of the University of New England, Armidale Teacher's College, a technical college, and several secondary schools. The local Art Gallery, with an excellent provincial collection, and the Folk Museum, containing relics of pioneer days, are both worth seeing. A half dozen motels and a good caravan park (which also has some new housekeeping cabins) provide comfortable accommodations.

The best way to reach Armidale is by air. The train, though air-conditioned and pleasant, is slow (about 9 hours to make the 350 miles). The New England Highway traversing the plateau is a well-maintained, two-lane road that slows you down through every town on the way, requiring 7 to 8 hours for the trip.

Gem fossicking—for topaz, diamonds, and

SIDE TRIPS from Sydney can include winery tours near Cessnook (above) in the Hunter Valley or relaxing at Shelley Beach (top right) on North Coast. Accommodations range from modern motor inns to old timers like the ornate Hotel Toronto (right).

SIDE TRIPS OUT OF SYDNEY   53

BARBECUED STEAKS provide an aroma-filled climax to a tour of the Madorama Sheep Stud Ranch near Berrima; coach excursions visit the ranch on day trips.

sapphires—is good in the vicinity of Glen Innes and Tenterfield at the northern end of the plateau. Some dredging has taken place in the area; rockhounds will find the best hunting grounds along stream beds.

New England National Park. Fifty miles east of Armidale, New England National Park is similar topographically to the Blue Mountains but is far less crowded and relatively undeveloped. Extensive trails wind through various zones of vegetation along the scarp of the tablelands. Visitors either camp or stay in one of the two cabins in the park or in the new little motel in nearby Ebor.

Some of the best scenery is found along the eastern escarpment, where the tablelands suddenly drop off to the lush, subtropical coast. If you go eastward through the park and the little town of Dorrigo, you will come across Dorrigo State Park—a lovely, rolling, pastoral plateau where you can picnic and take a nature walk through subtropical rain forests with giant trees, ferns, and overhanging vines to waterfalls and superb view points.

SOUTH TO ILLAWARRA

South of Sydney, Princes Highway (Route 1) winds along the coast through the industrial cities of Wollongong and Port Kembla and into the Illawarra, an area of uncrowded surfing and swimming beaches and miles of rich farm and dairy lands. Here resort towns mix with fishing villages; open pasturelands alternate with river valleys and cedar forests. The highway eventually rounds the southeast corner of the continent and heads westward to Melbourne.

Paved and well-maintained, the road is two-lane most of the way, though it becomes narrow and winding south of Kiama. The Sydney-to-Melbourne distance shows as 557 miles on the mileage charts, but it seems like many more miles because of the narrow roads, the many towns, and the sights to see.

Day trips out of Sydney show off the panorama of the coast, with stops in the Royal National Park, Wollongong, Port Kembla, Lake Illawarra, Kiama, and Kangaroo Valley.

Royal National Park

Only 20 miles south of Sydney, the Royal National Park is 36,800 acres of bushland with scenic drives, walks, and beaches. Popular with Sydney residents on weekends and holidays, the park lies between the Princes Highway and the ocean.

Scenic drives meander through the park, reached on turnoffs at Loftus, Waterfall, and Helensburgh. Park facilities are not highly developed, but you will find sites for camping and picnicking. Surfing beaches line the park's ocean edge.

The Illawarra Coast

South of the Royal National Park, the highway bends toward the coast. At Sublime Point, 1,200 feet above the sea, you get a sweeping view southward along the Illawarra coast as far as Kiama. You'll find another good view point just south of Sublime Point: the top of Bulli Pass.

In the waters off this stretch of coast, half of Australia's 74-million-ton fish catch is taken. Salmon fishermen congregate here, and you'll see their net dinghies and power boats anchored offshore and in the little ports along the way.

The coast road. The Princes Highway runs inland south of Wollongong; but if you take the coastside road south, you hug the ocean through Port Kemba and get to see Lake Illawarra and Shellharbour. The port is another industrial center, but Lake Illawarra is a 16-square-mile body of water used by water-skiers, fishermen, and swimmers.

The road runs between ocean and lake for several miles, then turns inland to follow the lake shore. The little fishing port of Shellharbour, just south of the lake, is a quiet, pleasant, seaside resort with a motel, caravan park, and campgrounds.

Kiama. Lighthouse buffs will be interested in the lighthouse in Kiama, built in 1886 and still in operation. At the foot of the lighthouse, a blowhole funnels

54   SIDE TRIPS OUT OF SYDNEY

ILLAWARRA FIG TREE (above) dwarfs visitors at Minnamurra Falls. Surf casting (right) is a favorite early morning pastime along the coast.

a huge jet of spray a hundred feet skyward.

The town is situated on the Minnamurra River; upstream about 11 miles, the river cascades in a waterfall set among some of the area's few remaining red cedar trees. Picnickers will find barbecue pits, and trails wind through the bush and rain forest.

South of Kiama, the coast road follows a tortuous route along cliffs and beaches through the little town of Geroa at the mouth of Crooked River; along Seven Mile Beach, famous as the take-off point for Kingsford-Smith's flight across the Tasman Sea in the "Southern Cross"; past the fishing resorts of Greenwell Point, Currarong, and Jervis Bay. The latter, though one of the best natural ports in the country, has never been developed commercially.

Kangaroo Valley, about 14 miles inland from the Princes Highway, combines rain forests, grazing land, and bush into some of the most beautiful countryside in Australia. Trails for hiking and riding are well developed. Camping facilities, cottages, and cabins are available in Kangaroo Valley Village.

Nowra, on the Shoalhaven River, has become popular in recent years with vacationists from both Sydney and Canberra. The river follows a rugged course through forest-covered ranges, and the sights include waterfalls, caverns, and interesting rock formations. A sizable town with more than 10,000 population, Nowra has a good assortment of hotels, motels, cabins, caravan parks, and campgrounds.

Bateman's Bay, 172 miles south of Sydney, marks the southern extremity of the Illawarra district. The bay was first sighted by Captain Cook in 1770 and named after Captain Bateman of the ship *Northumberland.* The small village has an old-world atmosphere and offers beautiful seascapes. Famous for its oysters and crayfish (which can be bought right off the boats), the town is popular with Canberra residents. Motels, a guest house and a half-dozen caravan and camping parks provide a variety of accommodations.

At Ulladulla, 30 miles north, you can watch Italian fishermen unloading their catches. Between the two towns, you'll see mullet fishermen on the beaches using gear and methods reminiscent of those their ancestors used hundreds of years ago.

Other trips from Sydney

If you've only a day to spend in Canberra (it's worth far more time), you can board one of the numerous Sydney-to-Canberra morning flights. To see as much as possible, make arrangements in Sydney to connect with a coach tour in Canberra. Some tours include several hours of bushland driving and a visit to a sheep station. For Canberra's highlights, see page 57.

Even though the Snowy Mountains area (see page 63) is closer to Canberra, many visitors reach the area from Sydney. Daily flights go into Cooma from Sydney, as do rail, bus, and tour services.

SIDE TRIPS OUT OF SYDNEY

DESIGNED CAPITAL city, Canberra borders on Lake Burley Griffin (above); trees line many city streets. Sailboats rendezvous at one of the lake's small bays (right). Snowy Mountains are visible from Scammel's Lookout (far right).

56   CANBERRA

CANBERRA—the nation's capital, city of grand design and artistic order

Most handsome of all Australian cities, Canberra reflects the country's national pride and international appeal. It is a planned city, designed and built—and landscaped as well—for the functions of government. Its architecture and atmosphere are unique and stimulating.

To the nation, Canberra represents the Commonwealth and headquarters for international diplomats. To its 186,000 population, the capital is an important city of great natural and man-made beauty. To the visitor, Canberra's grand design and artistic order appear less like a city than as a life-size model.

Broad avenues and residential streets are lined with trees—eight million have been planted—differing in form, color, and flowering season, making Canberra an all-year garden city. More than 50 embassies, legations, and offices of high commissioners give the capital a cosmopolitan flavor. Universities, museums, libraries, and scientific research institutes foretell a city of learning and culture.

Located in a valley of the Great Dividing Range, Canberra lies 147 air miles southwest of Sydney. Melbourne is another 292 air miles to the southwest. The major city of the 939-square-mile Australian Capital Territory (A.C.T.), Canberra can also be reached easily by rail or highway from either Sydney or Melbourne, and it makes a convenient stop between these cities.

Canberra's city area covers some 50 square miles (comparable to the city of San Francisco) in a valley traversed by the Molonglo River. The site, about 1,900 feet above sea level, was originally pasture land; around it rise gently contoured hills.

A PLANNED CAPITAL CITY

The late Walter Burley Griffin, Chicago landscape architect and associate of Frank Lloyd Wright, won the 1911 international competition and prize—$3,500—to design Australia's capital city. Griffin saw

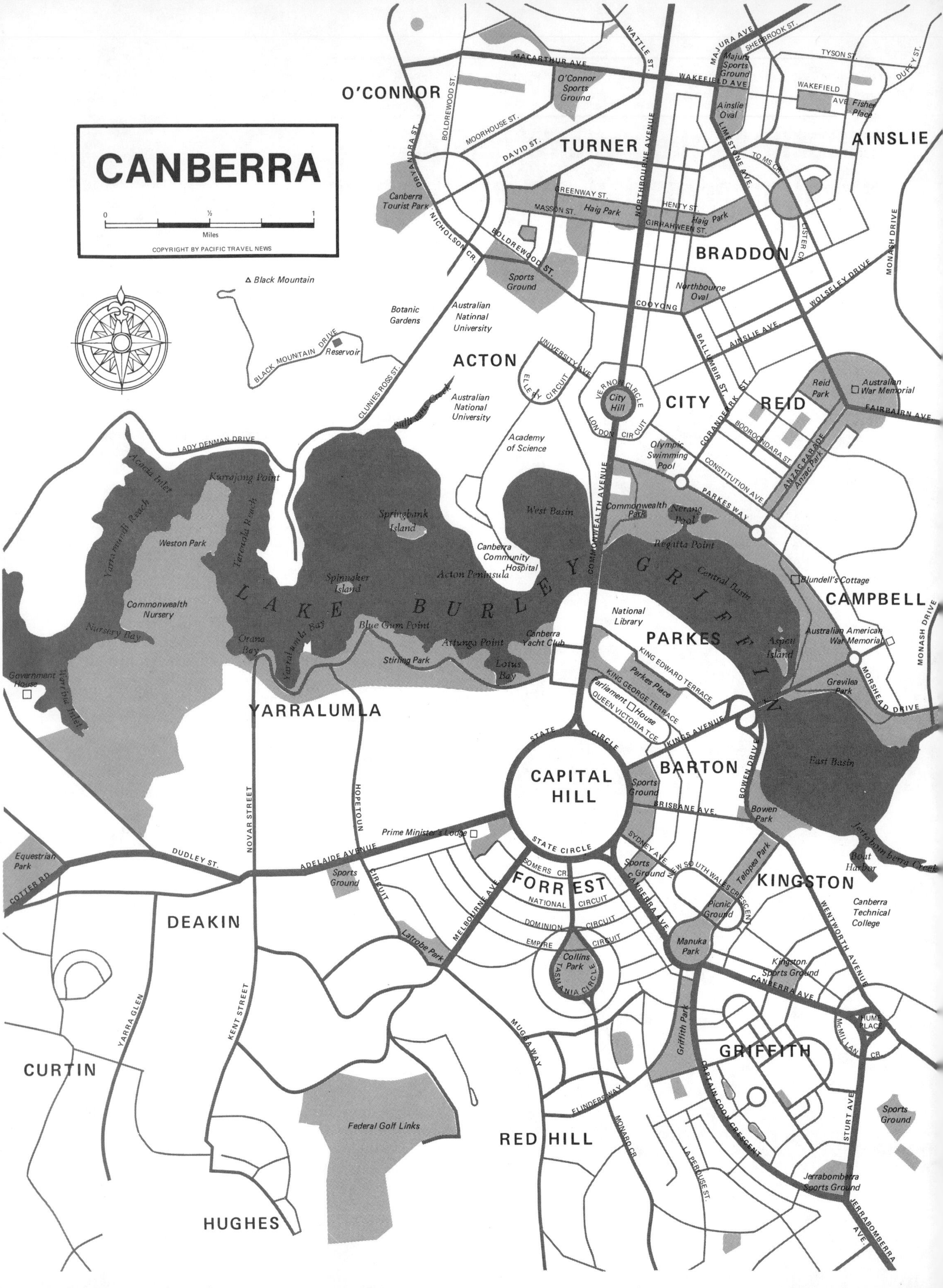

CANBERRA
0
½
1
Miles
COPYRIGHT BY PACIFIC TRAVEL NEWS
O'CONNOR
TURNER
AINSLIE
BRADDON
ACTON
CITY
REID
CAMPBELL
PARKES
BARTON
CAPITAL HILL
YARRALUMLA
FORREST
KINGSTON
DEAKIN
CURTIN
GRIFFITH
RED HILL
HUGHES
LAKE BURLEY GRIFFIN
MACARTHUR AVE.
WAKEFIELD AVE.
WATTLE ST.
MAJURA AVE
SHERBROOK ST.
TYSON ST.
DUFFY ST.
WAKEFIELD AVE.
Fisher Place
Majura Sports Ground
O'Connor Sports Ground
Ainslie Oval
BOLDREWOOD ST.
MOORHOUSE ST.
DAVID ST.
DRYANDRA ST.
NORTHBOURNE AVENUE
LIMESTONE AVE.
TOMS CR.
Canberra Tourist Park
GREENWAY ST.
MASSON ST.
Haig Park
HENTY ST.
GIRRAHWEEN ST.
NICHOLSON CR.
BOLDREWOOD ST.
LISTER CR.
MONASH DRIVE
Sports Ground
Northbourne Oval
COOYONG
WOLSELEY DRIVE
Black Mountain
Botanic Gardens
Australian National University
BLACK MOUNTAIN DRIVE
Reservoir
CLUNIES ROSS ST.
UNIVERSITY AVE.
ELLERY CIRCUIT
VERNON CIRCLE
City Hill
LONDON CIRCUIT
AINSLIE AVE.
BALLUMBIR ST.
Reid Park
Australian War Memorial
FAIRBAIRN AVE.
Sullivans Creek
Australian National University
Academy of Science
Olympic Swimming Pool
CORANDERRK ST.
BOOROONDARA ST.
ANZAC PARADE
Anzac Park
CONSTITUTION AVE.
PARKES WAY
LADY DENMAN DRIVE
Acacia Inlet
Kurrajong Point
Yarramundi Reach
Tarcoola Reach
Weston Park
Springbank Island
West Basin
COMMONWEALTH AVENUE
Commonwealth Park
Nerang Pool
Regatta Point
Canberra Community Hospital
Acton Peninsula
Spinnaker Island
Central Basin
Blundell's Cottage
Commonwealth Nursery
Nursery Bay
Blue Gum Point
National Library
Orana Bay
Yarralumla Bay
Attunga Point
Canberra Yacht Club
Aspen Island
Australian American War Memorial
Government House
Weriba Inlet
Stirling Park
Lotus Bay
KING EDWARD TERRACE
Parkes Place
KING GEORGE TERRACE
Parliament House
QUEEN VICTORIA TCE.
Grevillea Park
MORSHEAD DRIVE
STATE CIRCLE
KINGS AVENUE
East Basin
NOVAR STREET
HOPETOUN CIRCUIT
Sports Ground
BRISBANE AVE.
BOWEN DRIVE
Bowen Park
Prime Minister's Lodge
STATE CIRCLE
Jerrabomberra Creek
Boat Harbor
Equestrian Park
DUDLEY ST.
ADELAIDE AVENUE
SYDNEY AVE.
COTTER RD.
Sports Ground
SOMERS CR.
Sports Ground
NEW SOUTH WALES CRESCENT
Telopea Park
NATIONAL CIRCUIT
CANBERRA AVE.
Picnic Ground
Canberra Technical College
MELBOURNE AVE.
DOMINION CIRCUIT
EMPIRE CIRCUIT
Latrobe Park
Manuka Park
WENTWORTH AVENUE
Collins Park
TASMANIA CIRCLE
Kingston Sports Ground
CANBERRA AVE.
YARRA GLEN
KENT STREET
MUGGA WAY
HUME PLACE
McMILLAN CR.
Griffith Park
FLINDERS WAY
CAPTAIN COOK CRESCENT
STURT AVE.
Sports Ground
Federal Golf Links
MONARO CR.
LA PEROUSE ST.
Jerrabomberra Sports Ground
JERRABOMBERRA AVE.

the undeveloped bushland selected for the site as an amphitheater, in which Capital Hill, the city's focal point, together with City Hill and the Australian-American Memorial, would form a triangle. Construction of Canberra started in 1913, and it was formally declared the capital in 1927.

Concentric streets circle Capital Hill, from which boulevards radiate. The Molonglo River, flowing through the valley, has been dammed to form 7-mile-long Lake Burley Griffin, the "water axis" of the city. Capital Hill is joined to the other points of the triangle by two graceful bridges.

A dry and moderate climate

Canberra's climate is moderate, with rare temperature extremes. During a normal summer season (December, January, February), the climate ranges from warm to hot.

Average temperatures during spring and fall, the best seasons to visit, are usually pleasant—in the low 70s from September through November (spring); in the mid-70s from March to May (fall). Though rainfall is only about 23 inches annually, it's spread throughout the year.

Hotels where politicos stay

Canberra has nearly 40 hotels and motels concentrated in several districts: the downtown City Hill-Civic Centre area; surrounding Capital Hill; and north of the Civic Centre along the highway to Sydney. Nearby Queanbeyan has an additional 10 motels.

Larger and newer hotels near the city center are Noah's Lakeside International, beside Lake Burley Griffin, and the Canberra Rex, a mile north of the city center. Among the good, smaller downtown hotels and motels are the Canberra City TraveLodge, the Park Royal Motor Inn, Speros Motel, Kythera Motel, and Noah's Town House Motor Inn.

Accommodations in the Capital Hill area, several miles south of the Civic Centre, include the Wellington Hotel, Embassy Motel, and Manuka TraveLodge. Among the recommended hotels and motels in North Canberra is the Lyneham TraveLodge.

Your choice in restaurants

Although Canberra isn't noted for its night life, the city does have a number of excellent restaurants.
• The Lobby on King George Terrace, just across from Parliament House, is one of the most fashionable; many of its clientele are members of the government. The food is excellent; the decor, intimate.
• Bacchus Tavern, in the City Mutual Building on Hobart Place, serves French cuisine. Its charcoal broiled steaks are especially good, and the wine cellar is excellent.
• Maggie's in Civic Square, attractively decorated, features French cuisine.
• Noah's Town House Motor Inn features Continental cuisine combined with excellent service and an elegant decor.
• The Lotus, in the Kythera Motor Inn, is a different cup of tea—it features authentic Peking, Cantonese, Szechwan, and Shanghai dishes, superbly served.
• Neptune's Tavern, in Una Porter Center on Alinga Street, is the place to go for seafood—though they also serve steak and barbecued chicken dishes.
• The Charcoal Restaurant, at 60 London Circuit, specializes in steaks and boasts a fine wine cellar.
• Paco's Carousel Spanish Restuarant, on top of Red Hill (southwest of Capital Hill), serves Continental cuisine in a rotunda-shaped dining room with fine views of the city.

Getting around the city

Taxis operate from numerous ranks (stands) at hotels, in all of Canberra's shopping centers, and at other centers of activity. Avis and Hertz rental cars are available. In some of the major hotels, you'll find agencies where you can hire a car with a driver-guide. A public bus system serves the downtown area and suburbs, and motor coach tours are available.

SIGHTSEEING IN CANBERRA

Canberra's main thoroughfares radiate out from Capital Hill like the spokes on a giant wheel. Commonwealth, Kings, Brisbane, Canberra, Melbourne, and Adelaide are the main arteries.

The principal shopping and commercial district surrounds City Hill, about 1½ miles north of Capital Hill across Lake Burley Griffin. Commonwealth offices and many of the city's public buildings are spread east and west of the Civic Centre on both sides of the lake. The city's traffic axis is Commonwealth Avenue, which starts at Capital Hill, goes north across Lake Burley Griffin, and runs into City Hill; it continues north as Northbourne Avenue, becoming Route 23, the main highway to Sydney.

A city overview

To get the full effect of Canberra's grand design, begin your sightseeing from a viewpoint overlooking the city. Mount Ainslie (2,762 feet) is the highest point. Other peaks are Red Hill (2,368 feet), Black Mountain

(2,664 feet), and Mount Pleasant (2,175 feet).

For an all-encompassing view, take one of the half-hour flights over Canberra and the surrounding countryside; they leave the airport every half hour between 8:30 A.M. and 6 P.M. daily. (Phone for reservations.)

Another helpful stop is the Regatta Point Planning Exhibition in Commonwealth Park, which helps put Canberra's development into perspective. Located on the lake's north shore, just east of the Captain Cook Memorial Water Jet, this collection of models, pictures, and diagrams gives you a better understanding of the layout of this planned city. The exhibit is open daily from 9 A.M. to 5 P.M.

On and around the lake

Lake Burley Griffin, edged by more than a thousand acres of parkland, is not only Canberra's major natural scenic attraction but also the city's recreation center. Along its 22-mile shoreline, you can follow lakeside drives and walking paths, picnic in well-developed recreation areas, stroll across grassy open spaces, or go boating. You can take a sightseeing cruise, or see if the lake's trout are biting.

Shore development is relatively formal in the lake's central portion, between the Commonwealth Avenue and Kings Avenue bridges. Commonwealth Park, along the northeastern shore, has been landscaped to include marsh gardens and a children's play area. West Basin, just west of the Commonwealth Avenue Bridge, has a jetty where the lake cruises dock and where you can rent rowboats, canoes, and pedal boats.

At the lake's western end, near Scrivener Dam, the shoreline is more natural, with many trees, grassy banks, and wildlife. Weston Park, on a peninsula near Yarralumla Nursery, has picnic facilities.

Lake cruise. You can enjoy the city skyline and the lake breezes—and rest weary feet—while cruising on Lake Burley Griffin. The 1½-hour excursion operates daily from the Ferry Terminal on West Basin.

Water jet. A relatively recent addition to the lake scene is the Captain Cook Bicentennial Water Jet, a fountain located near Regatta Point, just east of the Commonwealth Avenue Bridge. Installed in 1970 as a memorial to mark the 200th anniversary of Captain Cook's voyages of discovery in the Australia area, the jet can send a water column more than 450 feet high.

Carillon. On the occasion of Canberra's 50th jubilee, the United Kingdom presented the city with a carillon—a 53-bell tower located on Aspen Island just west of the Kings Avenue Bridge. Housed in a graceful concrete tower, the carillon plays Australian, English, and Scottish tunes on a regular schedule each day.

Blundell's Farmhouse. History buffs will be interested in this pioneer cottage built in 1858 and still on its original site—on Wendouree Drive in Commonwealth Park. Three of its rooms have been furnished with pieces dating from the mid-1800s. The cottage is open daily from 2 to 4 P.M., and also from 10 A.M. to noon on Wednesdays.

Government House. Historic Government House, built by early-day Canberra Valley settlers as Yarralumla Homestead, is the official residence of the Governor General. It sits at the end of a tree-lined drive at the southwestern end of the lake. Although not open to the public, you can get a good view of the handsome building and its gardens from a lookout off Lady Denman Drive.

Yarralumla Nursery. Gardeners will be interested in visiting this nursery, located just off the Weston Park Road at the western end of the lake. More than 8 million trees and shrubs now gracing the city were grown from seed at the nursery.

Around Capital Hill

Parliament House, the residence of the Prime Minister, and many government office buildings are located within a mile radius of Capital Hill. Among the principal buildings of interest to the visitor are these:

Parliament House. With its 450 rooms sprawling over 3½ acres, "The House"—as it is known in the capital city—is an attractive white building set amid trim lawns, trees, and colorful gardens. Located northeast of Capital Hill, it faces Lake Burley Griffin. Inside, you can visit King's Hall with its fascinating collection of historical portraits and documents. To the right of King's Hall is the Senate Chamber; to the left, the House of Representatives.

In the daytime, the Australian flag is flown over the chamber that is in session. At night, lights are used: red for the Senate, green for the House. Each chamber has a visitors' gallery, where you can watch the proceedings. Parliament sits at irregular intervals, generally in March and early April, then again in May and June.

When Parliament is in recess, the House is open from 9 A.M. to 5 P.M. Monday through Saturday, 9:30 A.M. to 5 P.M. on Sunday. Conducted tours of the building are scheduled on the half-hour.

The National Library. Located north of Parliament House overlooking the lake, the National Library is an imposing building of great beauty.

Among its displays is the handwritten journal of Captain James Cook, recounting events on his voyage of discovery to Australia on board the *Endeavor* between 1768 and 1771. Another important document on permanent display is one of the three surviving originals of the Inspeximus issue of the Magna Carta, dated 1279.

The five-story building houses more than a million volumes, maps, plans, pictures, prints, photographs,

BLUNDELL'S FARMHOUSE (above) was one of Canberra's original buildings; cottage was built in 1858. Two city landmarks are Australian-American Memorial and Captain Cook Memorial Jet (right).

and film. The library's exhibition area is open Monday through Friday from 9 A.M. to 10 P.M.; on Saturday, Sunday, and public holidays from 9 A.M. to 4:45 P.M.

Embassies and legations. More than 60 countries have diplomatic missions in Canberra. Their embassies spread out through three suburbs south and west of Capital Hill—Red Hill, Forrest, and Yarralumla. Many of the buildings have been designed in the architectural style of the country they represent, lending an exotic flavor to this international section.

Prime Minister's Lodge. Just west of Capital Hill is the official residence of Australia's Prime Minister. Neither the building nor the grounds is open to the public, but you can see them from Adelaide Avenue.

The Civic Centre area

Across the Commonwealth Avenue Bridge and just north of City Hill is the civic and business heart of Canberra. The spirit of the community is symbolized by the Ethos statue in the middle of the handsome, brick-paved Civic Square; adjacent is a generous pool with a fountain in its center.

The city's theater and arts center is located on the square. Symphony concerts, ballet, opera, and major stage shows are presented in the Canberra Theatre,

PARLIAMENT HOUSE, seat of Australia's Federal Government in Canberra, presents an imposing facade overlooking the lake; Anzac Parade is in the foreground.

CANBERRA **61**

COPPER-DOMED Australian Academy of Science is one of Canberra's architectural highlights. A moat encircles the attractively landscaped modern building.

seating 1,200; intimate theater is performed in the 300-seat Playhouse.

Many government offices are located in this area, and several points of interest are in the vicinity. The A.C.T. Tourist Bureau is located just north of City Hill on London Circuit; visitors may obtain information Monday through Friday from 9 A.M. to 5:15 P.M. and on Saturday from 9 to 11:30 A.M.

Academy of Science. This copper-domed building, located off Marcus Clarke Street west of City Hill, is so modern in design it is sometimes called "The Martian Embassy." Though not open to the public, the Academy will interest visitors who enjoy contemporary architecture. Designed by architect Sir Roy Grounds of Melbourne, the building's dome is a copper-sheathed concrete shell 150 feet in diameter, resting on arches set in a pool circling the building.

The Institute of Anatomy. A block west of the Academy, this research center consists of two museums, one with Aboriginal displays, the other with biological exhibits. The ethnological section provides a better understanding of the primitive Aborigines and their customs. In the biological section, you'll learn more about the evolution of man and nature in this part of the world. Visiting hours are 9 A.M. to 5 P.M. Monday through Saturday, 2 to 5 P.M. on Sunday.

Australian National University. West of the Civic Centre, the University's lakeside is edged with green park land and the waters of West Basin. Sullivans Creek flows through the center of the campus, emptying into the lake at the head of Acton Peninsula.

Still developing, the campus already boasts many interesting buildings, and its parklike setting is inviting. Conducted tours of the campus leave the main entrance of University House at 3 P.M. Monday through Friday (except on holidays and Christmas week).

Botanic Gardens. You'll find plants native to Australia in the Botanic Gardens, lying west of the University along the lower slopes of Black Mountain. Six thousand native plants—representing more than 2,000 species—have been planted on the 100-acre site. This is not a play or picnic area; it is designed and operated for horticultural science study. Visiting hours are 9 A.M. to 5 P.M. daily.

East of Civic Centre

The area east and south of Civic Centre mixes interesting churches with military memorials. The Church of St. John the Baptist, on Constitution Avenue, dates back to 1841; its tombstones and memorials record much of the area's early history, and the adjoining schoolhouse contains relics of those days. To the north, All Saints Church in the Ainslie district, exemplifies modernized Gothic design.

National War Memorial. When you stand in front of Parliament House on the south bank of Lake Burley Griffin, you can look across the water and up the broad sweep of Anzac Parade to this handsome building, built as a memorial to men and women who gave their lives in the service of their country.

Anzac Parade is a parkway, bordered with Australian blue gums and a variety of New Zealand shrubs. The memorial houses relics, paintings, photos, and other records of every war in which Australians have served. The building is open daily from 9 A.M. to 4:45 P.M.

Australian-American Memorial. Standing at the head of King's Avenue, east of Blundell's cottage, this 258-foot aluminum spire commemorates the contribution made by the people of the United States to the defense of Australia during World War II. Surrounding it is a complex of buildings housing the Commonwealth Defense Departments.

The Royal Military College. In Duntroon, just east of the Australian-American War Memorial, you'll find Australia's West Point, where her regular army officers receive their training. The grounds are open for inspection at 2:30 P.M. Monday through Friday (except during January and February).

SIDE TRIPS OUT OF CANBERRA

Since Canberra is relatively new, most of the area's development is contained within its boundaries and those of its "satellite" cities and the neighboring town of Queanbeyan.

Anyone interested in city planning will want to visit some of the new suburbs. Twenty of them, with a future population of 95,000, are near the completion stage in Woden Valley, southwest of Canberra; another 25, with an estimated population of 120,000, are taking shape at Belconnen to the northwest.

The surrounding countryside remains almost as untouched as it was in 1911 when the site was selected as the location of the capital. A trip to a sheep station is easier from Canberra than from any of Australia's other major cities. Canberra also is the best base for visits to the following attractions:

Space tracking stations

Three space tracking stations, among the most advanced in the world, are located less than an hour's drive from Canberra. These are at Tidbinbilla (25 miles), Honeysuckle Creek (31 miles), and Orroral Valley (36 miles)—all of them key tracking stations on man's space probes. Check with the A.C.T. Tourist Bureau for current visiting hours.

Tidbinbilla Nature Reserve

Near the tracking station, this 12,500-acre reserve —surrounded by mountains reaching 5,000 feet high— provides an accessible site near Canberra to view Australian wildlife in natural surroundings.

Varieties of gum trees provide shelter for the squirrel-like sugar glider and his cousin, the feather-tailed glider, for koalas and kangaroos, and for a wide variety of native birds—including the brightly-colored crimson rosellas, the raucous kookaburra, and the magpie. Walking trails wind through the reserve, and you'll discover picnic areas and scenic outlooks. The koalas and kangaroos are kept in enclosures, open daily to visitors from 11 A.M. to 4 P.M.

The Snowy Mountains area

Some of Australia's most rugged and dramatic scenery is found about a hundred miles southwest of Canberra in the Snowy Mountains, the highest range on the continent.

Here six of Australia's largest rivers rise—the Murray, Murrumbidgee, Tumut, Tooma, Snowy, and Eucumbene. They rush down through fern gullies and lush forests, cutting deep valleys into mountains that are covered with snow in the winter, with wildflowers in spring and summer. Much of the area has been set aside as parkland, its development limited by the Government of New South Wales and the Snowy Mountains Authority.

Cooma is the gateway to the mountain country and the area's transportation center. The town is a half hour by air from Canberra, about an hour by air from Sydney or Melbourne, and easily reached by rail, bus, or car. Situated 66 miles from the Mount Kosciusko ski slopes, Cooma provides a starting point for tours visiting the park and the remarkable Snowy Mountains Hydro-Electric Scheme.

Snowy Mountains Hydro-Electric Scheme, in the Snowy Mountains, is one of the world's most extensive engineering projects—a vast undertaking diverting the flow of a river from one side of the mountains to the other and developing new agricultural and power resources.

Begun in 1949, the project has just been completed. Sixteen dams have been built and ten power stations installed, some of them buried in the hills. More than 90 miles of tunnels have been hewn through mountains, and 60 miles of aqueducts have been constructed. As a result, water from the abundant Snowy River has been diverted from the unproductive eastern slopes of the mountains into the Murray-Murrumbidgee river system on the west side, generating electricity and providing irrigation water for an additional thousand square miles of productive farmland.

The project has created a chain of lakes; the largest —Eucumbene—contains nine times the volume of water in Sydney Harbour. Planted with brown and rainbow trout, Lake Eucumbene is open for fishing the year around; with rainbows up to 7 and 8 pounds, it is considered the best trout fishing lake in the country.

The Snowy Mountains Authority has set up inspection tours for visitors. A number of companies in Sydney, Canberra, and Melbourne operate coach tours and air/coach tours including a visit to portions of the complex. Arrangements for a similar tour can also be made in Cooma.

Kosciusko National Park, covering 1½ million acres, is Australia's largest national reserve—used by residents of Sydney and Canberra as a summer and winter playground. Towering above the rest of the range at 7,316 feet is Mount Kosciusko—the highest peak in Australia—offering skiers excellent slopes during the relatively short season from June through September. Resorts are located in the southern part of the park at Thredbo Village, Perisher Valley, Smiggin Holes, Mount Kosciusko, Digger's Creek, and Wilson's Valley.

Summer activities center around hiking, fishing, trail riding, and viewing the hydroelectric project. The Yarrangobilly Caves, in the northern portion of the park and about 60 miles from Cooma, will interest spelunkers. The four large limestone caves that have been developed for park visitors are electrically lighted. Wildflowers in the park are at their best in January; fishing is good from September to April.

BROAD, TREE-LINED avenues like Collins Street (above) and electric trams typify Melbourne's famed Golden Mile. Top hats and morning dress (right) are in fashion at the famed Melbourne Cup. Parks along the Yarra River offer quiet sites near city skyscrapers (far right); rowers practice on the river in summer.

64 MELBOURNE

MELBOURNE—gracious and green, conservative and cultural

Melbourne is as different from Sydney as San Francisco is from Los Angeles. It's a difference in atmosphere and in surrounding terrain. Sydney is all rush and hustle. Melbourne moves at a leisurely pace. Sydney has the uneven shores of the Parramatta River, Melbourne the smooth banks of the serenely-flowing Yarra River. Melbourne is considered more conservative and more European in personality.

Second in size to Sydney among Australian cities and capital of the state of Victoria, Melbourne's population has climbed above 2.7 million. The city is considered Australia's financial and commercial center. More than half of the country's leading companies are headquartered there.

Some 550 air miles southwest of Sydney, Melbourne sits at the head of Port Phillip Bay, and is a port of call for many of the large cruise and passenger ships. Melbourne's proximity to water gives the city one major similarity with Sydney, however—easy accessibility to good beaches. St. Kilda Beach, Elwood, and Brighton beaches are no more than a half hour from downtown Melbourne.

Including its suburbs, Melbourne spreads far inland from Port Phillip Bay and the mouth of the Yarra River to the edge of the Dandenong Ranges; its total area covers some 714 square miles. Within this area are 59 separately named "cities," all part of the city called Melbourne.

Melbourne is a city for strolling. Wide, tree-lined boulevards invite dalliance and long pauses; public parks and gardens hint of waiting pleasures; well-stocked shops display their tempting wares. The boulevards most nearly capture the essence of the city, for spaciousness and greenery are part of Melbourne's charm. These broad, leafy avenues are flanked at intervals with smooth lawns and public gardens. Melbourne is surrounded by some 1,750 acres of parkland, luxurious greenbelts of generous proportions rare within the confines of a major city.

A CITY OF DIGNITY—AND GUSTO

Instead of the frenetic tempo usually associated with a metropolis, Melbourne has a quiet dignity; on all

MELBOURNE
0 ¼ ½ 1 1½ 2
COPYRIGHT BY PACIFIC TRAVEL NEWS
To Melbourne International Airport (Tullamarine)
Essendon Airport
Northland Shopping Center
GAFFNEY ST.
MURRAY ST.
MURRAY ROAD
SUSSEX ST.
Batman
Pascoe Vale
Preston
Coburg
COBURG
REYNARD ST.
KEILOR ROAD
BULLA RD.
Strathmore
Glenbervie
NICHOLSON ST.
PRINCESS ST.
Moreland
MORELAND RD.
MELVILLE ROAD
ALBION ST.
Anstey
Croxton
NORTHCOTE
Essendon
BUCKLEY ST.
TULLAMARINE FREEWAY
BRUNSWICK
ESSENDON
PASCOE VALE ROAD
SEPARATION ST.
Northcote
VICTORIA ST.
Brunswick
Moonee Valley Race Course
HIGH STREET
VICTORIA RD.
STATION ST.
FULHAM ROAD
Moonee Ponds
MT. ALEXANDER RD.
ROYAL PARADE
Merri
Dennis
Westgarth
RALEIGHS RD.
MARIBYRNONG RD.
BRUNSWICK RD.
Jewell
HOLDEN ST.
Ascot Vale
Rushall
HEIDELBERG RD.
Royal Park
EPSOM RD.
FITZROY
Zoo
LYGON ST.
Clifton Hill
LONGS RD.
Showgrounds
Yarra Bend National Park
ROSAMOND RD.
Flemington Br.
PARKVILLE
NICHOLSON ST.
BRUNSWICK ST.
ALEXANDER PARADE
MITCHELL ST.
RACECOURSE ROAD
Flemington RC
Flemington Race Course
SMITHFIELD RD.
FLEMINGTON ROAD
Victoria Park
BALLARAT RD.
Kensington
Macauley
JOHNSTON ST.
Melbourne University
CARLTON
ABBOTSFORD ST.
HODDLE ST.
GORDON ST.
Carlton Gardens
Collingwood
COLLINGWOOD
PRINCES HIGHWAY
S. Kensington
Exhibit Bldg.
DYNON RD.
VICTORIA PARADE
N. Richmond
Mid-Footscray
Footscray
N. Melbourne
RICHMOND
FOOTSCRAY RD.
LA TROBE ST.
LONSDALE ST.
BOURKE ST.
COLLINS ST.
FLINDERS ST.
SPENCER ST.
KING ST.
WILLIAM ST.
QUEEN ST.
ELIZABETH ST.
SWANSTON ST.
RUSSELL ST.
EXHIBITION ST.
SPRING ST.
Fitzroy Gardens
LANSDOWNE ST.
W. Richmond
WELLINGTON PARADE
HYDE STREET
To Geelong
MELBOURNE
BRIDGE RD.
Seddon
WHITEHALL ST.
Maribyrnong River
Victoria Dock
Spencer St.
BURNLEY ST.
SOMERVILLE RD.
Olympic Stadium
Richmond
SWAN ST.
Burnley
Yarraville
Yarra River
Government House
Olympic Park
E. Richmond
LORIMER ST.
SOUTHEASTERN FREEWAY
FOOTSCRAY
SALMA ST.
INGLES ST.
KING'S WAY
Botanic Gardens
CHURCH ST.
YARRA
Montague
PORT MELBOURNE
S. Melbourne
TOORAK RD.
S. Yarra
PRAHRAN
CROSSING
PUNT RD.
Spotswood
Graham
Albert Park
Hawksburn
WILLIAMSTOWN RD.
Albert Park
Port Melbourne
BLACKSHAWS RD.
Tasmanian Ferry Terminal
COMMERCIAL RD.
Yarra River
ST. KILDA RD.
WILLIAMSTOWN
MELBOURNE
Prahran
CHAPEL ST.
WILLIAMS RD.
Princes Pier
Middle Park
HIGH STREET
MASON ST.
SOUTH
Station Pier
Windsor
DANDENONG WATTLETREE RD.
St. Kilda
HOBSON BAY
HOTHAM ST.
ALMA ROAD
INKERMAN RD.
St. Kilda Pier
KOROROIT CK. RD.
ST. KILDA
BALACLAVA RD.
Railway Pier
Balaclava
Breakwater Pier
Williamstown Pier
ORRONG ROAD
BARKLY ST.
Ripponlea
Williamstown
NEPEAN HWY.
Point Gellibrand
Elsternwick
PORT PHILLIP BAY
Point Ormond
To Mornington

sides you sense the city's culture, graciousness, beauty, and unhurried growth and prosperity.

But, despite its leisurely pace, Melbourne is a city for *doing* as well as *seeing*. For instance, you'll surely want to visit the handsome, relatively new National Gallery on St. Kilda Road, viewing at close range the window waterfall and gazing up at the splendid stained glass ceiling in the Great Hall. You'll also want to stroll across the lawns of the King's Domain to the Sidney Myer Music Bowl, lingering, perhaps, to listen to an evening concert under the enormous aluminum overhang that appears to float in the air.

A moderate climate

Sydney jibes aside, Melbourne's weather is quite pleasant in all seasons, though the best time to visit is from November until April. Summer temperatures (December to March) range from 55° to 90°, cooling in winter (June to August) to the 40° to 60° range. Rainfall averages over 25 inches a year.

Ever-growing choice in rooms

The building boom in Melbourne is quickly evident. Along with the new office buildings, many new hotels and motor inns are being constructed. Although the city is in a period of transition, it appears that new developments are attempting to retain Melbourne's characteristic feeling of spaciousness.

The top hotels and motor inns—all located in and around the inner city—are the Southern Cross, Australia Hotel, the Melbourne Hilton, several Travelodges, Park Royal, John Batman Motel, Marco Polo Motel, Noah's Hotel Melbourne, Old Melbourne Motor Inn, Commodore Chateau, the Victoria, and the Hotel Windsor.

New hotels rise every year; your travel agent can provide up-to-date information. If you plan to be in Melbourne during the Melbourne Cup Week, at the beginning of November, or during the Moomba Festival in March, be sure to arrange your hotel reservations far in advance; the city is extremely crowded during both events.

Getting around Melbourne

Melbourne has kept her street cars (trams), an enjoyable and inexpensive way to explore the city. Buses, trams, and electric trains thoroughly cover the city and suburbs. For information on city transportation, check with the Transport Information Centre of the Victorian Government Tourist Office, 272 Collins Street, Melbourne; the phone number is 63-0141.

Taxis charge a flat A40 cents, plus A25 cents per kilometre. More than a dozen car rental agencies are listed in the pink section of the phone directory.

Dining choices galore

Cosmopolitan Melbourne has restaurants representing cuisines from around the world, giving visitors and residents alike a wide selection from which to choose.

Downtown restaurants. Among the leading restaurants located near the city center are these:

- The Legend Restaurant, 165 Lonsdale Street, adds to its excellent food and service (and exceptional wine cellar) a series of paintings by Leonard French depicting the legend of Sinbad the Sailor.

- Peanuts Gallery, 453 Swanton Street, serves peanuts and encourages patrons to drop the shells on the floor. All of this is a background to food specialties that include prawns in bacon, charcoal grilled steaks, and salads. Sunday nights are enhanced by a folk singer or band.

- Pamplemousse, top floor (20th) of the National Mutual Centre, 447 Collins Street. Well known for its view: the restaurant's balcony provides a 250° sweep of Melbourne. International menu includes smoked Canadian salmon and *escargots* from France.

- Florentino's, 80 Bourke Street. Italian and French cuisine served in warm surroundings of one of Melbourne's early buildings. No entertainment. Relies on excellent cooking and good wines.

- Mulligans, upstairs in the Eureka Stockade complex, Bourke Street. You must ring the restaurant's bell to enter, speakeasy fashion. Low lighting and old fashioned lamps give it an unpretentious, old-time atmosphere. Popular with businessmen at lunch.

- Lamplighter, 130 Bourke Street, specializes in provincial French cuisine. Decor attractively captures the mood of southern France.

- Lazar's, 244 King Street, has an interesting baroque atmosphere. Chamber music from about 7:30 to 9:30 P.M., then a combo comes on for dancing. Large menu selection featuring sea food and meat specialties.

- Fanny's, 243 Lonsdale Street, provides an old English atmosphere in a downstairs bistro; the upstairs restaurant is fancier with thick curtains, rich decor. Piano music.

- Frenchy's, 80 Jolimont Street. One of Melbourne's most fashionable restaurants, it offers the best in French cuisine and carries a large stock of vintage French wines.

- Le Chateau, 48 Queens Road, is housed in a fine old mansion. Menu offers wide range of continental dishes with emphasis on French.

Farther afield. Beyond the city center, many other restaurants are worth a visit. Here are some local favorites:

- Maxim's, 60 Toorak Road, South Yarra, is regarded by many Melbournians to be the finest restaurant in

Australia. No attempt is made at decor, except for the mural after Renoir at the end of the east room. Quality and a "club" feeling are what Maxim's offers —along with fine food, correctly cooked and presented with care.

- The Two Faces, 149 Toorak Road, South Yarra. This is a simple but attractively converted basement, decorated with wine bottles and wrought iron grilles. The imaginative cuisine includes fondue Bourguignonne and an excellent wine list. Locals claim it's the best restaurant in Australia.
- The Pickwick, 176 Toorak Road, South Yarra, reproduces the atmosphere of Charles Dickens' England. The menu features Continental cuisine.
- Smacka's Place, 55 Chetwynd Street, North Melbourne. An easy-going atmosphere with jazz music provided by Smacker himself. Bistro-style meals with steaks, casseroles, fish, and salads.
- Jimmy Watson's, 333 Lygon Street, Carlton. A Melbourne institution, this long-established, very popular restaurant is essentially a wine shop. It's the haunt of journalists, advertising men, TV personalities, and students from the nearby universities. For food, you select from a lavish smorgasbord and a variety of hot dishes.
- Bernardi's, 34 Punt Road, Prahran. Open seven days a week for lunch and dinner, with dancing Monday through Saturday. A ten minute taxi ride from city center or 15–20 minutes by tram.
- Leonda, 2 Wallen Road, Hawthorn. Located two miles from the city in a delightfully rural setting on a bank of the Yarra River. Elegant atmosphere with Latin American music.
- Tolarno's French Bistro, 42 Fitzroy Street, St. Kilda. Operated by restaurateur Leon Massoni and his wife Vivienne, this place specializes in French cuisine and features an excellent variety of Australian and overseas wines. Atmosphere and dress are casual; lunch and dinner are served 7 days a week.
- Didjeridoo, 417 Beach Road, Beaumaris, a 30-minute taxi ride from the city. This restaurant's decor has an Aboriginal theme, using Aboriginal art from Arnhem Land. Australian seafoods are featured on the menu. You're entertained by strolling musicians and folk singers nightly except Mondays, with dancing Friday and Saturday nights.

Nighttime entertainment

A swinging night life hasn't been part of the Melbourne scene since the boom days of the Australian Gold Rush, when Lola Montez entertained the diggers. But you'll find a few night clubs in the larger hotels, and entertainment and dancing are offered by many restaurants. Though you'll find nothing as bright or bizarre as Sydney's King's Cross district, Melbourne's brightest lights and busiest nighttime activity are centered in the suburbs of St. Kilda and Toorak. Try the Distillery in the Chevron Hotel on St. Kilda Road and Silvers on Toorak Road—they're both open until 3 A.M.

Melbourne is Australia's theater capital; and you'll find good fare offered by road companies from the United States, Europe, and the United Kingdom performing in its three legitimate theaters. International dance and ballet companies stage performances throughout the year, and local little theater productions are popular.

If you're visiting Melbourne in spring or summer (September to March), you can take advantage of the free concerts—symphony, pop groups, ballet—at the Sidney Myer Music Bowl. The bowl, in the King's Domain on St. Kilda Road, has a tentlike roof of aluminum and steel housing the sound shell and stage; it is open on the sides, so the effect is like attending an outdoor concert. The Melbourne Symphony Orchestra schedules its concerts each year from March to October.

The shopping scene

Melbourne is Australia's major fashion center; and tree-shaded Collins, Bourke, and Flinders streets are noted for their smart shops, arcades, department stores, and fashionable boutiques.

The huge Myer department store on Bourke Street, the largest department store in the Southern Hemisphere, reflects the buying habits and life style of the Australian. The most exclusive shop—for women's wear, men's wear, and household goods—is Georges, on Collins Street. Glossy boutiques and shops specializing in imported couturier clothes cluster in the side streets and distinctive arcades off Collins and Bourke streets. Here, too, you can find shops offering tax concessions to overseas visitors.

Suburban shopping highlights. Beyond the city center, you can explore the inner suburbs such as South Yarra, Prahan, Toorak, and Camberwell; all have an assortment of boutiques, small fashionable shops, and antique dealers specializing in Victoriana.

Mock-Tudor-style buildings make Toorak distinctive. An arcade in Prahan, called the Gallery, is worth a visit; built in 1880 and recently restored, the Gallery has a glass-domed ceiling with shops opening off both sides of the arcade. One of the shops, The Cellar, offers a fine wine collection—providing a pleasant setting for the wine connoisseur interested in learning more about Australia's better wines.

Opals and antiques. Though you'll find opals for sale in most major Australian cities, you may find the greatest variety of opals—mounted and unmounted —in Melbourne at the Australian Gem Trading Company. Located on Little Collins Street, it is the largest gem company in Australia.

And the antique buyers say that Melbourne is the best city for antiques in the country. You'll find a great assortment of Victoriana, as well as some 18th century French pieces and maps and prints relating to early Pacific area exploration.

Among the best antique shops are these: J. S. Allen & Sons and Regency Antiques, both specializing in antique silver; John D. Dunn, a dealer in early oak, Jacobean and European antiques and a specialist in early silver; Joshua McClelland, whose owner is Australia's leading connoisseur of Oriental antiques; and Kozminsky Galleries, which specializes in antique jewelry and silverware.

SIGHTSEEING IN MELBOURNE

For a bird's-eye view of Melbourne—the grid of wide, tree-lined streets, tall steeples, and the gently curving Yarra River—go to the observation deck of the National Mutual Building, at the corner of William and Collins streets. Open on weekdays from 10 A.M. to 4 P.M., it provides a 360° view of the city.

Another good Melbourne viewpoint is the 21st floor of the ICI Building, on Nicholson Street between Victoria and Albert streets. The scenic lookout is open daily except Sundays. A guide points out the city's main features and tells you a little about Melbourne's growth, from its origin as John Batman's village to its present position as Australia's second largest city.

The Golden Mile

Within an inner city center, about a mile square, stands the government, business, and commercial hub of the city, its chief shopping center, the main hotels, and theaters. Melbournians term this inner city their "Golden Mile," its perimeters being the Yarra River on the south, Spencer Street on the west, La Trobe Street on the north, and Spring Street on the east.

Within these boundaries are some of the city's "main streets"—Collins, Bourke, Flinders Street—and as you walk the streets of this area, you discover the characteristics of each. Collins Street is all brass plates, flagstone, shade trees, and gay, tilted umbrellas flowering above sidewalk cafes (Collins is also the heart of the banking area). Bourke Street bustles, forgetting a formerly raffish reputation in the rush of commerce. Between these streets run many arcades, a delight to the perennial browser. This inner city area still retains vestiges of its 19th century character.

As you stroll about, you may want to include some of these places in your sightseeing:

Gallery of Handicrafts, Arts and Crafts Society of Victoria, 99 Cardigan Street, Carlton. The gallery displays an interesting collection of Australian ceramics, weaving, and hand-made jewelry.

Gallery of Primitive Art, 5 Crossley Street. This gallery has a fine collection of primitive art, including Sepik carvings from New Guinea. Open Tuesday through Saturday.

Ye Olde Mitre Tavern, on Bank Place, a few yards north of Collins Street. One of Melbourne's oldest pubs, it has a cozy atmosphere and a long tradition as a gathering place of lawyers, artists, and writers.

Stock Exchange of Melbourne, 351 Collins Street. Melbourne is Australia's financial center, and you can stop here between 10 A.M. and 3:30 P.M. to watch some of the day's trading from the visitors' gallery.

St. Paul's Cathedral, Flinders Lane. Designed by William Butterfield, the church is a good example of post-Gothic revivalist architecture. Melbourne's second Anglican cathedral, it replaced Old St. James in 1891.

Young & Jackson's Hotel, 1 Swanston Street. A painting, "Chloe," has lured clients to the bar of Young & Jackson's for more than sixty years. Since its first appearance in Melbourne at the Exhibition in 1881, the portrait of this beauty has excited much attention.

State Library of Victoria, Swanston Street. This institution, which began as the old Melbourne Public Library, is now known to scholars the world over. It contains more than 800,000 volumes and a notable collection of Victoriana—including more than 18,000 paintings, drawings, prints, and artifacts.

Institute of Applied Science Museum, Swanston Street. An intriguing collection of working models and the H. V. McKay Planetarium are special features of

TENTLIKE ROOF shields concertgoers at Sidney Myer Music Bowl; the arena is open on the sides. Many of the events held here during the summer are free.

MELBOURNE 69

this museum. You can attend a night demonstration at the Science Museum Observatory. The museum is open 10 A.M. to 5 P.M. Monday to Saturday, 2 to 5 P.M. on Sunday.

National Museum, Russell Street. Here you can obtain a special insight into things uniquely Australian—Aboriginal weapons, domestic articles, and ceremonial objects; mammals, birds, reptiles, and minerals. The collection includes the famous Australian race horse, Phar Lap. Museum hours are 10 A.M. to 5 P.M. Monday to Saturday, 2 to 5 P.M. Sunday.

Old Melbourne Gaol, at the corner of Russell and La Trobe streets. Some of Australia's most distinguished criminals have been housed in this jail, including Ned Kelly, the legendary bushranger. The Old Gaol, now open to visitors daily, has been carefully renovated to memorialize its harshest days.

St. James Old Cathedral, at the corner of King and Batman streets. The church formerly stood on Little Collins Street until it was moved to its present site in 1914. It served as Melbourne's Anglican cathedral for more than 50 years, until superseded by St. Paul's in 1891. This historic old church still retains its original box pews and furnishings, including a baptismal font donated by Queen Victoria.

Flagstaff Gardens, on King Street opposite St. James Cathedral. Melbourne's oldest public gardens were laid out in the 1840s. A plaque marks the site of the old signal which announced the arrival of ships at Williamstown.

Old Treasury Building, Spring Street bordering on the Treasury Gardens. One of Melbourne's handsomest public buildings, it was erected from 1859 to 1862 and is an excellent example of Italian Renaissance.

North of city center

Two of Melbourne's oldest suburbs—Carlton and Parkville—lie north of the city center and offer some interesting contrasts, brought about by the impact of the young and the mod.

Carlton. Victorian architecture still graces this lovely suburb—beautifully proportioned terrace houses with lacy cast-iron balconies, wide tree-lined streets, and grassy squares. The district is spiced with a dash of Greenwich Village, a strong measure of new Australians from Italy, and numerous trendy, dissenting young people—most of them students at the University of Melbourne or Monash University. The latter school, 16 miles from city center, is worth visiting for its striking stained glass window—24 feet in diameter—in the University's Great Hall, designed by Melbourne artist Leonard French.

On Saturdays, the young people stroll along Lygon Street, the main shopping area, dressed in a provocative assortment of garments bought in the Flea Market or one of the area's small "opportunity" shops. Following the weekly prominade, they congregate about mid-day at Jimmy Watson's (see page 68) to "rap" and drink wine.

Between bouts of sightseeing, you may wish to catch your breath in Carlton Gardens, a 60-acre park of lawns and flowers. Its Exhibition Building, topped by an exotic dome and minarets, was constructed for the International Exhibition of 1880. In 1901 the first Federal Parliament gathered here, and the building remained the seat of Parliament until 1927, when the government moved to Canberra.

Parkville. Adjoining Carlton, this suburb is the site of the University of Melbourne. Founded in 1854, it was Australia's second university—but the first to admit women. As you stroll around the campus, you'll discover the Percy Grainger Museum, displaying the personal effects of the noted composer-pianist, and some striking murals by Douglas Annand. The avenue of palms leading to the main entrance was planted with seedlings brought back from the Middle East by Australian soldiers after World War I.

To the east—gardens and sports

Some of Melbourne's loveliest gardens and busiest sports arenas lie east of the Golden Mile.

Fitzroy Gardens and the adjacent Treasury Gardens, at the east end of Collins Street, were laid out in the late 1850s and are shaded by magnificent elms. Here, amid lawns and flower gardens, you can see the

NATIONAL GALLERY of Victoria is an architectural showcase containing Australia's finest art. Chandelier inside entrance is visible through water curtain.

MOOMBA!... IT MEANS "HAVE FUN"

Each March, as summer yields to autumn, the dignified dowager on the Yarra tosses gravity aside and kicks up her heels in the week-long Moomba, a zesty celebration of the arts, sports, and the sheer fun of living. Moomba is the Aboriginal word for "have fun," and 2½ million Melbournites and their guests do just that.

There's something for everybody: an open-air art show in Treasury Gardens, where you might find a budding Sidney Nolan; water-ski championships and regattas on the Yarra; a Queen of the Pacific contest with lovely girls from countries all around the Pacific; an international book fair; horse shows; racing. There's more still—theatrical and musical performances for every mood and taste...ferris wheels, carousels and clowns...a grand procession on the final Monday. And to wind it all up, a spectacular finale of fireworks explodes above a floodlit water revue along the River Yarra.

FESTIVAL PARADE is a high point; coach delivered mail in the outback more than a century ago.

---

delightfully whimsical Fairy Tree—carved by the late Australian sculptress, Ola Cohn—and a miniature Tudor village that delights children of all ages. Nearby is a conservatory, open daily from 10 A.M. to 4:45 P.M.

In the Treasury Gardens, surrounded by lawns and covered with ivy brought from England, is one of Melbourne's historic monuments—Captain Cook's Cottage. It was brought to Melbourne from Great Ayton, Yorkshire, in 1934 to commemorate Melbourne's first centennial the following year. The cottage was probably built by Cook's father around 1755. Though it cannot be verified that James Cook lived in the house as a youth, he knew it well and often returned there to visit his father.

Melbourne Cricket Ground, a couple of blocks north of the Yarra River, is about a 10-minute walk from the east end of Collins Street. Australia's biggest sporting arena, it accommodates more than 120,000 people and was the main stadium of the 1956 Olympic Games. One block toward the river, across Swan Street, are other arenas and sports fields built for the Olympics, including the swimming stadium, soccer field, and bicycling track. The oval is also the home of Australian Rules football (see page 28).

The Melbourne Cricket Club was formed in 1838, a mere three years after the settlement of Melbourne. The Cricket Museum on the grounds has a wealth of cricket memorabilia, much of it contributed by the Englishman Tony Baer, who began his cricket collection in London. The collection covers the history of the game—in paintings, etchings, cartoons, glassware, wood carvings, score cards, even the bats and caps of such famous cricket players as Don Bradman, Jack Hobbs, and Leary Constantine.

South of the Yarra

South of the city center, across Princes Bridge, you'll find more parklands, several historical sites, and the stunning new National Gallery of Victoria.

The National Gallery of Victoria, 180 St. Kilda Road, is the first stage of the exciting, eye-catching new Victorian Arts Centre. You approach the gallery over a bridged moat, which surrounds the museum on three sides; you then pass a unique water curtain that helps to cut glare and cool the building. The stained glass ceiling in the Great Hall soars above like a colorful floating cloud. The breathtakingly beautiful work of Leonard French, it took six years to construct.

The Gallery contains Australia's finest art collection, including not only a comprehensive display of Australian art and paintings but also a fine collection of rare Oriental porcelain, and works by impressionist, postimpressionist, and English painters.

When complete, the Arts Centre will have two concert halls, two theaters, and studios housed under a 432-foot spire. Hours are Tuesday to Sunday from 10 A.M. to 5 P.M.; Wednesday to 9 P.M.; closed Mondays except on public holidays.

The King's Domain rises gently from the banks of the Yarra River to St. Kilda Road, merging with Alexandra and Queen Victoria Gardens and the Royal Botanic Gardens to form a huge parkland—more than 530 acres of gardens, lawns, and recreation facilities.

MELBOURNE 71

ROYAL BOTANIC GARDENS (left) are only a short walk from the city center. Como House (above), overlooking Yarra River, is fine example of colonial architecture.

Here you'll also find the Sidney Myer Music Bowl and La Trobe's Cottage (the first Government House), one of numerous prefabricated buildings shipped from England in the late 1830s during Melbourne's first decade. Only two of the structures are known to have survived the years. The cottage, which originally stood across the Yarra at Jolimont, is a small weatherboard building. It served as the state's first Government House, where Governor Charles La Trobe lived during his term of office from 1839, until 1854. Restored by the National Trust, the cottage retains many of its original furnishings; it is open daily from 10:30 A.M. to 5 P.M.

In the southwest corner of the King's Domain is the Shrine of Remembrance, Victoria's impressive memorial to her dead in the two world wars and in Malaysia, Korea, and Vietnam. It is designed so that on the 11th day of the 11th month, at the 11th hour, sunlight falls upon the Rock of Remembrance. From the top of the memorial, you have a fine view across the parks and the Yarra River to the heart of the city.

The Royal Botanic Gardens, south of King's Domain, is one of Melbourne's oldest parks. Governor Gipps early approved a "public domain for the purpose of cultivating indigenous and exotic plants," but the site was not selected until 1845.

Stroll through its glades with their dense growth of majestic, venerable trees—some older than the city itself, some planted by famous personalities such as Prince Albert, Dame Nellie Melba, Alfred Lord Tenny-

ON ANZAC DAY, crowds gather at Shrine of Remembrance, Victoria's memorial to countrymen lost in war. Rooftop view looks across parklands to the city.

son, and the Duke of Edinburgh. On a walk around the lake you can find the red gum tree under which Melbournites celebrated their "separation" from New South Wales in 1851. Wild ducks and black swans congregate on the three lakes in the Botanic Gardens. In the southwest corner, the National Herbarium contains tropical and subtropical plants.

Como House, off Williams Road, South Yarra, is one of Melbourne's oldest residences. This stately Georgian mansion overlooks the Yarra River; it had remained in the possession of the Armytage family, descendants of the original owners, until purchased by the National Trust in 1959. Much of the original furniture remains.

The gardens, laid out following suggestions of the famous botanist Baron von Mueller, were once the scene of annual cherry picking parties (if the trees did not produce a sufficient crop, the boughs were hung with ripe cherries purchased for the event).

THE SPORTS SCENE

Melbourne may be the most sports-minded city in this sports-loving country. Tens of thousands flock to football, horse races, and cricket matches. And they're activists as well—you'll find a wide choice of sports facilities if you prefer to participate.

For the spectator

In addition to the "big sports" like horse racing and football, you can watch greyhound racing (at night under the lights at Olympic or Sandown Park stadiums), lawn bowling tournaments at many of the parks around the city, polo matches, surf carnivals (on beaches to the south, facing Bass Strait), and top-notch tennis matches (at Kooyong, scene of many Davis Cup games).

The daily papers list scheduled events, or you can check with the Victorian Government Tourist Bureau on Collins Street.

Australian Rules Football is at its best in Melbourne. If you're visiting during the season (usually April to September), you won't want to miss a game of this exciting, long-kicking mayhem, which evolved from a Gaelic form of football (see page 28).

Soccer adds to the excitement of the summer season. On January and February nights, the Ampol Cup contests are played in Melbourne.

Horse racing is still the major draw, and not just the Melbourne Cup, number one classic of the Australian turf, which is held the first Tuesday in November. Melbourne's four courses—Flemington, Caulfield, Moonee Valley, and Sandown—pack in enthusiasts on weekends almost the year round. Trotting (harness racing) fans enjoy a long season from October through July; most races are held at the Royal Agricultural Society Showgrounds in Ascot Vale.

The Melbourne Cup is more than a horse race to the Australians. That first Tuesday of November has a particularly glamorous aura, climaxing an event-filled season. The champagne flows. Huge sums are wagered. The finest bloodstock in the nation parades in the paddock; prize money in excess of A$100,000 is at stake. The grandstands blaze with color. The gentlemen wear grey top hats and dark morning suits, while the ladies command attention in wacky, wonderful hats, lavish confections months in the making.

Cup Day and Cup Day alone commands universal interest and enthusiasm, causing a suspension of business over the length and breadth of the land (and in Aussie-occupied offices around the world).

Cricket is regarded by some visitors as a stodgy ritual, performed by solemn men in white. A visit to a match at the Melbourne Cricket Ground may be an eye-opener. International test matches are played from December to February. You'll also find the game being played in many of the city's parks.

Golf. February's the month for the Victorian Open. Check with the Victorian Golf Association, 6 Riddell Parade, Elsternwick, or with the Victorian Government Tourist Office for specific dates.

Active sports

If you'd rather play than watch, Melbourne provides plenty of opportunities, ranging from surfing to table tennis. You have to travel south to the Bass Strait beaches for surfing, but you'll find a huge table tennis facility in Albert Park, St. Kilda, just a few miles south of the city center. Other sports in which you can participate are these:

Golf. Golfers may choose from six public courses, all welcoming visitors. Private clubs will usually grant guest privileges if you can arrange for an introduction by a member or if arrangements are made through your home club.

Tennis. Players should contact the Secretary of the Lawn Tennis Association, Victoria (at 489 Glenferrie Road, Kooyong) for information on private clubs offering guest privileges. Public and private tennis courts for hire are listed in the pink section of the Melbourne phone book.

Boating. You'll find superlative boating and sailing outside Melbourne—at Sandringham, Black Rock, Mordialloc, and Frankston—but you'll also find sailboats for rent at Albert Park Lake in the nearby suburb of St. Kilda.

Beach sports. Melbourne's best beaches—St. Kilda, Elwood, Brighton, Sandringham, and Frankston—are all within a half hour of downtown by car or train.

DANDENONG RANGES are a short drive from Melbourne through forests and farmlands (above). Reconstructed stores brighten Sovereign Hill Historic Park in Ballarat (right). Lighthouse at Cape Nelson rises above Victoria's south coast (far right).

74 SIDE TRIPS OUT OF MELBOURNE

EXPLORING VICTORIA—mountains, rugged coasts, gold towns, the Murray

Melbourne makes an excellent excursion center; in less than a day's journey you can travel along the scenic Victoria coast or inland to the mountains and Gold Rush towns.

Swimmers, skin divers, and surfers will head for the ocean, where inviting beaches await. Lakes and bays offer superb boating and fishing. Nearby mountains accommodate skiers on snowfields more extensive than those in Switzerland.

In Victoria's national parks you can enjoy the richness of Australia's wildlife and flora in terrain varying from volcanic plains to dramatic mountains to rain forests tangled with lianas and giant ferns. Vivid history lives on in the Gold Rush towns of Ballarat and Bendigo and in the old ports along the Murray River.

The nearest point of departure for Tasmania (see page 85), Melbourne is little more than an hour's flight from the slopes of the Snowy Mountains (see page 63). Good highways, frequent jet service to main centers, and excellent rail and bus services make touring easy. The Victorian Government Tourist Bureau, 272 Collins Street, Melbourne, can advise you on excursions and assist you in booking them.

CLOSE-IN MOUNTAINS

In less than an hour from downtown Melbourne, you can be walking through the deep fern gullies of the Dandenong Ranges, listening to the mimicking calls of the lyrebird. Good roads lead from the city through attractive suburbs and open country to the gentle hills of this pleasant area, as well as to other close-in mountain areas around Healesville and in Kinglake National Park. These areas are easily accessible from Melbourne by road or rail, and bus tours include them on frequent schedules throughout the year.

The Dandenong Ranges

Melbourne is blessed with the Dandenong Ranges, a forested, low-lying range of mountains less than 30

SIDE TRIPS OUT OF MELBOURNE   75

minutes from the city center. Barely more than 1,500 feet at their highest point, they still provide a topographical backdrop for the city's northern and eastern suburbs. Here native bush combines with the trees and shrubs planted by an ever-increasing population of Melbournites seeking homesites in the woods and fresh mountain air.

Mount Dandenong, highest point in the ranges, gives sweeping views toward Port Phillip Bay and Melbourne across patches of farmland and forested slopes concealing numerous townships. At the summit a restaurant takes full advantage of the vista. Amid the greenery you catch the glint of Silvan Reservoir, Melbourne's largest water storage facility, distributing nearly 300 million gallons daily to the city.

The William Ricketts Sanctuary, near Mount Dandenong, has an eerie beauty. As you walk along trails between the giant ferns, the sculpted forms of Aborigines—carved by Ricketts from the stumps of trees—seem almost alive in the filtered green light of the rain forest.

Sherbrooke Forest, south of Mount Dandenong, is perhaps the gem of the Dandenongs, a favorite with bush ramblers—and one of the best places in Australia to watch the lyrebird. The lyrebird is a remarkable mimic; the male displays his beautiful tail in the courtship ritual (see page 23). Road signs remind you to watch: "Drive Carefully—Lyrebirds Cross Here".

Ferntree Gully National Park, 21 miles east of Melbourne, in the foothills of the Dandenongs along the Burwood Highway, has magnificent ferns and plentiful wildlife; you may see swamp wallabies, platypuses, and echidnas, as well as lyrebirds.

The Puffing Billy is a famous old narrow-gauge steam locomotive pulling a little train through wooded hills, fern gullies, and flower farms between Belgrave and Emerald. You can hop aboard a few miles beyond the Ferntree Gully Park. The trip takes 1½ hours and operates only on weekends and public holidays.

Sir Colin Mackenzie Wildlife Sanctuary

One of Australia's most attractive wildlife sanctuaries will be found near Healesville, 39 miles northeast of Melbourne. At the Sir Colin Mackenzie Wildlife Sanctuary, in conditions closely resembling their native habitat, live koalas, kangaroos, wombats, emus, and—in a glass-sided tank—duck-billed platypuses. You can visit the Sanctuary on half-day tours leaving Melbourne daily throughout the year; the excursion travels through the Dandenongs to the refuge, returning via Maroondah Reservoir.

Kinglake National Park

Waterfalls and magnificent mountain ash trees, some 300 feet tall, are highlights of this 14,079-acre park on the southern slopes of the Great Dividing Range, 40 miles north of Melbourne. Impressive Mason's Falls tumbles 140 feet down Sugarloaf Peak. From the summit of Bald Hill, visitors have magnificent views across the forest and fern gullies toward Melbourne and Port Phillip Bay.

Lyrebirds, kangaroos, wallabies, and many unique species of birds make their home in the park. If you have always wanted to see a platypus in its natural habitat, watch for them there, particularly in early morning or late afternoon.

COASTAL EXCURSIONS

South of Melbourne are the sunny, sheltered beaches and broad, open waters of Port Phillip Bay, edging the Mornington Peninsula. East of this peninsula lies Western Port Bay, with French Island in its center and Phillip Island (see page 82) protecting the entrance. Farther to the southeast is the continent's southernmost tip, Wilson's Promontory, a narrow strip of land jutting into Bass Strait like an arrow pointing toward Tasmania.

The beach world east and west of Port Phillip Bay

MORNINGTON PENINSULA beaches, easily reached from Melbourne, are sandy, tree-lined playgrounds for residents of the city and its suburbs.

is one of dramatic seascapes, rugged headlands, and an amazing number of beaches, some with well-developed resorts, some virtually untouched.

Mornington Peninsula

The beaches of the Mornington Peninsula, which divides Port Phillip from Western Port Bay, are Melbourne's playground, easily reached by electric train and shoreline highway. Along Port Phillip Bay from Frankston to Portsea, translucent waters and tree-sheltered beaches attract large numbers of avid weekend yachtsmen, swimmers, fishermen, and sun-worshippers. In the towns of Mornington, Mt. Martha, Dromana, Rosebud, Sorrento, and Portsea, visitors find accommodation in hotels, flats, cottages, motels, and caravan-camping parks. For sports-loving vacationers, amenities include good golf courses and tennis courts, boats to hire for sailing and fishing, water-skiing, and excellent surfing along the beaches facing Bass Strait.

At Arthur's Seat, near Dromana, a chair lift transports sightseers to the summit for panoramic views of both bays, Phillip Island, and the orchards and small farms of the peninsula itself.

Collins Bay, at Sorrento, is a good spot for picnicking and shell collecting; rock hounds can hunt for gem stones in outcroppings along the beach near Shoreham, on Western Port Bay.

Wilson's Promontory

Jutting into Bass Strait southeast of Melbourne, this mountainous and windswept peninsula is one of Victoria's largest parks. It has a grandiose beauty. Heavily-wooded mountains descend to the edge of an ocean fringed by white sand and massive rocks. Deep gullies shelter pockets of rain forest. From the peaks you gain sweeping views across the strait and to Gippsland. Wildlife roams the forests and heathlands, and in spring, wildflowers add brilliant color.

Holiday lodges and caravan and camping areas at Tidal River Camp provide accommodations for leisurely enjoyment of this wild beauty. You can also visit the park on a day trip from Melbourne; check with the Victorian Government Tourist Office for more information.

Ninety Mile Beach

East of Wilson's Promontory is an unbroken stretch of beach extending northeast, in an almost straight line, for nearly 90 miles. Named for its length, Ninety Mile Beach is relatively undeveloped; this pristine stretch is superb for surfing, surf fishing, and undisturbed beach walks. Fishermen try for salmon, trout,

PUFFING BILLY, an old steam train filled with families on a Sunday excursion, chugs across a wooden trestle through the Dandenong Ranges.

WILSON'S PROMONTORY lighthouse settlement stands on a rocky headland below South Peak; the Moncoeur Islands lie a short distance offshore.

SIDE TRIPS OUT OF MELBOURNE 77

snappers, greybacks, tiger flatheads, and flounder. Inland are some of Victoria's richest dairylands, combined with coal fields and industrial development.

The best points of access to Ninety Mile Beach are at Port Albert, about 135 miles southeast of Melbourne at the southwestern end of the beach, and at two towns at the other end—Seaspray and Paynesville. Modest beach accommodations are available in these towns.

The Gippsland Lakes

Good highways lead from Melbourne to Gippsland, a popular resort district in southeastern Victoria, known for rich farmlands, forests, rivers, and large navigable lakes.

Paralleling the shoreline inland from Ninety Mile Beach, the lakes stretch for more than 50 miles. Some of them are separated from the ocean by only a narrow ribbon of land. All of the lakes are connected, inviting long lazy days of cruising between Lakes Entrance at their eastern end to Sale, some 80 miles west. Swimming and fishing are excellent. In the tidal waters you'll find bream, perch, mullet, and skip-jack; lakes and streams abound with blackfish, perch, and bream. From many of the lakes you can hike over extensive dunes to Ninety Mile Beach; a more direct access route is by bridge from Lakes Entrance across North Arm.

AUSTRALIA'S GOLDEN BONANZA

The story of Australia's Gold Rush begins on the banks of California's Sacramento River in 1849, where an Englishman, out to gain his fortune in the California gold fields, recognized the similarity of the Mother Lode terrain to a valley in the mountains behind Bathurst, New South Wales. Though 18 years had passed since Edward Hargreaves had seen that valley, he returned to Australia, struck out across the Blue Mountains—and immediately found gold beside Summer Hill Creek.

News of the discovery emptied the cities; and Melbourne, drained of population, offered a £100 reward to the first person to find a gold field within a hundred miles of town. In July, 1851, gold was discovered at Clunes, and in August, at Ballarat—the richest alluvial gold field the world has ever known. Discoveries at Bendigo and Mount Alexander followed soon after.

The gold was easily won. So rich were the alluvial deposits that the output of Bendigo and Ballarat alone nearly equalled all of the California fields. By the middle of 1852, adventurers from all over the world were pouring into Melbourne and fanning out across the Victorian bush—"fortyniners" from California, New Englanders, Texans, Irish, English, Europeans, and Chinese—100,000 in one year alone. Port Phillip Bay became a "forest of masts"; at one time, approximately 500 ships were anchored in Sandridge, many empty, deserted by their crews who had set off to seek their fortune in the fields. Almost overnight towns sprang up in the bush—canvas and clapboard cities, replaced with surprising swiftness by ornate, neo-classical stone structures.

Today you can easily reach this historic area from Melbourne by daily coach or rail service. Full-day coach tours depart every Thursday and Sunday for Ballarat and Sovereign Hill and every Tuesday and Saturday for Bendigo. Information on the tours is available from the Victorian Government Tourist Bureau, 272 Collins Street, Melbourne.

Ballarat, in hilly country 70 miles west of Melbourne, was a small farming community until Thomas Hiscock found gold near Buninyong cemetery in 1851. Its alluvial gold fields were the richest in the world—it was here that the "Welcome Nugget," weighing 2,217 ozs. and assayed as 99.2% pure gold—was discovered.

In 1854, Ballarat witnessed Australia's only civil war, the Eureka Stockade rebellion. A group of some 150 diggers, angered by oppressive government policies and the arrogance of the police, declared themselves independent. Though they were overwhelmingly defeated, their rebellion resulted in sweeping reforms.

The city retains much of its Victorian atmosphere. Among its many interesting sights, you can visit the Eureka Stockade Memorial, site of the original stockade; Adam Lindsay Gordon's Cottage; the Botanic Gardens, containing the famous Begonia House (center of the annual March begonia festival); and "Ercildoone," a pioneer homestead built by the Learmonth Brothers around 1859. Competitions in music and drama are held in Ballarat in September and October.

Nearby at Smeaton, north of Creswick, Smeaton House is an excellent example of early pioneer architecture of the late 1830s.

More than 20 hotels and motels, as well as guest houses, trailer parks, and campgrounds, provide comfortable accommodations for visitors.

Sovereign Hill Historical Park, about a mile beyond Ballarat, evokes memories of the Gold Rush period. Set near land once mined by the diggers, the park marks the first phases in re-creating many aspects of the miners' lives—windlasses, shafts, a horse-drawn *arrastre* (drag-stone mill) to crush the ore, a Chinese joss house, the Gold Commissioner's tent where the hated licenses were issued, shanties, blacksmiths' shops, and the Colonial Bank of Australia. In the "New York Bakery" (a restaurant), waitresses dress in the

78 SIDE TRIPS OUT OF MELBOURNE

Accommodations. The Gippsland Lakes have numerous small resort towns and villages; the main ones are Lakes Entrance and Paynesville. Either town is easily accessible from Melbourne by car or by a rail-bus combination via Bairnsdale. Both resort towns are small fishing villages with modest accommodations, ranging from campgrounds to small hotels. Lakes Entrance sits at the eastern end of the lakes, commanding their outlet to the sea.

Excursions. You can take launch trips from either town, and you'll find every type of craft available for hire, including well-equipped four and six-berth cruisers. You can book craft through the Victorian Government Tourist Bureau, 272 Collins Street, in Melbourne.

You can also take a day tour from Melbourne to Tarra Valley and Bulga national parks, both west of Lakes Entrance, where you will find a wonderland of ferns, waterfalls, and the pink heath that is the floral emblem of Victoria.

Southwest Riviera

Another interesting excursion from Melbourne takes you to the Bellarine Peninsula, jutting eastward into Port Phillip Bay from the mainland, and on to the rugged grandeur of Victoria's Southwest Riviera.

Route 1—the Princes Highway—and fast rail service connect Melbourne with Geelong. From here you can travel by bus or coach or explore by car along

---

costume of the era. Today you can purchase a "Miner's Right" for a more moderate sum and pan for gold yourself; you can also have your name printed by hand-operated press on a "Wanted" bulletin.

There are no overnight accommodations at Sovereign Hill.

Bendigo, 95 miles northwest of Melbourne on the Calder Highway, ranked second in gold production to Ballarat. Its record year was 1856, when 661,749 ounces were taken from the fields. Today, Bendigo is a prosperous agricultural center, with the third largest sheep market in the country.

Many Gold Rush buildings survive, including the old log jail. In the Bendigo Art Gallery you can enjoy a fine collection of Australian and French impressionist paintings. An annual highlight is the Easter Fair, at which the Chinese community parades its dragon as one of the main events. Australia's biggest track meet is held annually at the Sports Centre in March.

If you decide to stay in the area, you can choose from 25 hotels and motels, several trailer parks, and campgrounds.

Beechworth, an old mining town about 150 miles northeast of Melbourne (via the Hume Highway to Wangaratta), had a role in the saga of Australia's notorious bushranger, Ned Kelly; he was imprisoned in the town's jail in 1881. The museum in Beechworth contains an outstanding collection of pioneer relics.

Castlemaine and Maldon, northwest of Melbourne on Highway 79, are two small gold mining towns well worth visiting. Maldon, on the slopes of Mount Tarrangower, is the only town entirely protected by the National Trust of Victoria. Its Folk Museum, housed in the old Council Offices, contains a wealth of Gold Rush memorabilia, and the post office was the childhood home of the novelist Henry Handel Richardson. You'll find ample and varied accommodations in both Castlemaine and Maldon.

"MINERS" at Sovereign Hill demonstrate use of sluicing cradles and pans (left). Headframe still stands over the mine shaft at mist-shrouded Sovereign Hill (above).

SIDE TRIPS OUT OF MELBOURNE

OLD PADDLE STEAMER (upper left) takes visitors on a sightseeing tour along the Murray River. Blacksmith demonstrates 19th century methods (left) at Emu Bottom pioneer settlement. Windswept cliffs rim Airey's Inlet along the Great Ocean Road (above). Sea, river, and rock fishing are nearby.

the Great Ocean Road. An all-day tour leaves Melbourne Wednesdays at 9:00 A.M., traversing the Great Ocean Road as far as Lorne and allowing visitors to sample the magnificent southern coast.

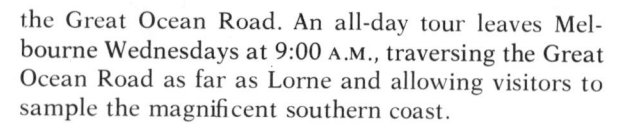

Geelong. Victoria's largest provincial city (with a population exceeding 120,000), Geelong is located 45 miles southwest of Melbourne. Though basically a regional commercial center—wool-selling headquarters and busy port—Geelong is an attractive city with extensive parklands. About 60 hotels and motels provide accommodations, making it a good base for exploring the Bellarine Peninsula and the scenic southwest coast.

Bellarine Peninsula. Resorts on the northeastern shore of the peninsula are pleasant and attractive; visitors enjoy good fishing, sheltered swimming beaches, and facilities for tennis, golf, and water sports. Surfing is best on the southern beaches, below Point Lonsdale.

You'll find comfortable accommodations in hotels, guest houses, and motels in the Portarlington area (inside Port Phillip Bay), Queenscliff-Point Lonsdale (on the headland at entrance to the Bay), and in Ocean Grove and Barwon Heads (both on the ocean side of the peninsula). Campers will find well-equipped parks in most of the local towns.

The Great Ocean Road. One of Victoria's most scenic routes is along the Great Ocean Road, following the coast southwest of Melbourne for nearly 200 miles. The highway begins just south of Geelong at Torquay and winds south and west to Warrnambool. Linking more than a dozen resorts, the Great Ocean Road skirts sheer cliffs, parallels miles of golden sand beaches, and traverses the forested slopes of the Otway Ranges.

At Torquay you'll find excellent surf, and 8 miles beyond at Anglesea, on a protected stretch, good swimming and fishing. Airey's Inlet is popular with sportsmen; Fairhaven attracts Melbourne's surfers.

The Otway Ranges meet the ocean at Lorne. Here the scenery is superb; you can bushwalk through groves of giant eucalyptus and fern filled valleys, surfcast, or laze away the days on a wide, golden strand.

Beyond Apollo Bay, the road turns inland, crossing the Otway Ranges, and returns to the ocean south of Port Campbell, where brown, yellow, and orange cliffs have eroded into a series of natural bridges and rock stacks. The twenty-mile stretch of coast comprising Port Campbell National Park is one of the most beautiful in Australia; offshore islands support many birds, including some of the largest penguin rookeries in Victoria. The national park maintains a good camping area near Port Campbell. At the resort town of Warrnambool, center of rich dairy farming country, you can rejoin Princes Highway and return to Melbourne along the inland route or continue along the coast to the old town of Port Fairy and to Portland, an important old whaling town with numerous interesting historic sites.

For sharp contrast to the coastal scenery, turn inland from Port Fairy or Portland to Hamilton; these roads cross the world's third largest lava plain and Victoria's richest wool and wheat producing area. From Hamilton it is 112 miles east to Ballarat (see page 78) and another 70 miles back to Melbourne.

VICTORIA'S RUGGED WEST

West and northwest of Melbourne the countryside varies—from rolling farm and grazing lands to rugged hills and forested mountains. Among attractions you can sample are pioneer settlements, vast sheep stations (some operated as guest ranches), onetime boom towns recalling Victoria's gold rush, and bush and wildlife reserves displaying Australia's special brand of native beauty and offering excellent hiking and camping opportunities. To learn more about Ballarat and other towns associated with Victoria's gold rush days, see page 78.

Emu Bottom

Beyond Tullamarine Airport—and only about 15 miles northwest of downtown Melbourne—Emu Bottom is a pioneering homestead of the 1830s, restored to its original style, including furnishings of the period. This is a "working model" homestead; you see sheep sheared by hand blades and a blacksmith working his metal, using century-old methods. Recipes once prepared for pioneer families are cooked on the premises and served by the "lady of the house" in period costume.

Sheep station at Naringal

Much of Australia's wealth has been shorn from the backs of sheep, and at Naringal—the historic 6,000-acre sheep station a hundred miles west of Melbourne—you can watch the Australian farmer at his work and, if you like, participate in the duties of the station yourself.

Guests are accommodated as they would be at guest or dude ranches in the western United States. You can visit for just a day or make a longer stay—to watch sheep musterings and shearing, have a picnic in the bush, play tennis, swim in the station pool, go fishing or hunting, or simply use the station as a restful base for making trips to the coast and mountains.

Day tours by coach from Melbourne include a visit to the station and watching a shearing. It's an easy day's drive via Ballarat from Melbourne, or you can fly by light aircraft to Naringal's own airstrip.

The Grampians

The stark sandstone ridges of the Grampians—the western verge of the Great Dividing Range—rise in wild grandeur from the surrounding plains some 170 miles west of Melbourne. With towering cliffs eroded into weird forms, heaths carpeted by wildflowers in spring and summer, and cascading waterfalls, the Grampians offer fascinating opportunities for bush walking and some stiff challenges to rock climbers.

To enjoy the wildflowers at their best—more than 700 species of flowering plants have been recorded in the area—you should visit the mountains between late September and late October.

Kangaroos, emus, and koalas still inhabit the Grampians, and platypuses may be seen in the streams.

In season, all-day tours from Melbourne give you an opportunity to enjoy the region's wildflowers, scenery, and wildlife. If you want to linger in the area, you'll find comfortable accommodations in Hall's Gap in the heart of the Grampians.

THE MURRAY RIVER VALLEY

Australia's most important waterway—the Murray River—flows westward from the mountains of northeastern Victoria, through a quiet pastoral land of orange groves and farmsteads, delineating the state's border with New South Wales. Once the great trade route of the paddle steamer era, its waters now provide irrigation and hydroelectric power for New South Wales, South Australia, and Victoria.

You can drive along the river on the Murray Valley Highway, paralleling the water from Albury northwest to Mildura, near the South Australia border. Or you may prefer a leisurely cruise on the river in an old paddlewheeler (see page 102).

Two river towns

Once a roistering river port, Echuca sits at the junction of the Murray, Campaspe, and Goulburn rivers 128 miles north of Melbourne. The town still retains a memorial of its rambunctious days: the paddle steamer *Adelaide*, moored at the river bank. Neighboring marshes provide good fishing and duck hunting. Barmah State Forest, a well-known birdwatching territory, lies only 20 miles northeast.

Another site of special interest to birdwatchers is the town of Kerang. Located on the Loddon River, at the junction of the Murray and Loddon highways,

SIDE TRIPS OUT OF MELBOURNE 81

SUMMERTIME TOUR—TO WATCH A PARADE OF PENGUINS

One of the most enjoyable short tours out of Melbourne is the summer excursion to Phillip Island, 90 miles off the southern tip of Victoria, where colonies of penguins emerge from the sea each evening, returning to their burrows following the day's hunt for food.

The parade begins at dusk. Spotlights play across the sand, picking up one dark form, then another, and another, as up from the surf they strut, squadron after squadron. The day's fishing is over, and the fairy penguins of Phillip Island return to their rookeries overlooking Bass Strait.

Eudyptula minor is the world's smallest penguin, 8 to 10 inches tall. Though several species visit the Australian coast, the fairy penguin is the only one to breed there, nesting amid grass tussocks, in crevices, and in burrows—sometimes as many as two hundred penguins to the acre.

Excursion to the rookeries, at Summerland Beach on Phillip Island, can be made between October and April. Tours leave Melbourne daily at approximately 1:30 P.M., returning nine hours later.

FAIRY PENGUINS *parade up beach on Phillip Island nightly during the summer months.*

---

its surrounding marshlands are home for enormous flocks of ibis. Reedy Lake is thought to be the world's largest ibis rookery.

Swan Hill

One of Australia's most imaginative folk museum villages—Swan Hill—is located on the Murray River 210 miles northwest of Melbourne. The Swan Hill Folk Museum, Pioneer Settlement, and the paddle steamer *Gem* recreate a 19th century inland river town; the site is worth a day of browsing.

Focal point of the Museum is the paddle steamer *Gem,* which serves as museum entrance, art gallery, restaurant, and administrative center. The museum is open daily from 9 A.M. to 5 P.M.

Working exhibits are located in a log cabin, station homestead and blacksmith's shop; a steam locomotive and several horse-drawn vehicles recall the era's transportation. You can see everyday household and agricultural items used by the pioneers, including farm implements and windmills. Tradesmen demonstrate craft skills in blacksmithing, sign painting, and wood turning. Members of the settlement staff dress in period costume.

After you have explored this inland waterway town, you can take a cruise on the paddle steamer *P. S. Pyap.* Weekday trips leave the wharf, at the Pioneer Settlement on Horseshoe Bend, at 1:30 and 3 P.M. You cruise the Murray River around its sweeping bends, beneath overhanging red gums, and past historic homesteads.

Daily rail services link Swan Hill and Melbourne, and coach tours of the Murray Valley pass through the town. Accommodations are available in five hotels, four motels, and a camper-trailer park.

Other valley attractions

Near Swan Hill is the pioneer *Tyntynder Homestead,* built in 1846; it evokes the gracious living of the 1840s, when paddle steamers plied the Murray and the homestead was the area's social center. Exhibits include an unusual collection of local relics of the time.

About 20 miles from Swan Hill, just over the border into New South Wales, you can spend an interesting day at Mel Ness Sheep Station watching sheep shearing and mustering on a 6,000-acre ranch. Kangaroos abound on the station, and a barbecue luncheon is available for guests.

For more information on tours to the Murray Valley, consult the Victorian Government Tourist Bureau in Melbourne.

Mildura

This prosperous small city is the center of an irrigated fruit growing area and the homeport of the paddlesteamer, *Melbourne.* Afternoon cruises depart Mildura wharf daily, except Saturday, at 2 P.M. and return at 4 P.M. year around. A longer cruise aboard the

SIDE TRIPS OUT OF MELBOURNE

paddlesteamer, *Wanera*, leaves from Wentworth just west of Mildura. The three-day cruise departs every second Monday at 10 A.M. returning at 4 P.M. Wednesday. Book passage through the Victorian Government Tourist Bureau in Melbourne.

Mildura lays claim to the longest bar in the world: 285 feet of drinking space—a claim you can verify for yourself at the Working Men's Club. Additional attractions are the "Rio Vista" Art Gallery, good fishing, and a koala colony on Lock Island. The town's library was a gift from Andrew Carnegie in 1908. Accommodations include several hotels, guest houses, and holiday apartments, in addition to four camping and camper-trailer parks.

Located 356 miles northwest of Melbourne, Mildura can be reached by air, rail, or on coach tours of the valley.

Hattah Lakes National Park, 50 miles south of Mildura at the intersection of the Calder and Murray Valley highways, is the home of many varieties of water birds, including large nesting colonies of ibis. In the spring you'll find a profusion of wildflowers.

SKI COUNTRY

Melbourne residents enjoy the ski areas of the Snowy Mountain area (see page 63), but Victoria also has its own ski country in the Southern Alps, stretching south and west from the Snowy Mountains. Here the terrain is gentle, with long, fast, hazard-free runs —ideal for ski touring. Powder snow is virtually unknown in the area; the best skiing comes during the latter part of the season (late August and September), when the snow has been compacted.

Years of light snowfall make some of Victoria's resorts chancy—but you can generally count on good snow from mid-June to mid-September at Mount Buller, Mount Buffalo, Mount Hotham, and Falls Creek.

Most of the area's resorts operate the year round. In the spring, the mountains are a patchwork of alpine flowers. Summer activities include camping, trout fishing, horseback riding, hiking, and mountain climbing. Information on the Australian Alps may be obtained from the Victorian Government Tourist Bureau, 272 Collins Street, Melbourne.

Mount Buller

Australia's busiest ski resort is Mount Buller (5,907 foot elevation), only 150 miles by road from Melbourne. Visitors may stay at two relatively new facilities: the Kooroora Hotel or the seven-story Arlberg Motel. More than 150 private lodges and chalets dot the area.

Fourteen ski tows transport skiers up the mountain; ski runs descend three sides of the peak. One of the ski schools has French instructors.

Mount Buffalo

With an elevation of only 5,654 feet, Mount Buffalo presents snow conditions that are less predictable than those at the other three major resorts. Located about 200 miles from Melbourne, the resort area has two hotels, several smaller commercial chalets, and two ski tows, including a 1,600-foot chairlift.

Mount Hotham

The most reliable snowfall in the entire region occurs at Mount Hotham (6,109 foot elevation), but this is also the most difficult of the four resorts to reach. Distance from Melbourne is 232 miles. Mount Hotham is close enough to the Mount Buffalo ski area (both use the same road) that you can stay in one and ski at both. Hotham Heights, on the slopes of the mountain, has a hotel and two chalets, a handful of apartments for weekly rental, and three modern ski tows.

Falls Creek

The ski village at Falls Creek nestles in a natural bowl deep in the heart of the Bogong High Plains, 236 miles from Melbourne. The bowl not only forms a natural trap for sunshine (promoting spring skiing) but also provides excellent beginners' slopes. The resort's international-standard runs are the site of an annual international race, the Ross Milne Memorial Slalom, held in July or August. A carefully integrated system of seven ski tows—a chairlift, two Pomas, and four T-bars—can lift 5,500 skiers per hour. Accommodations are available in about a dozen lodges in the area, all quite new.

MOUNT BULLER offers après-ski entertainment on the terrace of the Arlberg Motel, overlooking the ski slopes. Melbourne is only 150 miles away.

YACHTS TIE UP at Constitution Dock (above) after annual Sydney to Hobart race. Summer market (right) offers items from art to fruit. Excursion boat winds along Derwent River (far right) from Hobart to New Norfolk.

84 TASMANIA

EXPLORING TASMANIA—Australia's lush, green island state

Although the island state of Tasmania lies only 150 miles south of Melbourne across Bass Strait, it is a world apart from the rest of Australia. Steeped in history, the island's 400,000 people prefer to be called Tasmanians rather than Australians, and they refer to the rest of Australia as "the mainland." An old-world atmosphere, reminiscent of England, emanates from white stone cottages, winding lanes, hawthorn hedgerows, and Georgian architecture.

With the highest rainfall of any Australian state, most of Tasmania is covered by dense vegetation. Winter dusts mountain tops with snow, and spring brings a scent of apple blossoms—the island's green, grass-covered hills and deep valleys nurture miles of apple orchards. Clear streams merge into wide rivers spawning enough trout to attract fishermen from around the world. Forests cover about 47 percent of the land, with much of the southwest corner an unexplored wilderness.

Most Tasmanians would rather not mention that grandfather or great-grandfather was a convict, even though a sixth of the island's inhabitants are direct descendants. The island was settled in 1803 as a British penal colony, then called Van Diemen's Land. Most of its development was done by convict labor under military supervision; approximately 70,000 prisoners were sent here between 1803 and 1850. The convict traffic stopped in 1853. The island was renamed Tasmania in honor of its discoverer, the Dutch explorer Abel Tasman, in 1855.

THE HOLIDAY ISLAND

Only 190 miles wide and 180 miles long (the smallest of the Australian states), Tasmania is a delightful area for the overseas visitor—and a favorite holiday retreat for Australians as well. The island's excellent network of roads makes most destinations easily accessible by car and coach tour. Planes and car-ferries connect Tasmania with the mainland.

FISHERMAN casts his line into the Derwent. Tasmanian rivers and lakes are Australia's best fishing waters, abounding with rainbow, brown, and Eastern brook trout.

EMPRESS OF AUSTRALIA (above), one of two car ferries plying between the mainland and Tasmania; book a year ahead.

OUTDOOR DINING has leisurely charm at New Norfolk's Old Colony Inn, built in the early 1900s as residence for district's military commander.

To the island by plane or ship

Whether you enter Australia at Sydney or Melbourne, Tasmania is only a short flight by domestic air carrier. Fly-drive packages are available that include air fare between mainland capital cities and Launceston, accommodations, car, and free touring allowance.

If you are touring Australia by car, you cross Bass Strait by passenger-car ferry. The *Empress of Australia* operates between Melbourne and Devonport, while the *Australian Trader* sails between Sydney and the Tasmanian ports of Hobart, Bell Bay, and Burnie.

Tasmania's weather

Tasmania's climate is generally mild in summer and cool in winter. The warmest months, January and February, seldom find temperatures above the mid-70s. In July and August, winter in the southern hemisphere, snow falls above 3,000 feet.

The best season to visit Tasmania is between November and May. Australians flock to the island from mid-December well into February, during school vacation periods, and again for the Easter holidays. You should make reservations well in advance during those periods.

Traveling around the island

You'll find it easy to travel around the island of Tasmania. Visitors who prefer to set their own schedule will find several car rental agencies in Hobart and other Tasmanian towns.

Excellent bus service connects the main island towns, with daily service between Hobart, Devonport, Queenstown, Burnie, and Launceston. Tasmanian Railways operates daylight trips between Hobart and Wynard, via Launceston and Devonport, except Sunday.

For a change of pace, you can cruise from Hobart up the Derwent River to New Norfolk. Intrastate air service now links main cities and towns throughout the state; air tours and charter service are available in Hobart and Launceston.

HISTORIC HOBART

Your first stop will probably be Hobart on the southeastern coast, the historic capital of Tasmania and the second oldest city in Australia (1803). Hobart provides the best base for touring the island.

Surrounding one of the world's finest deep-water harbors, the city covers the broad lower valley of the Derwent River, a few miles inland from Storm Bay. If you arrive by ferry, the trip up the Derwent is memorable. Providing a spectacular backdrop to the city is Mount Wellington—snow-covered in winter, forested and green the rest of the year. The 14-mile ride up to the Pinnacle, the 4,166-foot summit, rewards you with an unobstructed view of the harbor, the tree-lined streets of Hobart, and a good portion of south and central Tasmania, as well.

Hobart is a sea-minded city. From downtown office buildings, people can gaze out their windows to watch the frequent arrivals of merchant ships. Along the harbor, ships' bows loom over the side streets; and fishing vessels, hung with nets and green glass buoys, create a picture postcard setting.

Getting settled

Hobart's best hotel, the Wrest Point Hotel-Casino, overlooks the Derwent River at Sandy Bay, about a mile from the city center. Guests can enjoy golf, yachting, and boating, in addition to the hotel's heated swimming pool and tennis and squash courts.

Other good downtown hotels are Hadley's Orient, the Downtowner, and the Town House.

Several motels also offer comfortable accommodations: the Derwent Village, on the banks of the Derwent River, six miles north of Hobart; the Jason, on the river's eastern shore, five miles from the city center; the Panorama, on the Tasman Highway overlooking the harbor; the new TraveLodge Motel, in downtown Hobart; and the Shoreline, at Howrah across the river.

For the economy-minded traveler, Tasmania boasts about a dozen youth hostels (see page 11), where the

HOBART'S SKYLINE mixes towering new office buildings with historic structures. Wrest Point Hotel-Casino, left, is the capital's leading hotel and Australia's first gambling casino.

overnight charge is less than a dollar. For a complete listing of Tasmanian hostels, contact the Youth Hostel Association, Box 174B, 105 Macquarie Street, Hobart.

Restaurants. For a city its size (150,000), Hobart has a surprisingly wide variety of good restaurants—ranging from the rather elegant dining room atop the Wrest Point Casino and the Room at the Top of the Downtowner to the Good Intent and Dirty Dick's Steak House, both in the old Battery Point section of town. The latter is unlicensed (no liquor) but serves fine steaks in interesting surroundings.

Other good restaurants are the Ball and Chain, the Beef Eater, the Chart Room, the Don Camillo, the Gaslighter, the Golden Bamboo, the Hill Top, the Mona Lisa, Vader's Cellar, and the Village Motel Restaurant.

After dark. Night life is pretty much limited to hotel dancing, though the Wrest Point Riviera and the Carlyle hotels do offer floor shows.

Less than a five-minute drive from the city center is Australia's first gambling casino, the Wrest Point Casino Hotel, a 21-story tower adjoining the Wrest Point Riviera. Topped with a restaurant and cocktail bar, it has rooms for 600 guests and a main gambling casino accommodating up to 300 would-be winners. You can keep busy with baccarat, black jack, French and American roulette and *chemin de fer*.

APPLE ORCHARDS abound in the Huon Valley. Cygnet (above) is one fruit-growing center; apples are sold throughout Australia and exported to England.

POUNDING SEAS have left their mark on the coast at Eaglehawk Neck, a narrow strip of land joining the Tasman Peninsula to the mainland of Tasmania.

Shopping in Hobart

Articles made from the island's natural resources make interesting mementoes. Most Tasmanian souvenirs fall into these categories: gemstones, wooden products, pottery, metalwork, framed work (mainly dried flower arrangements), shellcraft, and antiques. Leatherwork is increasingly popular, and you'll find handbags, wallets, and key cases.

Hobart's two main downtown department stores are Fitzgerald's, 91 Collins Street, and The Myer Emporium, fronting both Liverpool and Murray streets. Each store has a special counter with a comprehensive selection of local souvenirs. Other shops of special interest to visitors are Ward's Souvenir Shop on Murray Street, Ashton's on Liverpool Street, and the two locations of Rembrandt's.

EXCURSIONS FROM HOBART

Radiating from Hobart are regions displaying Tasmania's diversity. To the southwest lies the Huon Valley, source of most of Tasmania's apples. Westward is a wilderness area so rugged that it remains unpopulated and virtually unexplored. Northwest of Hobart are the mountains and national parks. The sheep-raising Midlands Valley stretches due north from Hobart toward Launceston. Farther afield, there's good skiing in the inland mountains of the lightly-inhabited northeastern corner; resort towns and white sand beaches are scattered along the east coast. The Tasman Peninsula off the southeastern coast was the site of the Port Arthur penal colony.

You can explore many of these areas on day trips from Hobart.

Orchards and seascapes

Topping the excursion list is the day trip from Hobart through the Huon Valley, Tasmania's principal apple orchard district. On a 90-mile loop trip southwest from Hobart—heading for the valley on Route 1 (the Huon Highway) and returning on Route 6 along the D'Entrecasteaux Channel—you combine orchard views with seascapes. Along the way you can take a side road to the top of Mount Wellington.

The island's first apple tree was planted in 1788 by the botanist accompanying Captain Bligh on the *H.M.S. Bounty*, when the ship anchored at Adventure Bay off Bruny Island south of Hobart. Tasmanian orchards produce about three-fourths of Australia's overseas apple exports—big, crisp Tasman Prides—most of which are sent to England.

Highway 1 continues south beyond the Huon District past dairy farms, sawmill towns, and tiny seaside hamlets. From the end of the road at Southport, you can drive west about five miles into the hills to Hastings Caves—open for spelunkers daily.

Also southwest of Hobart lies Hartz Mountains National Park, a superb hiking area of forests and lakes, with peaks rising above 4,000 feet and providing sweeping views over southern Tasmania.

Mount Field National Park

Another easy one-day trip from Hobart by bus or car is through the Derwent Valley, lush with apple orchards and hopfields, to Mount Field National Park, with its 40,000 acres of mountains, rain forests, lakes, and streams.

You drive northwest through New Norfolk, the largest town in the Derwent Valley. About 25 miles beyond is Russell Falls; here you'll enjoy the sight of a beautiful series of cascades dropping 160 feet into a lush gorge, green with rain forest plants and tree ferns. Between July and October, Mount Field is a popular ski resort.

Wilderness toll road. Beyond the park, the Gordon River Road continues westward about 50 miles into the wilderness, along a route that many people consider Australia's most spectacular mountain highway. Every turn of the road (and there are plenty of them) reveals another range of mountains.

At the end is Lake Pedder, a natural lake now filled beyond its natural shoreline as part of Tasmania's hydroelectric system. You can also see the primitive western country surrounding Lake Pedder National Park on air tours from Hobart.

The big "if" is weather: rainfall in the area is heavy, and a spectacular drive in clear weather becomes a waste of time if it is raining.

Port Arthur's old penal colony

The last of the penal settlements, Port Arthur occupies the tip of the Tasman Peninsula, 63 miles southeast of Hobart. Guides show visitors through the ruins of this monument to misery, abandoned in 1877, relating its history with gusto and gory details.

Severe punishments were inflicted on some of the colony's prisoners who returned to crime in Australia. Most of the prisoners, however, spent their time learning some trade and were later released to become useful citizens of the infant colony.

Many of the colony's graceful buildings were constructed with convict labor. Ruins of the since-burned settlements include the prison church, the exile cottage, commandant's residence, and the lunatic asylum (now a museum). On Eaglehawk Neck, the peninsula's narrow land bridge, vicious dogs were chained to prevent prisoners from escaping.

Sea sculpturing. Within a few miles of Eaglehawk Neck, the sea has carved several interesting sights. Stretching from the rugged cliffs into the sea is the

EAGLEHAWK NECK is narrow isthmus separating Tasman Sea from Norfolk Bay. Area has small resorts, good beaches, boats for fishing, variety of spectacular scenery.

LION STANDS GUARD over the prison ruins at Port Arthur. Abandoned in 1877, the penal colony southeast of Hobart was the scene of inhuman punishment.

SIX-ARCHED STONE BRIDGE spans the Coal River near Richmond. One arch frames Australia's oldest Roman Catholic Church, built in 1823. Bridge is the country's oldest.

Tesselated Pavement, a vast plaza of rectangular paving blocks laid out by nature in one of her more orderly moods.

Nearby is an impressive blowhole, as well as Tasman's Arch, a bridge of land carved over the centuries by the crashing waves, now far, far below. At Devil's Kitchen you look straight down into a cauldron of churning, roaring surf, hemmed in on three sides by sheer cliffs.

Taranna Lodge. Shoppers interested in antiques will want to visit nearby Taranna Lodge on the shores of Norfolk Bay. Built in the 1840s, the lodge was used by government officers and others visiting Port Arthur on official business. Later, the lodge served as a hotel before it became the Taranna Post Office.

Currently being restored as the Norfolk Galleries, it houses an interesting collection of old furniture, porcelain, sterling, and Sheffield plate, as well as paintings and lithographs by early Australian artists.

The Midlands

Ross, Longford, and Oatlands—in the Midlands—and the town of Richmond, across the Derwent 15 miles northeast of Hobart, are probably the best preserved of Tasmania's villages. Founded in 1814, Ross is noted for its three-arched bridge built by convict labor; a village store operated by the same family for more than a century; and the Scotch Thistle Inn, restored as a restaurant.

Longford is known for its historic church and village green. This rich agricultural district supports the largest herd of stock in the entire state.

Oatlands, 52 miles north of Hobart, was established in 1826 as a military camp and stopping place for coaches traveling between Hobart and Launceston, to protect travelers against the notorious bushrangers (highway robbers). Topiary tree figures line both sides of the road northward to Antrill Ponds.

Richmond's special features include the six-arched stone bridge, Australia's oldest span, built across the

---

TASMANIAN ABORIGINES... A VANISHED RACE

Abel Tasman, the Dutch discoverer of Tasmania, thought the island was inhabited by a race of giants. When his men went ashore near the future site of Port Arthur, they heard strange voices and saw trees with foot notches cut at such distant intervals that only a giant could use them.

The Aborigines of Tasmania were not giants as feared, but they were different from the native tribes on the mainland. Physically, their hair was fuzzy and worn in rattails thickened with a mixture of animal fat and red ochre that hardened like a natural helmet. They wore no clothes, and they lived in caves, hollow trees, and tent-like huts. Their bodies were decorated with red ocher, scars, and shell necklaces. Food was shellfish, lily roots, wallabies, fruits, and berries. They had no dingoes (dogs) or boomerangs. Anthropologists believe they may have been Melanesians who sailed from the New Guinea vicinity, two or three thousand which then divided into about twenty tribes.

The early settlers so mistreated the Aborigines that in 1830 the Governor decided to end the problem by rounding up the primitive tribes and isolating them on another island.

The round-up, or "black line" sweep, as it was called, was described by Charles Darwin six years later in *The Voyage of the Beagle:*
"Martial law was declared and the population commanded to assist in one great sweep of the island to capture the whole race. A line of three thousand soldiers and settlers formed across the island (like an India tiger hunt) to drive the Aborigines down onto Tasman's peninsula. This failed when the natives slipped through the line at night. Shortly though, a party of thirteen from two tribes, came in and gave up in despair. The rest of the natives were persuaded to follow the original thirteen. They were removed to an island and provided with food and clothes. Most eventually died from a variety of chest complaints."

A few returned to Tasmania, but Trugannis, the last of her race, died at Hobart in 1876. All that remains of the Tasmanian Aborigines today is the habitat group in the Tasmania Museum and Art Gallery in Hobart.

Coal River in 1823; the oldest Roman Catholic Church in Australia, completed in 1837; and the Richmond Gaol (jail), built in 1825, with walls three feet thick.

ELSEWHERE ON THE ISLAND

Beyond the Hobart area, scenic highway routes lead to Tasmania's other towns and attractions.

Launceston, the state's second largest city, is the hub of northern Tasmania. From here you can make a number of excursions to coastal resorts and the lake district in the center of the island. Fine beaches and rich farmlands line the northwestern coast, while the wild region of the west holds some of Tasmania's most spectacular scenery.

The Launceston district

Set in pleasant, hilly countryside 40 miles inland at the head of the Tamar River estuary, Launceston is a small, provincial city of 66,000. Three scenic highways and good bus and railway connections, link it with Hobart in the south. The city has a half-dozen hotels and motor-inns including Overton House, a restored 128-year old Victorian house now incorporated into the Colonial Motor Inn.

The town's parks and private gardens are among the best in Australia. European trees, particularly oaks and elms, and flowering shrubs flourish in Launceston's mild, moist climate. This countryside reminds many travelers of rural England, but the resemblance is due more to the English trees and hedge plants, introduced by early settlers, than to the land itself.

In ten minutes you can walk from the city center to famed Cataract Gorge, an awesome rocky corridor

LAUNCESTON, Tasmania's second largest city, provides an excellent base for touring the lake district and the excellent beaches and resorts along the island's northeastern coast.

CAMERON STREET, Launceston (above) offers access to one of the city's parks. Tree ferns lend tropical beauty to Russell Falls (left), near entrance to Mount Field National Park.

TASMANIA **91**

HISTORIC HOMESTEADS abound throughout Tasmania. A favorite stop is Entally National House, built during the early colonial period at Hadspen, south of Launceston.

OLD WHALING PORT of Bicheno, on Tasmania's eastern coast, provides a natural harbor for fishing fleets; catches include scallops and tuna. You can arrange for a fishing trip.

chewed out by the South Esk River. The rapids are especially exciting after a heavy rain in the highlands. On the north face of the gorge, a pathway leads along the face of the cliff about a mile to Cataract Cliff Grounds and Park. You can cross the river on a chair lift or by a suspension bridge leading to a picnic area, Olympic-sized swimming pool, and children's wading pool, with kiosk and changing rooms nearby.

Entally House. Eight miles south of Launceston at Hadspen, Entally House is an excellent example of early colonial architecture. Built in 1820, the restored mansion was once the home of a Tasmanian premier. The building is furnished with antiques of exceptional quality. Early horse-drawn vehicles are displayed in the outer buildings of the estate.

The Great Lake, 75 miles southwest from Launceston, is one of Australia's leading trout fishing resorts. Lying 3,333 feet above sea level, the 15-mile-long lake is also part of Tasmania's hydro electric system. Visitors' galleries are located at power stations around the lake.

East coast resorts

Tasmania's east coast, paralleled by the Tasman Highway, is famed for its mild climate, beautiful beaches, fishing, and swimming facilities.

Of numerous popular coastal holiday resorts, the principal ones are St. Helens, Scamander, Bicheno, Coles Bay, Swansea, and Orford. You'll find good motel accommodations at all of them except Coles Bay, which has an excellent older guest house with cabins—the Château—that is popular with families.

St. Helens, 161 miles northeast of Hobart, and 104 miles east of Launceston, has a large sheltered bay popular for fishing and boating. Good surf beaches line the open coast, and forest streams wending from the north and west offer excellent trout fishing. Crayfishing boats anchor in Binnalong Bay, a favorite fishing area. St. Helens Point, a high headland, offers magnificent views of the coast.

Bicheno and Triabunna on the coast are old whaling towns where people still make their living from the sea. You can arrange for deepwater fishing trips with the local fishermen.

At Coles Bay you can explore secluded coves, swim from snow-white beaches, scale rocky cliffs, or stroll leisurely along quiet, bush-edged trails. The small guest house stands at the base of The Hazards, thousand-foot-high hills of red granite.

Tasmania's largest park

The largest wildlife sanctuary and scenic reserve in Tasmania is Cradle Mountain-Lake St. Clair National Park in the Central Highlands, covering an area of 525 square miles. From Devonport on the north coast, the park is a three-hour drive. Lake St. Clair, at the southern end of the park, is 105 miles north of Hobart on the Lyell Highway.

A favorite among hikers is the 55-mile, 5-day trek through the park from Waldheim Chalet at Cradle Mountain to Cynthia Bay at the south end of Lake St. Clair, with overnight stops at huts along the way.

The wild western coast

The most unusual and fascinating part of Tasmania is the island's wild western coast. The region varies from the unexplored wilderness of the southwest to the bare stark hills of the Queenstown area, and from the savage magnificence of Frenchman's Cap National Park to Marrawah in the far north, with its Aboriginal rock carvings.

A danger in the mountains is a Tasmanian phenomenon called the "horizontals." Saplings grow about 50 feet high, blow over, and lie parallel to the ground—but about 40 feet above it. This creates an area that looks like solid ground, but the man who falls through is trapped in a veritable dungeon from which escape is very difficult.

A good way to glimpse the territory is to take the Lyell Highway into Queenstown, 158 miles northwest of Hobart, and a boat trip up the Gordon River from Strahan.

Queenstown. This is the largest township on the west coast (about 5,000 people), prospering from nearby copper fields. Before the turn of the century, the surrounding hills were green and covered with forests and dense underbrush. But when the smelters were installed to process copper ore, the timber was cut for fuel, and sulphur fumes denuded the slopes. Heavy rains washed away the topsoil, and the rocks became stained in shades of chrome yellow, purple, grey, and pink. Ore processing was changed in 1922, and plant life is now returning.

A wilderness boat trip. The only developed port on the west coast is Strahan, about 26 miles west of Queenstown, on the northern shore of Macquarie Harbour. Fishing boats and ships handling lumber sail in and out of the port.

Strahan is the departure point for a one-day boat trip across Macquarie Harbour and up the Gordon River into a solitude unbroken except by the sounds of the wilderness. You cruise 20 miles upriver, through stretches of thick rain forest that are still relatively unexplored.

The northwest corner. From Queenstown you can travel north on the Murchison Highway through rugged mountains to Burnie on the northern coast. A timber and agricultural center, the town is the terminus for the Sydney-Tasmania ferry.

From Burnie, Highway 2 heads west to Marrawah, where Aboriginal rock carvings dating back to the Ice Age can be seen in caves overhanging the beach.

QUIET, DESERTED BEACHES stretch for miles along Tasmania's scenic western coast. At Ocean Beach, near the town of Strahan, you have the magnificent shore to yourself.

Emu Bay Railway. Rail fans will enjoy a ride on the diesel-powered ore train, operated by the Emu Bay Railway between Burnie and Primrose Station, Rosebery. You ride on bench seats in the "guard car" at the rear of the train. The scenic 85-mile trip approximates the route of the Murchison Highway. You can make arrangements at the offices of the Emu Bay Railway in Burnie.

For the sports minded

Tasmania is world famous for its trout-stocked lakes and streams. All waters are open from November 1 to April 30, including some scenic back country with seldom-fished waters. Brown trout up to 20 pounds have been taken on the northwest coast; the highlands are known for wet and dry-fly lake fishing, while southern Tasmania specializes in stream fishing under rugged conditions. Some fine streams are less than 25 miles from Hobart. Deep sea fishermen will find bluefin, tuna, mako, and other sharks off the southern and southeastern coasts.

Other sports facilities include golf courses in Hobart and Launceston, open the year around; tennis courts and bowling greens in all cities; the sweeping beaches of the northwestern and eastern coasts for swimming; lakes, rivers, and the ocean for boating and yachting; skiing in winter at Ben Lomond in the north and Mount Field in the south; and the outstanding hiking trails in the national parks.

Spectators can enjoy cricket matches in the summer and football (Australian rules) in the winter. Horse and greyhound races are held in Hobart and Launceston and motorcycle scrambles near Launceston. Wood chopping carnivals are held at agricultural shows in the spring and autumn.

TORRENS LAKE (above) is part of the greenbelt encircling Adelaide. Flinders Ranges (right) north of Adelaide typify the country's dry interior. Adelaide is a city of wide streets (far right), parks, gardens, and fountains.

94 SOUTH AUSTRALIA

SOUTH AUSTRALIA—graced by Adelaide, the Murray River, wine country

Much of the state of South Australia is desert and semidesert, but not so the southern section—a delightful prosperous region of wheat, wool, wine, and fruit orchards surrounding Adelaide, the capital.

Along the coast are miles of beaches bordering attractive gulfs, bays, and harbors. Inland is the Barossa Valley, the country's main wine producing region. To the north and east the Flinders and Mount Lofty ranges offer colorful mountain scenery, sparkling reservoirs, and opportunities to see native birds and wildlife in natural surroundings. You can tour wineries, attend colorful festivals, enjoy uncrowded resorts, and explore rural towns and villages.

South Australia was developed on a how-to-colonize plan created by Edward Gibbon Wakefield, a philosopher, while serving time in Newgate Prison in London. Even though he had never been to the country, Wakefield described the plan in *Letter from Sydney*, his book dealing with the art of colonization in Australia. He detailed errors made in settling New South Wales and laid out a plan for the future colonization of Australia. Land was the key, he said, and it should be sold to land owners at a sufficiently high price to compel laborers to work until they had saved enough to buy land. This would enable the colony to survive without convicts. To some degree, Wakefield's philosophy was followed in the colonizing of South Australia, and its residents take pride in the fact that their state was not settled by convicts.

With a population of 879,000, Adelaide contains nearly three quarters of South Australia's population. Elizabeth (about 33,000 people), Whyalla (33,500), Mount Gabier (18,000), and Port Pirie (12,600) are the other large towns in the state.

ADELAIDE, CITY OF PARKS

Situated on the banks of the Torrens River between the Mount Lofty Range and the waters of Gulf St. Vincent, Adelaide is a graceful city. It owes its quiet

SOUTH AUSTRALIA 95

charm to a town plan carefully laid out in 1836 by Colonel William Light, the new colony's Surveyor-General. Although his critics charged that the new city was "nothing but a military containment," the plan had an orderliness that has turned Adelaide into one of Australia's most beautiful cities.

The heart of Adelaide is a square mile of streets centering around Victoria Square. Surrounding this inner city are 1,700 acres of green parklands, separating the downtown district from the residential and manufacturing areas. The Torrens River runs through the northern green belt of parklands, where one finds the Adelaide Oval (for cricket), the Adelaide Festival Centre, the municipal golf course, tennis courts, football fields, hockey grounds. The river widens on the west to mile-long Torrens Lake Gardens—formal gardens, grassy meadows, a great collection of trees, ponds, restaurants, and beautiful Torrens Lake with its rowboats and graceful black swans.

Parklands surrounding the inner city contain numerous children's playgrounds and lawn bowling greens, as well as a zoo, botanic gardens, and a municipal swimming pool.

Hotels and motels

Adelaide has over 30 hotels and motels in the city and suburbs. Among those most favored by overseas visitors are the Adelaide TraveLodge, the Australia Hotel, Grosvenor Hotel, Hilton Motor Inn, Noah's Arkaba Hotel, Parkroyal Motor Inn, South Terrace TraveLodge, Town House, Meridien Lodge, Earl of Zetland, Royal Coach, and Flinders Lodge.

Dining and entertainment variety

Although Adelaide retained legal restraints on hard liquor for many years, today it is easy to drink, dine, dance, and watch a floor show. Hotel facilities include restaurants, cocktail lounges, music, and special shows; and you'll find a varied assortment of lounges, restaurants, and espresso bars tucked away on side streets, in basements, and along arcades.

In recent years Adelaide's restaurants have gained fresh sophistication from the city's newly arrived citizens—Lebanese, Chinese, Italian, Yugoslavian, French, German, American, Hungarian, Greek, Spanish, Indonesian, Dutch, and Sri Lankan. From among the many fine ones, here are a few restaurants that set the pace:

Henry Ayers, North Terrace, is Adelaide's most elegant restaurant. It is situated in a section of Ayers House, a magnificent old colonial villa that was once the home of one of the state's earliest premiers. Paxton's, in the same building, is a popular bistro specializing in steaks and Lebanese dishes. It also features an excellent luncheon smorgasbord.

- Arkaba Steak Cellar, on Gilbert Place, is housed in an old wine cellar, with an intimate atmosphere.
- Lord Kitchener's Indian Kitchen, on Unley Road, is housed in an old cottage; it specializes in regional curries with spiced side dishes.
- The Magic Flute, in North Adelaide, has a French menu with some Swiss dishes; it is furnished with large round wooden tables and offers classical background music.
- Decca's Place, on Melbourne Street, is housed in an attractive cottage and features Continental and Hungarian cuisine. Surrounding the restaurant is a vine-covered courtyard, where ripening grapes hang during the summer and a splashing fountain offers cool sounds.
- Los Amigos, on Chesser Street, is a basement restaurant with white-washed walls, Spanish furniture; it features Spanish cuisine.
- Benjamin's, on the north shore of Torrens Lake, is pleasantly situated facing the lake and parkland; it offers Continental cuisine, seafood, and wine cellar.
- Swain's Seafood Restaurant, on Glen Osmond Road, Frewville, is the only restaurant in Adelaide serving seafood exclusively.
- Charlie Brown's, on Port Road in Hindmarsh, specializes in Italian peasant food.
- Festival Theater Restaurant, on King William Road, presents international cuisine in the surroundings of Adelaide Festival Theater.
- The Samurai, on Melbourne Street, is a Japanese restaurant with a representative menu and an excellent plum wine aperitif.
- The Adelaide Oyster Bar, in a basement on Grenfell Street, is one spot where you can get your fill of fresh oysters opened in front of you.

Touring starts at Victoria Square

To explore the city on foot or by car, begin in the center at Victoria Square, where Queen Victoria's statue stands in a parklike setting of trees. Surrounding the square are some excellent examples of early Adelaide architecture: the Treasury Building, St. Francis Xavier's Cathedral, the Magistrate's Court House, and the Supreme Court.

Chief among the city's attractions are the following:

King William Street, with its median strip of lawns and flowers, is the widest capital city road in Australia. Lining it are most of the banks, insurance offices, and travel agencies, as well as the town hall and the post office.

It is the city's avenue for parades, festivals, and other public events. The city's families gather here in November to watch John Martins Pageant, marking the official opening of the Christmas season. In past years Adelaide's citizens have watched their troops march down the street during three wars to the Cross of Sacrifice in Pennington Gardens.

North Terrace, a tree-lined boulevard bordered by cultural and civic buildings, provides at its western end near King William Street most of the air and rail terminals, Parliament House, the Grosvenor Hotel, and Adelaide's oldest church, Holy Trinity. Its eastern half has an almost continental atmosphere with shade trees, lawns, and gardens. Here also are Government House, the Adelaide Museum, Art Gallery, the State Library, the University of Adelaide, the Royal Adelaide Hospital, and the Botanic Garden. Rundle Street is the major shopping center, with large retail stores, boutiques, cinemas, coffee lounges, snack bars, and colorful fruit carts. At the eastern end are sporting goods shops and photographic equipment suppliers.

The business district lies north of Victoria Square in the area of King William, Currie, Grenfell, Franklin, and Flinders streets. The town hall and post office, diagonally opposite each other on the corner of Franklin and King William streets, have clock towers that surprisingly always agree on the time.

Light's Vision—a memorial to Colonel Light, who laid out the town plan—crowns Montefiore Hill north of the river, overlooking the city.

Central Market, just west of Victoria Square, is a huge, roofed food center, sprawling over 4 acres with row upon row of stalls laden with abundant produce displays—fresh garden vegetables piled high alongside grapes, cherries, apricots, peaches, oranges, plums, and pears. Delicatessen and butcher stands lend their own aromas with hearty cheeses, plump sausages, geese, ducks, and turkeys. Bakery stalls will tempt you with fresh breads, cookies, cakes, and other sweets.

City tour. A half-day city and garden tour takes in most of Adelaide's highlights, including the parks and Botanic Gardens, North Terrace, and Torrens Lake. You see the city view from Light's Vision monument and ride through the city's suburbs. Along the way you pass many holdovers from another century—old stone houses, cottages, schools, churches, and pubs.

Good buys—opals and antiques

One of the thriving local industries is the manufacture of opal jewelry, with stones from South Australia's own mines, making Adelaide one of Australia's best cities for opal shopping. Look for small workshops tucked away on back streets—little factories where opal is polished and cut on the premises to make custom jewelry. Most of the major jewelry stores and department stores also stock a good range of opal jewelry.

Antique hunting can be combined with enjoyable sightseeing in North Adelaide's Melbourne Street. An enterprising, aesthetically-minded resident persuaded a group of imaginative shopkeepers (antique dealers among them) to join with him in restoring

VICTORIA SQUARE FOUNTAIN, at the end of King William Street, marks Adelaide's center. The square is a good starting point for exploring the city.

SUNLIGHT filters through the vines shading the courtyard of Decca's Place, a favorite dining spot. Many Adelaide restaurants feature cuisines from around the world.

SOUTH AUSTRALIA 97

FUTURISTIC ADELAIDE FESTIVAL CENTRE soars above Torrens River where excursion boat Popeye *waits for passengers.*

OUTDOOR ART exhibitions are just one feature of Adelaide's biennial Festival of Arts, when the entire city joins in a 3-week cultural festival.

part of Melbourne Street into a charming area of shops, restaurants, boutiques, and galleries. Brick-paved walkways, shaded by arbors with climbing vines, lead to numerous small shops, all adhering to a code of quality and design.

Antique dealers are found throughout the city and suburbs. Among the best are these: Antique Galleries, Unley Road, for a wide range of antique furniture; Artist's Market, Unley Road, specializing in porcelain; Investigator Gallery Antiques, Magill Road, with a wide range of Oriental antiques. Items ranging from the antiquities to Victorian bric-a-brac can be found at Megaw and Hogg on Leigh Street, J. G. Elder in North Adelaide, Moghul Antiques on Pirie Street, and Bagot Antiques, North Adelaide.

Authentic Aboriginal artifacts can be obtained from the Aboriginal Artists Centre, 125 North Terrace.

Twenty miles of beaches

Adelaide's beaches stretch for 20 miles along the coast, the nearest ones only 5½ miles west of the city center. Extending from Outer Harbor in the north to Marino in the south, the principal resorts are Largs, Semaphore, Grange, Henley, Glenelg, Seacliff, and Marino. They can be reached by bus, train, or streetcar from the city. In addition to water sports, you'll find facilities for tennis, golf, and lawn bowling.

In the early morning, racehorses are exercised along the beaches, and members of the "icebergers" have their early dip every day of the year. Even on cool evenings and winter weekends you'll find the locals on the beaches. On summer weekends when swimmers and sun worshippers can barely find elbow room, the coastal waters bloom with the brilliantly colored sails of hundreds of yachts.

Festival city

Biennially—in March of even numbered years—the Adelaide Festival of Arts brings together some of the world's finest performing talents. Opera and ballet, jazz and symphony concerts, folk dancing, comedies and dramatic plays are presented during the 22-day cultural festival. Art and sculpture fill the galleries and spill over into outdoor exhibits. Floral displays provide color in the gardens. Processions and pageantry complete the festival's calendar.

Focal point for the festival is the recently completed Adelaide Festival Centre, alongside the Torrens River, containing a multipurpose theater, drama and experimental theater, outdoor amphitheater, and restaurant.

Other principal celebrations held annually are the Tunarama Festival at Port Lincoln (January); the Schutzenfest at Hahndorf, a shooting contest (January); the Great Eastern Steeplechase at Oakbank in the Mount Lofty Ranges (Easter); the Vintage Festival in nearby Barossa Valley (April during odd-numbered years); the Royal Agricultural Show (September); John Martin's Christmas Pageant (2nd Saturday in November); and surf carnivals (semimonthly November to April).

EXCURSIONS FROM ADELAIDE

The vast stretches of desert comprising most of the northern and western parts of South Australia are for that special breed of vacationer—the adventurer interested in dry lake beds, salt bush, moonlike stretches of rocky plain, ghost towns, and opal mines.

But the countryside surrounding Adelaide is varied and interesting, ranging from Kangaroo Island offshore to the southwest, to nearby mountains and the rich farmlands of the Murray River valley.

Numerous half-day and full-day excursions travel to the major attractions—among them the opal fields at Coober Pedy and Andamooka (see below), the world's largest silver-lead-zinc mine at Broken Hill, actually in New South Wales (see page 103), and the vineyards, wineries, and orchards of the Barossa

---

OPAL FOSSICKING AT COOBER PEDY

With a little luck, a rockhound can have a heady day digging for opals at Coober Pedy, about 600 miles north of Adelaide. All you need to become a weekend opal fossicker are a Miner's Right (costing A$1), a pick and shovel, a strong back, and a constitution able to withstand desert temperatures.

Miners at Coober Pedy and nearby Andamooka (a hundred miles away) dig out more than A$8 million worth of opals annually. They pock-mark the ground with small crater-like surface diggings and sink mine shafts running underground at a shallow angle. The Coober Pedy field has yielded a 135-ounce opal, and the Andamooka field was the source of the 220-ounce "Desert Flame of Andamooka". As an amateur, you can sift through the piles of old rubble and scratch into the walls of abandoned mines.

To the casual tourist seeking an outback experience, the arid, lunar-like landscape and the unusual little town of Coober Pedy have appeal enough. The town has no streets, no street signs, and no trees (except one made of metal posts). Two motels (the Opal Inn and the Desert Cave Motel), a small market, and a couple of restaurants mark the downtown area. Nearly half of the 3,000 residents live underground (even the church is underground). Thus, the name of the town: Coober Pedy, Aboriginal for "white fellow live underground."

This underground way of life is one fascination of Coober Pedy. You can visit the church and the Opal Cave, a three-room cavern where you can see opals cut and polished and see one of the world's finest opal collections. Opals, mounted and unmounted, are available in Coober Pedy at prices considerably lower than in the larger cities.

Above ground, it is impossible to distinguish on sight persons who have struck it rich and those living off credit. But the wealthy miner often lives in a dugout dwelling as luxurious as a city apartment, with several rooms, wall-to-wall carpets, stereo, and cocktail bar. The largest such dugout, Aladdin's Cave, has 11 rooms and a shop covering 3,420 square feet. All miners—successful or hopeful—work their claims between 3 and 10 A.M. when temperatures are relatively cool (in summer, mid-day heat can climb to 120°).

More than 100 million years ago, the sea covered this area of Australia, laying down sediment and entrapping the silica solutions that developed into opals. The gems are found in foot-thick seams of sandstone, below layers of rock and jasper.

You can get to Coober Pedy from Adelaide by bus or by Opal Air, which operates eight-seater Cessnas on a regular schedule. Coach tours and one-day air tours are also available from Adelaide. For details, contact the South Australian Tourist Bureau, 18 King William Street, Adelaide.

In addition to Coober Pedy and Andamooka, you can visit gem mining areas at Lightning Ridge in far northern New South Wales (home of the famous black opals) and in the Anakie District of Queensland, an important sapphire-producing area where good stones can still be found near old diggings and where visitors can fossick around in established workings.

MINER ASCENDS from underground home in Coober Pedy; some dugouts are luxurious.

Valley (see below). Below are several additional places worth a visit.

Mount Lofty's miniature mountains

The foothills of the Mount Lofty Ranges are only 4 miles from the city, sweeping along Adelaide's eastern skirts and providing views over the city and countryside. The rounded, low-lying hills, fertile and well-wooded, catch most of the winter rains, swelling the creeks and rivers and filling the valley reservoirs.

Mountainside villages have gradually become city suburbs as more and more people choose to live among the hills and trees, and careful zoning has avoided development on hills facing the city. Away from the main roads, numerous townships follow the seasons with pruning, ploughing, fertilizing, and harvesting. Sheep graze on steep hillsides, and cattle roam among huge old eucalyptus trees.

Though only a miniature mountain range, the Mount Lofty Ranges embrace four recreation parks, a couple of wildlife sanctuaries, several historical buildings, a wildflower garden, miles of walking trails, and numerous picnic areas.

Six miles south of Adelaide is Belair Recreation Park, six square miles of bush surrounding the old Government House. Built as a summer residence in 1860, the century-old building has been restored and is now a museum containing Victorian memorabilia.

At Cleland Conservation Park, Torrens Gorge Wildlife Park, and in another park with the delightful name of Humbug Scrub, you can mingle with kangaroos, emus, koalas, wombats, and a variety of Australian birds.

Ol' Man Murray

Rising in the Australian Alps between Melbourne and Canberra, Australia's longest river—the Murray—flows northwest for most of its 1,609 miles, forming the boundary between Victoria and New South Wales for much of its route. Southeast of Adelaide, the river widens into silt-laden Lake Alexandrina before entering the sea at Encounter Bay.

Constantly changing its course over the centuries, the river has left a wide swath of rich bottom land now used for orchards, vineyards, and dairy farms. Protected by a series of weirs and locks, the river towns serve both as farming centers and river resorts.

Goolwa. A drive through the Mount Lofty Ranges past Aldgate, Macclesfield, and Strathalbyn leads to the historic old river port of Goolwa on Lake Alexandrina. In the river trading days, Goolwa was the last port of call, and many buildings remain from this time. On the approaches to Goolwa, you'll find a picnic area in a bird sanctuary where you can walk among pelicans, geese, swans, and ducks.

A launch cruise on the *Aroona*, through a series of locks, takes you past the dam that created the lake at the mouth of the Murray. The return route is through orchards and rich dairying country.

River cruises. Houseboats for river cruising may be rented at riverside resort towns; minimum booking period is usually two days. Information is available from the South Australia Tourist Bureau office in Adelaide. For a more carefree journey on the Murray, book passage on the *Coonawarra* or the *Murray River Queen* (see page 102).

Wine Country

Australia's greatest wine making region, the Barossa Valley, lies only 30 miles northeast of Adelaide, a pleasant trip through rolling pastoral lands. Here, in a valley 18 miles long and about 5 miles wide, is produced about a third of Australia's wines.

The three main towns in the area are Tanunda, Angaston, and Nuriootpa—though numerous smaller settlements cluster around them and contribute to the valley's wine production. The towns have retained an old world look, with solid stone houses, old German cottages, and carefully cultivated gardens set along scrupulously clean and neat tree-lined streets. At the center of each community is a Lutheran Church, its square tower and belfry standing above the surrounding buildings. Many of the wineries are still family owned; some boast chateau-like buildings and clock towers reminiscent of the wine growing districts of the fatherland.

The original settlers were from Prussia and Silesia, members of Lutheran communities who migrated so they might practice their own religion. They planted the first vines in 1847 near Tanunda and Rowland Flats. Although generations removed, the present-day population retains many old German customs. Many of the names are German. The Lutheran religion predominates. Brass band competitions are held in Tanunda each November. Old artifacts created by 19th century German craftsmen in colonial days are still to be found.

The best time to visit the Barossa Valley wineries is from mid-February through the end of April. In odd numbered years, the Barossa Valley celebrates the vintage with a large scale festival in late March or early April. Contributing to the carnival atmosphere, suntanned girls in German costume compete for the title of Vintage Queen, and the Tanunda Liederfel Choir performs. Processions, dancing, feasting, wine sampling, a grape picking contest, and winery inspections add to the activities.

An old whaling port

The largest and most popular seaside resort near Adelaide is Victor Harbour, 52 miles to the south on

SEAL BAY on Kangaroo Island is a breeding ground (left); part of this unspoiled island is a nature preserve. Grape pressing championships are one of the highlights at the Vintage Fair in the Barossa Valley (above).

a beautiful, sheltered section of Encounter Bay. The road from Adelaide winds through the vineyards of McLaren Vale and the almond groves of Willunga. Whaler's Haven, near the harbor, is a museum with relics of early whaling days.

Nearby Granite Island, joined to the mainland by a causeway, is buffeted by giant rollers crashing against its windward side, throwing spray high into the air. On the island's harbor side, you can swim and study the marine life in sheltered pools along the causeway.

Granites and glaciated rocks from the Glacier Age stand exposed in many areas around Victor Harbour. You can examine the rocks in comfort at Glacier Rocks Tea Room in the Inman Valley, 8 miles from the town. From the restaurant, you have a magnificent view of the valley; near the swimming pool are excellent examples of striated glacial rocks.

Unspoiled Kangaroo Island

Seventy miles southwest of Adelaide, Kangaroo Island offers a wild yet serene coast, combined with fishing, swimming, sailing, and pleasant resorts. Much of the island's original character remains—abundant wildlife, sweeping beaches, secluded coves, unspoiled rivers, and wind-sculptured boulders. Ninety miles long, it varies in width from 34 miles to a mile at its narrowest point.

When the white man arrived about 1802, Kangaroo Island was uninhabited. Because the mainland Aborigines had not developed boats sturdy enough to cross the channel, they held the island in awe, referring to it as Karta, Island of the Dead. However, evidence indicates habitation by an earlier race, probably pre-Australoid and similar to the Tasmanian Aborigines. Seal hunters and escaped convicts began to occupy the island about 1816.

Transportation. Access to Kangaroo Island is just 40 minutes by air from Adelaide; by sea, a passenger/car ferry takes six hours. On the island, sightseeing buses leave from Kingscote, American River, and Penneshaw, the principal resorts on the northeast coast.

Towns. Largest of the island resorts is Kingscote, offering many safe beaches, a seafront swimming pool, long jetty, and the island's main shopping area. American River, southeast of Kingscote, is a holiday resort in a woodland setting. The waterway is not really a river, but an arm of the sea separating Dudley Peninsula from the rest of the island. Penneshaw, on

SOUTH AUSTRALIA **101**

RIVER TRIP ON A PADDLEWHEELER

For a memorable trip penetrating the heart of rural South Australia, one of the five-day cruises up the Murray River by paddlewheeler is hard to top. You travel more than 200 miles upstream on Australia's great waterway, seeing parts of the country seldom visited by tourists.

The diesel-powered paddlewheeler, *Murray River Queen*, has fully air-conditioned cabins for 70 passengers, a spacious sun-deck, dining room, bar, reading room, and television lounge. The *Coonawarra*, with accommodations for 42 passengers, is a stalwart survivor of the old transport system. She offers a similar style of holiday but with a little less luxury. The *Murray River Queen* operates from Goolwa to Swan Reach and return, the *Coonawarra* from Murray Bridge to Morgan.

During the lazy, sunny days, your boat glides past great stands of gum trees, towering sand and limestone cliffs, lagoons teeming with river birds and wildlife. You may even see some of South Australia's huge aquatic lizards—2 to 4-foot reptiles—eyeing you from their sunny perch on the river bank. Your vista includes wealthy river towns, vineyards, orchards, rich farmlands, and the relics of outpost settlements. At night the boat ties up at century-old landings under towering, gnarled ancient gum trees.

Fishing gear is provided (licenses are not required.) Fares for the five days range from A$58 to $72.

PADDLEWHEELER Coonawarra *cruises leisurely up the tree-lined Murray River on 5-day excursions.*

Dudley Peninsula, looks 8 miles across the strait (called Backstairs Passage) to the mainland. An attractive town with a white sandy beach, jetty, and sheltered anchorage, it has a rocky promontory populated with fairy penguins. These birds are smaller than their Antarctic cousins, standing only 8 to 10 inches high.

South Coast Road. If you have time for further exploration, the South Coast Road takes you past seal breeding grounds at Seal Bay, Vivonne Bay with its crayfishing fleet, the limestone caves at Kelly Hill, and to Flinders Chase, a fauna and flora reserve covering most of the island's western end. Here you'll find kangaroos, wallabies, emus, and Cape Barren geese. If you stop for lunch at the picnic grounds, you may be joined by kangaroos and goanna lizards.

Mount Gambier's crater lakes

Mount Gambier, a large commercial center on the coast about 300 miles southeast of Adelaide, takes its name from an extinct volcano rising above the town. Inside the mountain crater are several small water-filled basins—three beautiful crater lakes.

The superb setting of these lakes has almost been overshadowed by the enigma of Blue Lake. Annually at the end of November, Blue Lake mysteriously changes color overnight, from slate grey to bright blue. Between March and June, it slowly reverts to its former winter grey, confounding skeptics and puzzling scientists.

The two other crater lakes, in close proximity, can be seen on a scenic drive out of Mount Gambier. The lakes are exposed portions of the countryside's water table, the craters acting as natural basins with water constantly percolating into them through the limestone formations.

Nearby are huge limestone quarries yielding almost pure white building stone; east, centered around Hamilton, lies one of the world's largest lava plains.

The colorful Flinders Ranges

The Flinders Ranges, extending northward some 500 miles, provide a great slice of the Australian outback. Here are mountains with colorful cliffs, granite peaks, razor-backed ridges, and steep gorges—many of them cut by creeks and cooled by deep waterholes that are surrounded by stately gums. A large number of Australia's native animals and birds live in these parts. Beginning about 120 miles north of Adelaide, the range disappears into the desert about a hundred miles east of Marree.

Tours and accommodations. Five to 13-day coach tours, leaving Adelaide weekly, provide the easiest way to visit the Flinders Ranges. Driving is not recommended. Secondary roads are primitive and treacherous after heavy rains, and flash floods are not uncommon. If you do drive, obtain information locally in advance and tell someone where you will be going.

Good hotels, motels, trailer parks, and campgrounds are available at Wilpena Pound, Arkaroola, and other towns throughout the ranges. Wilpena Pound, a small resort set in a basin amid colorful, rugged peaks and majestic gum trees, boasts a motel with swimming pool. This area is famous for pound quartzite, created eons ago and protected from erosion by huge sandstone formations. It is the most spectacular rock found in the Flinders.

Ghost farms. Throughout the region you'll see ruins of towns and farms, some of them reminders of an attempt to grow wheat (by farmers who trusted the idea that "rain follows the plough"). Abandoned shepherds' cottages and remains of mining equipment will also be found. Copper mining has been discontinued in Blinman, an old mining town high in the mountains; but the local hotel, now more than a hundred years old, still provides bed and board.

Arkaroola. In the northernmost part of the Flinders, Arkaroola is another resort area centered around a sheep station and a sanctuary for kangaroos, wallabies, and emus. It has a small luxury motel, caravan park, shopping center, and service station. In good weather you can take the road branching off just east of Blinman, passing outstations and homesteads on its way north through Balcanoona to Arkaroola.

Four-wheel-drive vehicles are available for trips into the surrounding bush from Arkaroola. You can even turn pioneer and sign up for a 10-day safari by camel from Mt. Serle Station through semi-desert country to Lake Eyre.

Eyre Peninsula—grain, ships, and tuna

The Eyre Peninsula, lying between Spencer Gulf and the Great Australian Bight, forms a giant triangle with Port Augusta in the northeast, Ceduna in the northwest, and Port Lincoln at the southern tip. The peninsula is cut up by grain fields and sheep farms, with steel factories and shipyards along the coast.

The coast surrounding Port Lincoln is long and deeply indented, with great seas for yachting, quiet inlets for swimming, sweeping beaches with rolling waves for surfing, and rocky shores for seals and seabirds. Fishermen usually find the sea generous, whether tackled from beach, jetty, rock, or boat. Record-sized white shark—up to 2,664 pounds—have been taken from the deeper waters offshore.

Port Lincoln is the home of South Australia's tuna fleet, and the fish has become the local symbol. The town's major event is the Tunarama Festival, held the last weekend in January.

Daily air service from Adelaide is available, or you can take the bus from Adelaide via Port Augusta. If you drive, take Highway 1 north from Adelaide to Port Augusta, then the Lincoln Highway south toward Port Lincoln. Your route passes through Whyalla, site of Australia's largest ship-building yards. Motels, hotels, and guest houses are located in Port Lincoln, and a trailer park nearby also provides accommodations.

Broken Hill—city of silver

To the world's mining community, Broken Hill represents one of the greatest mineral discoveries of the past hundred years. Chanced upon in 1883 by a range-rider, it has since become known as the world's largest silver-zinc-lead lode—500 feet wide and as much as 2,000 feet deep.

Although Broken Hill is located in New South Wales (739 miles west of Sydney), it is only 30 miles over the border from South Australia and most easily reached from Adelaide (250 miles southwest). Ansett Airlines operates six weekly flights from Adelaide, and connecting flights fly through Sydney and Melbourne. Several coach tours of the outback stop in Broken Hill.

The country around Broken Hill is a dry stretch of the famous Australian outback, with only nine inches of rainfall yearly. Despite this, the town is green with parks, gardens, playgrounds, and sport fields.

Mine tours can be arranged if you are intrigued with huge, mechanical earth movers and with the miners' lifestyle.

SHEEP GRAZE at Wilpena Station in the Flinders Ranges, below St. Mary's Peak. A small resort and campgrounds offer accommodations amid these rugged mountains.

SOUTH AUSTRALIA 103

PERTH (above) as seen from King's Park, a short walk from downtown. Members of a life-saving club (right) scan the waters off Perth's beaches. New Norcia Monastery (far right) was established by Spanish monks in 1847.

104 WESTERN AUSTRALIA

WESTERN AUSTRALIA—booming Perth, surrounded by a vast frontierland

The vast state of Western Australia, covering approximately a million square miles, comprises almost a third of the Australian continent. It stretches from the northern tropics, at the edge of the Timor Sea, more than 1,500 miles to the southern coast, and from the Indian Ocean on the west inland for a thousand miles to the borders of the Northern Territory and South Australia. Because of its distance from the populous eastern cities, most tourists fail to include Western Australia on their itinerary. But this wide open, empty country has its own special appeal. Among the state's scenic highlights are hundreds of miles of sunny, uncrowded beaches; the spectacular highlands of the Kimberley Plateau, the Hamersley and Darling ranges; and wildflower fields stretching almost into infinity. An incredible mineral development has superimposed industrial development onto the natural scene on a mammoth scale.

Three gigantic deserts sweep across the western part of the continent. The Great Sandy Desert starts on the Indian Ocean and stretches east and south between the Kimberley Plateau and the Hamersley Range. The Gibson Desert lies in the heart of the continent, and the Great Victoria Desert covers a massive chunk of Western Australia. Along the edges of these wastelands, irrigation schemes have added millions of acres to Australia's farm and grazing lands.

Perth, Western Australia's capital city, stands alone as the state's only major city. All other settlements are small towns or villages. Though Perth and some of these smaller towns are modern in appearance, this is still a frontier land.

PERTH—A BOOMING CAPITAL

Situated on the Swan River, Perth is 12 miles upstream from the river's mouth. The metropolitan area-including Fremantle, Australia's main west coast port-has a population of about 800,000 and extends west to the Indian Ocean and inland some 25 miles to the foothills of the Darling Range.

The city of Perth was planned during the horse and buggy era, adapted itself to the automobile age, and now is being replanned for the next century. Modern freeways encircle the city and giant cranes tower above the skyline, as one tall building after another goes up. This growth is softened by half a dozen parks—city gardens with ornamental lakes and flower beds—and by the colorful array of flora and fauna contained in national reserves outside the metropolitan area. The drive along the Swan River is one of the loveliest in the country, with grassy, tree-shaded banks and the stunning black swans that are a feature of the city's rivers and lakes.

Mediterraneanlike climate

Perth has a mild, Mediterranean climate, the best of any Australian capital city, with an average temperature of 73° in February, the hottest month, and 55° in July, the coldest month. Annual rainfall averages 36 inches, with a dry season extending from November to March.

How to get there

Daily flights (TAA and Ansett-AA) link Perth with Adelaide and Melbourne, with connections to Sydney. Air-conditioned trains run on weekdays between Adelaide and Perth, via the gold mining town of Kalgoorlie; the 1,622 mile rail trip across the Nullabor Plain takes about 46 hours. The only transcontinental road connecting Perth to the eastern part of the continent is the Eyre Highway (not first class and not recommended for tourist travel).

Accommodations and restaurants

At last count, Perth had 25 hotels and motels in the metropolitan area—and this total increases every year. Those most used by tourists are located within a half-mile of the city center.

Hotels and motels. Restaurants and swimming pools are standard at Perth hotels. Downtown favorites include these: Sheraton Perth, Koala Park Towers, Perth TraveLodge, Town House Motor Hotel, Riverside Lodge, and Parmelia.

Across the Narrows Bridge, in South Perth (a mile from downtown) you'll find the Freeway Hotel, overlooking the Swan River; another mile south is the Westos Motor Inn. Your travel agent can help you with a complete list of accommodations.

Surprisingly, the Parmelia Hotel in downtown Perth ranks as one of Australia's best. Some world travelers even place it alongside such famous hostelries as Claridge's of London and the Ritz in Paris. It is a pleasant, luxurious change from the every-day hotel, with elegant furnishings, unusual objets d'art, and highly-regarded restaurants.

Restaurants. Perth has plenty of good restaurants, and food is relatively inexpensive (about half the price of a comparable meal in Sydney). On Hay Street, Perth's "restaurant row," you'll find a broad variety of international restaurants. In the downtown area, here are several favorite restaurants:
• LeCoq D'Or, 645 Hay Street. French provincial cuisine and decor are featured; a good selection of wines.
• Garden Room in the Parmelia Hotel on Mill Street. One of the city's most elegant restaurants, where you'll enjoy continental cuisine and an excellent wine cellar.
• King's Park Garden Restaurant. Good continental cuisine in a parkland setting overlooking the city.
• Luis on Sherwood Court, Esplanade. An elegant French restaurant with a friendly atmosphere. A favorite with the locals.
• Heidelberg Restaurant, 473 Hay Street. An excellent place to try some of the good local German foods.

Other restaurants you may wish to try are these:
• El Sombrero, on the waterfront facing Matilda Bay, Crawley. Mexican cuisine and decor with dining inside or out under the stars.
• Le French Taverne, 135 Stirling Highway, Claremont. Provincial French cuisine and decor, good selection of local and imported wines.
• The Oyster Beds, out over the Swan River at East Fremantle. Featured are five choices of oyster entrees and other seafood, including dhufish. The latter is a firm, succulent fish, found only in Western Australian waters; it's served fried or grilled and covered with mussels and hollandaise sauce.

Discovering Perth

Perth is an attractive city following the modern pattern: old buildings shaded by new high-rise office and apartment buildings. Four main streets, running east to west, comprise the heart of the city: St. George's Terrace, Hay, Murray, and Wellington streets.

St. George's Terrace has insurance companies, banks, and offices mixed with small shops, theaters, federal and state offices, real estate agents, and professional offices. At the western end of the street is the Barracks Archway; preserved after the building was torn down for a freeway, it now serves as a memorial to the early colonists. Hay and Murray streets are known for restaurants and the big department stores. At the corner of Hay and Barrack streets is the Perth Town Hall, built with convict labor in the style of an English Jacobean Market Hall.

Here are some of Perth's points of interest:

London Court. A strange experience awaits visitors strolling through the commercial area; this street is right out of the 16th century. London Court was built in 1936 by a civic-minded benefactor and is reminiscent of the Elizabethan era. Lining the street are some 50 shops, with living quarters on the upper floors of the buildings.

The Perth Art Gallery and Museum. Located on Beaufort Street, north of the commercial area, the museum has a comprehensive selection of exhibits from the state's gold rush days.

King's Park. Other city parks may be devoted to carefully manicured gardens, but King's Park comprises a thousand acres of bushland. In this natural setting about a mile southwest of the central district, you can enjoy a myriad of wildflowers—labeled with odd and descriptive names such as bacon and eggs, kangaroo paw, cocker's tongue, one-sided bottle-bush, and white spider orchid. Mount Eliza, at the edge of the park, provides views of Perth, the river, and the distant Darling Ranges.

The University of Western Australia. Three miles from Perth on the Stirling Highway, the university campus covers 150 acres. Buildings are low and rambling, constructed in Spanish style reminiscent of the old California missions. In the summer, symphony concerts are held outdoors in Somerville Auditorium, and plays performed in the Sunken Gardens.

Shopping malls

Perth boasts a delightful array of shopping arcades. Along the Hay Street promenade, shoppers relax on seats beneath large umbrellalike shades. Where cars once parked, small trees—planted in movable pots—add a softening touch of greenery. Other shopping streets will be closed to traffic, creating more pedestrian malls with small shops and sidewalk cafes. Already shoppers roam walkways like Plaza Arcade, City Arcade, Piccadilly Arcade, and Terrace Arcade; cars use underpasses or are detoured around the arcades.

Other shops on Hay Street include five of the city's seven big department stores: Aherns, David Jones, Walsh's, Big-W, and Cole's. Perth's other big stores—Boan's and Myer's—are located on Murray Street.

Sports events

Cricket and tennis matches, Australian rules football, yachting and rowing races, lawn bowling and horseracing provide a choice of spectator sports in Perth. Three metropolitan race courses and a night trotting track, Gloucester Park, host the horse races. Many events take place at Perry Lakes Athletic Stadium and the aquatic center at Beatty Park, both sites of the VIIth British Empire and Commonwealth Games held in Perth in 1962.

LONDON COURT in downtown Perth has Tudor-style architecture reminiscent of Elizabethan era. Some 50 small shops offer varied shopping opportunities.

Several public golf courses welcome visitors, and you'll find an abundance of tennis courts.

The beach world

A thousand miles of white sand beaches extend from near Geraldton (300 miles north of Perth) to Esperance on the southern coast. Major beach resorts, accessible by rail and highway, are at Geraldton, Bunbury, Busselton, Albany, and Esperance.

Perth residents use the Swan River for all forms of aquatic sports—yachting, speedboat racing, swimming, diving, and water-skiing. The most popular ocean beaches near Perth are at Fremantle, Cottesloe, and Scarborough.

EXCURSIONS FROM PERTH

Perth has enough attractions to fill a two or three day visit, but you'll have seen only a small part of Western Australia. Short side trips from Perth can take you west to an offshore island resort or east to the Darling Ranges. Longer trips allow visits to the southwest forest country, wildflower areas, and subterranean caves. To the northwest are coastal towns, fishing villages, and tours through the mining country.

Coach and plane excursions cover this vast region in tours varying from one to 11 days. The Western Australia Government Travel Centre on Hay Street or your travel agent can help arrange these trips.

Rottnest Island

This popular summer resort, 12 miles offshore from Fremantle, attracts armadas of private launches, boats, and yachts all season long. Only 7 by 3 miles in size, it is a low-lying island, with sand dunes rising more than 60 feet above the sea.

In 1917 Rottnest was declared a permanent public reserve and wildlife sanctuary. Its attractions are the sea, sun, sand, a rich marine life, and the rare marsupial known as the quokka—which looks like a giant rat. Dutch seamen, who first landed here, saw the quokkas and named the island "Rats' Nest."

You can visit Rottnest Island on an all-day river and sea trip from the Barrack Street jetty, or you can take a 25-minute flight from Perth. In the summer, daily motor launch service is available.

The Darling Ranges

A trip to the Darling Ranges, 15 miles east of Perth, takes you through the 4,000-acre John Forrest National Park. Scenic drives wind through the park; facilities include a swimming pool, picnic areas, and sport grounds. Hilltop viewpoints provide sweeping vistas out across the plains to the sea.

This wooded country, laced with streams and ablaze with wildflowers in spring, was once an Aboriginal camping ground. Nearby is the Mundaring Weir (dam), starting point for a 350-mile pipeline to the eastern gold fields.

Yanchep Park

This 6,000-acre bushland reserve preserves not only wildlife and flora but also beautiful limestone caves. Only 34 miles north of Perth, the park has a good hotel, golf course, tennis courts, artificial lake, and swimming pool.

The caves are in limestone cliffs rising more than 270 feet above Loch McNess. Launch trips on the lake follow a meandering course cut through the cliffs. In Crystal Cave, the main grotto, an underground stream reflects images of stalactites and stalagmites in the crystal clear water.

New Norcia Monastery

When the Spanish visited Western Australia in the 19th century, 82 miles north of Perth, at New Norcia, they left a reminder of their passing—a monastery. Situated on a river bend, it evokes visions of medieval Spain and provides a striking contrast with the surrounding land—and with any other architecture you'll see in Western Australia. Regular bus service is available from Perth, or you can reach New Norcia by driving north on Highway 1.

The main task of this early settlement was—and still is—to care for the Aborigines of Western Australia. On the vast grounds is an orphanage for the children, gardens, orchards, and a large flock of sheep. The Benedictine monks will be happy to show you around. The monastery's library has medieval manuscripts, its art gallery some rare paintings.

Wildflower country

Botanists and flower lovers find Australia's southwest a veritable paradise; few places in the world can boast such a profusion of wildflowers. Most of them are found nowhere else in the world, a phenomenon attributed to Western Australia's having been isolated for centuries. As a result, many native plants evolved in an unchanged habitat, and primitive forms have survived in the lovely plants blooming each year. So famous are these wildflowers that books have been written about them and tours organized especially for viewing and studying them.

COUNTRYSIDE around Perth bursts into magnificent springtime bloom, with acre upon acre of wildflowers. Tour companies offer wildflower excursions.

From August to October large areas are carpeted with spring wildflowers. The most notable places are King's Park near Perth; Albany on the southern coast; the Nullabor Plain, 600 miles east of Perth; and Geraldton, on the coast about 300 miles north of Perth.

East to the gold fields

A ghost town safari or mining tour into the desert east of Perth takes the history buff back more than 80 years. During the 1890s gold rush, some 200,000 prospectors ranged over the gold fields of western Australia, looking at every rock for the glint of gold. When pay dirt was found, Coolgardie and Kalgoorlie became boom towns, producing the purest gold the world has ever seen. Though they are within a few miles of one another, when the gold rush faded their fates separated: one virtually disappeared; the other survived. Tours of the area can be arranged at the Western Australia Government Travel Centre.

Coolgardie: ghost town. Coolgardie is probably Australia's most famous ghost town. All that remains today of what was once a roaring boom town of 15,000 is the old Denver Hotel, a few crumbling stone buildings, and some collections of gold field relics. The largest piece of gold found here weighed 2,000 ounces.

Kalgoorlie: active gold mine. Despite its age and the ravages of the desert, Kalgoorlie remains an active mining town. In its heyday, miners from around the world congregated in more than a hundred crowded pubs. Now the pubs have decreased to a busy few, but the town's broad streets remain, shaded by drought-resistant trees planted decades ago. Some handsome buildings dating from the early days of the gold rush are still in use, and the atmosphere of a desert mining town remains strong—an odd mixture of permanent and makeshift buildings.

More than 34 million ounces of gold were scraped out of the earth here at the turn of the century. Today the take is greatly reduced, and though miners have to sink shafts down 4,000 feet to find gold, Kalgoorlie is still a productive mine.

Cave country

On the continent's southwestern tip, near Augusta, are limestone caves so numerous and varied that the

---

LITTLE SICILY ON THE INDIAN OCEAN

The port of Fremantle, 12 miles from Perth, is Australia's western gateway to the Indian Ocean. This is a sailors' town, where ships from around the world dock bow to stern; it's a port of entry where immigrants get their first look at Australia; and it's a fishermen's settlement, where Sicilian fishermen continue the work habits and religion of their ancestors.

Captain Charles H. Fremantle landed at the mouth of the Swan River in 1829, beginning the British settlement of Western Australia. Within a year, 50 ships arrived, carrying 2,000 settlers, and building began.

Fremantle still retains the feel of those early days —narrow streets, a city square with a fountain, benches where one can relax in the shade of Norfolk Island pines. Sea breezes are heavy with the aroma of the day's catch, strong odors mixing with the subtle incense of sandalwood logs awaiting shipment to the Orient. Office buildings along the wharves face the sea and carry the names of shipping and trading companies. Old sea captains warm themselves in the sun and swap yarns embracing the ports of the world.

But the overlay is strictly modern—from the sparkling new Port Authority Building to the automated wharves, facilities making Fremantle one of the world's most efficient ports.

In addition to the freighters, passenger liners, grain ships, and other big ocean-going vessels, you'll find fishing boats from all over the world—tuna boats from Japan, Russia, and the United States; whalers from Norway; marine biology research vessels from several countries—all of them harvesting or probing the rich waters of the continental shelf off Western Australia.

The Sicilian fishermen have transplanted a bit of the Mediterranean to a small harbor a short distance from the freight wharves. Each morning they gather here, reclaiming their territory from the gulls. The nearby fish market exudes a festive, carnival atmosphere, offering an old merry-go-round and tree-shaded lawns where you can sit and watch the boats in the harbor. Try the local crayfish—tender, succulent, and sweet.

In the spring, when the new fishing season begins, the Blessing of the Fleet resembles a scene from an Italian fishing village. Tall, brown-faced men, the distant look of the sea in their eyes, gather with their families at the Roman Catholic Church. The somber-faced women are clad in black; boys and girls dress in Sicilian costume. After Mass the priest leads the congregation down to the harbor for the blessing of the fleet. Flowers and flags decorate the working boats, two of which proudly carry treasured Madonnas from Sicily and the local belle chosen Queen of the Fleet.

You can join the relatives and friends at the wharf to wave the fishermen out to sea as the sound of Italian hymns floats over the harbor.

region is a spelunkers' heaven. Nature has formed vast subterranean caverns decorated with stalactites, stalagmites, and shawls (thin sheets of limestone projecting at right angles from the cave walls). Beautiful underground rivers flow through some of the caves, their waters colored with iron oxides and manganese. Altogether, about 120 caves have been discovered; but only four have been developed for the tourist, with walkways and lights for easy viewing.

NORTH OF PERTH

The vast, open country stretching north of Perth is a land of adventure for rockhounds, sportsmen, photographers, and seekers of the frontier. This strange, exciting region, formed in ancient times, is unbelievably spacious and vividly colorful. Its coastal and mountain scenery is starkly different from that of Australia's eastern and southern states; its plateau country is rugged and untamed.

Along the coast

Along the road between Perth and Port Hedland—more than 1,200 miles—you go through only three towns of any size: Geraldton, Carnarvon, and Roeburne.

Geraldton, 300 miles north of Perth, is the state's second busiest seaport (after Fremantle). A highly prosperous community, Geraldton services wheat farms, tomato plantations, and sheep ranches spreading out to the east. It sits on the shore of a harbor that has been dredged and deepened to accommodate the large freighters taking on cargoes of iron ore, brought by rail from recently opened mines farther north and inland.

The country's largest crayfish-fishing fleet also berths here; each year these fishermen catch more than A$18 million of crayfish in the offshore waters.

The town's sandy beaches, coastal scenery, and excellent climate have also made it a popular resort area. Five motels, three of them on the beach, provide comfortable accommodations. Fishing is good, especially off the Abrolhos Islands 40 miles west. Launch excursions can be arranged to the islands

Carnarvon lies at the mouth of the Gascoyne River some 600 miles north of Perth. Riverside acreage east of town is well irrigated, and the region's fruits and produce—bananas, pineapples, oranges, beans, tomatoes, and melons—are trucked to Perth markets over the North West Coastal Highway. The Carnarvon area has a number of attractions: blowholes shooting spectacular bursts of ocean water into the air; banana plantations to tour; Jubilee Hall, housing a comprehensive shell collection; offshore fishing; wildflowers galore in the spring; and at Brown Range, four miles south of town, is the Overseas Telecommunications Station, open to visitors between 9 A.M. and 5 P.M. daily.

Exmouth lies west of the North West Coastal Highway on North West Cape, a peninsula thrusting into the ocean about 850 miles north of Perth. One of Australia's newest towns, it was built to house personnel at the United States Navy's radio communication base at the end of the cape.

The cape and Exmouth Gulf, which it shelters, offer sweeping beaches, game fishing, crabbing, prawning, and crayfishing. The Cape Range forms a spine down the peninsula's center, providing a jagged profile that adds rugged beauty to the terrain. Near the town enormous canyons and caves contain examples of primitive Aboriginal art.

Onslow, a small seaport town near the mouth of the Ashburton River, north of Exmouth, lies some 45 miles west of the main coastal highway. It is the nearest port for the Barrow Island oil fields, lying offshore about 60 miles north, and it also serves an expanding wool-growing area. Fishing in the Onslow area is excellent.

Roebourne, 1,085 miles north of Perth, is situated at the mouth of the Harding River, a few miles inland from Cossack, an abandoned pearling port. Roebourne is hardly more than a village, but it's an important center for surrounding farms and ranches. Cossack makes an interesting short side trip; its rough-hewn stone houses were built by the pearling community in the mid-1800s.

Nearby Dampier, about 30 miles west of Roebourne, is a company town, the seaport and railhead for the Hamersley Iron Company. Here you can see gigantic freighters being loaded with iron ore destined for Japan.

Whim Creek, about 40 miles north of Roebourne on the coast highway, was a bustling copper town in the 1880s. All that's left is a small hotel; locally it's known as the "pub with no town."

Port Hedland, destined to become one of the world's major mineral-shipping ports, is one of the most exciting places in Australia's northwest. It marks the northern end of the North West Coast Highway, more than 1,200 miles from Perth.

Before the iron-ore boom in the Hamersley Ranges, even the shallow-draft coastal tramp steamers that once came into port would sit in the mud when the tide went out. Now, after extensive dredging, Port Hedland is a deepwater port bristling with new construction. Originally built on an island in the harbor, the town has outgrown available space, and a new town is under construction five miles inland. The town's vitality stems from its tremendous growth and the exciting hustle and bustle of construction, ore-loading, and other industrial operations in such a remote area.

The Hamersley Ranges

The reason behind all the development and growth in this remote corner of Australia is the mineral wealth of the Hamersley Ranges, lying about a hundred miles south of Port Hedland. The geologic processes that created these mineral deposits also formed some of the area's spectacular scenery. The Fortesque River has cut deeply into the Hamersley Ranges, exposing rock formations reddened by an extremely high iron oxide content.

Tom Price. When the Hamersley Iron Company was formed in 1962, a modern town was established at Mount Tom Price. The town owes its existence to one man, Tom Price, an official of the Kaiser Company who first became excited over the iron wealth of this region. He died the day the company was formed, and soon afterward the town and mountain of iron were named for him.

The people of Tom Price and the Hamersley Iron Company have created here a little island of comfort —modern homes set amid lawns and gardens, public swimming pools, tennis courts, and modern shopping centers. The company also keeps its residents happy with company-subsidized stores, special tax concessions, and educational allowances. Crime is unknown. The menu in the town's hotel offers everything from Sydney rock oysters to French snails.

Wittenoom. About 50 miles north of Tom Price is Wittenoom, site of an abandoned asbestos mine. The mine road into the site is rough but passable, and the trip is worth the trouble to see some of the most beautiful scenery in the outback. The rolling scrub country on your route is gashed with deep red gorges, and wildflowers splash the hillsides with color during the spring.

Tours into the area

A variety of tours departing from Perth accent the state's frontier aspects; trips range from one to 11 days. Perth-based MacRobertson Miller Airlines offers a variety of northwest excursions. Coach tours usually run nine to eleven days, making a loop through the region. You'll also find interesting tours operating out of Carnarvon, Wittenoom, and Kununurra.

The Kimberley Plateau

Tucked into the northern corner of Western Australia, the broad, high plains of the Kimberley Plateau are broken by meandering, tree-lined rivers and solitary peaks shaped like ancient pyramids. Slightly larger than California in area, the region has a population of only 6,000 people scattered over half a dozen small townships, vast cattle ranches, and small bauxite mining settlements.

In an area where distances are so huge, air travel has not been lost on tour promoters. New itineraries blossom from year to year, with most tours including the major scenic spots and all the principal towns of the area—Broome, Derby, Fitzroy Crossing, Halls Creek, Kununurra, and Wyndham.

But for some, the huge new irrigation project called the Ord River Scheme may be attraction enough. Hub of the activity on this grand project is the new town of Kununurra, 60 miles inland from the port of Wyndham, terminus for the Great Northern Highway. The Ord River Scheme harnesses the Ord and other northern rivers for irrigation purposes, lessening the area's dependence on summer rains and creating Lake Argyle, Australia's largest man-made lake. Tourist facilities here include the Lake Argyle Inn resort complex and a launch for lake cruises.

PORT HEDLAND has new motels and hotels with swimming pools (above) for visitors. Ore ships dock at Dampier (right); mining company personnel in tropical shorts supervise loading.

WESTERN AUSTRALIA

BRISBANE (above) spreads out along banks of Brisbane River. Vintage vehicles are displayed at Gilltrap's Auto Museum (right), Kirra. Tall, sleek government building contrasts with architecture of Ann Street church (far right).

112 QUEENSLAND

SUBTROPICAL BRISBANE—centerpiece for a beach-lined playground

Subtropical Brisbane, Australia's third largest city and the capital of Queensland, is a busy port 630 miles by road (465 by air) north of Sydney. Yet within a few hundred miles of this large urban center, you'll find as varied a topography as almost anyplace else in Australia.

Some of the world's finest beaches line the coast north and south of Brisbane. Not far inland, the northern ranks of the Great Dividing Range stand sentinel over the entire length of Queensland. About 80 miles west of the capital, the western foothills of the Great Dividing Range soften into the Darling Downs, 3½ million acres of rolling wheat and grazing lands, where some of Australia's finest cattle, sheep, and race horses are bred.

The Downs gradually merge into plains, and still farther west the land eventually dries out to become part of the great Australian outback.

But on the north coast and along the river valleys to the south, dense tropical rain forests flourish, cleared in many places to provide growing room for sugar, pineapples, and other tropical crops. Mountain resorts and national parks lie within easy reach of Brisbane. Shimmering at the mouth of the Brisbane River is Moreton Bay, dotted with myriad timbered islands where wildflowers and orchids thrive.

BRISBANE, CITY ON THE RIVER

The busy port city of Brisbane lies 18 miles up the Brisbane River from the Pacific Ocean and about 60 miles north of the New South Wales border. Winding through the city in deep, graceful curves, the river is Brisbane's most colorful thoroughfare. Bridges and ferries, tugboats, freighters, ocean liners and pleasure craft, busy quays, and warehouses add up to a scene of never-ending activity and interest.

Six large bridges and eight ferry crossings link the north and south sides of the river. The center of the city occupies a river-bordered peninsula on the north shore, bisected by Queen Street.

QUEENSLAND 113

Brisbane's population, about 850,000, has spread from the river banks up and down the foothills in all directions, and the city now covers almost 400 square miles—an area larger than that of New York City. Dotting the hilltops are some of Australia's most beautiful homes, built to blend with the tropical background; avenues are bordered with gardens, parklands, and flowering trees.

The best time to visit

Most of Brisbane's 40-inch annual rainfall comes during the summer months—December, January, and February—when the high temperatures average in the upper 80s. The best months to visit are from April through November, when the average temperatures range between 50° and 70°.

How to get there

Transportation services to Brisbane are excellent. Ansett Airlines and Trans-Australia Airlines operate frequent daily flights from Sydney and Melbourne; air services connect Brisbane with most other principal Australian cities. The flight from Sydney takes an hour and ten minutes.

The Brisbane Limited Express train operates between Brisbane and Sydney—one train in each direction daily, leaving in late afternoon and arriving the next morning. The trip takes about 15½ hours.

Two highways link Sydney and Brisbane: the New England Highway takes an inland route; the Pacific Highway follows the coast. You can drive the distance in 13 to 14 hours.

Three motorcoach lines operate air-conditioned express coaches daily between Sydney and Brisbane; the coach trip takes nearly 18 hours.

Your choice of accommodations

You have your choice of several first-rate hotels and motels in Brisbane. The new Lennons Plaza Hotel, on Queen Street, offers a dining room, cocktail lounges, bar and grill, and convenient shops. A swimming pool sparkles among the attractions of the 191-room Gateway Inn, on North Quay overlooking the river. Sauna enthusiasts can indulge themselves at the Crest International, on King George Square, which also features a variety of shops. Your travel agent can give you more information on these and other Brisbane hotels.

Brisbane also boasts a number of excellent motels within a mile of the city center: the Metropolitan, on Leichardt Street, and the Ridge Motor Inn, at the corner of Leichardt and Henry streets, both featuring swimming pools; the Parkroyal Motor Inn, at the corner of Alice and Albert streets, just across from the lovely Botanic Gardens; Noah's Tower Mill Motor Inn, on Wickham Terrace in the Wickham Park area; the Zebra Motel on George Street; the TraveLodge, on Main Street, Kangaroo Point; and the Coronation Motel, in Milton, about a mile out of town.

Brisbane's restaurants

Local menus feature fresh seafood from Pacific Ocean waters and fresh fruits—strawberries, pawpaws, custard-apples, mangoes, passion fruit, bananas, and pineapples—from Queensland's "salad bowl" area near Brisbane.

The city's hotels provide some of the best restaurant fare, but here are a few additional restaurants you might like to consider:

Leo's, on Edward Street; Rendezvous, on Alice Street; and Two Seasons, on Queens Street, all feature fine continental cuisine. You can enjoy German dishes at the Heidelberg, on Edward Street; while Mama Luigi's, on St. Paul's Terrace, serves Australian and Italian specialties. Scaramouche at the corner of North Quay and Turbot Street combines a friendly atmosphere with tempting French cuisine. Queensland seafood specialties are available at Gambaro's at 36 Caxton Street, Petrie Terrace, a short cab ride from the city center.

If you're in the mood for a theater-restaurant, the Playhouse or the Living Room are ideal choices. For delightful views to complement your meal, try Top of the State, a revolving restaurant at the corner of Albert and Turbot streets; the Kiosk, atop Mount Coot-tha; and Room at the Top, in the Tower Mill.

Shopping suggestions

Should your travel notes include a reminder to "pick up something for Uncle John," Brisbane's department stores are a good place to start your shopping. The main stores are Allan & Stark and Finney Isles & Co. (Finneys), Queen and Adelaide streets; Barry and Roberts, Queen Street; Waltons Stores and McWhirter's (Myer Emporium), Brunswick and Wickham streets, in a suburb called The Valley.

Numerous gift shops specialize in souvenir items —rugs, garments, and bags made from hides and skins; curios from Queensland woods; and jewelry from local gemstones. You'll find the best selection of native handicrafts and artifacts at Queensland Aboriginal Creations on George Street.

Antique hunters will have a field day in Brisbane and its suburbs. Ian Still features a variety of New Guinea and Oceania primitive art in addition to a mixed stock of antiques. More than 20 other dealers round out the antique scene in Brisbane.

Sightseeing in Brisbane

One of the best ways to get acquainted with a city and its people is a leisurely walking tour taking in some of the city's highlights. Your hotel or the Queensland Government Tourist Bureau can supply a city map and other information.

City center highlights. Like most state capitals, Brisbane has its share of dignified government and civic buildings and monuments. You can see many of the city's highlights on a downtown walk.

The mammoth City Hall, at Adelaide and Albert streets in the heart of the city, is a good place to get your bearings. You ascend its 300-foot clock tower by lift; from the top, Brisbane looks like an architect's model. In the City Hall you can view an impressive collection of paintings and historic treasures. The building also houses a grand organ, said to be one of the finest in the Southern Hemisphere.

A short walk will bring you to Parliament House, at the corner of Alice and George streets. Opened in 1868, this building is an imposing example of French Renaissance architecture.

The Oxley Monument, an obelisk between Victoria and William Jolly bridges, marks the spot where Lt. John Oxley landed in 1823, establishing the site of Brisbane. You'll find the Anzac War Memorial in Anzac Square, its Eternal Flame of Remembrance burning brightly, surrounded by 18 Greek columns.

Collector's items. If you enjoy seeking out a city's museums and galleries, Brisbane has much to offer. The Queensland Museum, at Gregory Terrace and Bowen Bridge Road, is open from 10 A.M. to 5 P.M. daily except Sunday, when the hours are 2 to 5 P.M.; admission is free. Natural history displays include material on the Aborigines and their customs and implements, as well as collections of shells, corals, and marine life of the Great Barrier Reef.

The Queensland Art Gallery (M.I.M. Building, 160 Ann Street) is open from 10 A.M. to 5 P.M. daily except Sunday when the hours are 2 to 5 P.M.

Visitors with a special interest in art may wish to visit the Ray Hughes Gallery, McInnes Galleries, the Town Gallery, and Philip Bacon Galleries. A colony of arts and crafts showplaces has grown among the old narrow streets of Spring Hill close to the city. The Queensland Government Tourist Bureau can provide a list of interesting places to visit on a stroll through this district.

Design Art Centre features pottery and applied arts as well as paintings and drawings. Jewelry, sculpture, and paintings by Australian and international artists are on view at Grand Central Gallery.

Reminders of the past. Several buildings still remain from Brisbane's early settlement days. A door lintel at the Old Government Stores, on William Street, bears the Royal Crown and the date 1829. Convict labor built the Wickham Terrace Observatory as a windmill to grind maize and wheat for the settlement. When completed, though, the mill had to be powered by a treadmill—there wasn't enough wind!

TREASURY BUILDING, part of Brisbane's dignified government center, is illuminated during the Christmas and New Year holidays and for special events.

The proclamation establishing Queensland as a separate colony was read from the balcony of the Deanery, St. John's Cathedral, on Ann Street; the building was built in 1853.

Early Street, 75 McIlwraith Avenue, Norman Park, re-creates a pioneer town. From 11 A.M. to 5 P.M. daily, visitors may inspect an old-time pub, a coach house, a settler's cottage, and an Aboriginal *gunyah* (primitive shelter).

You can also visit Brisbane's oldest residence, Newstead House in Newstead Park, now the headquarters of the Royal Historical Society. Visitors are welcome Tuesdays through Thursdays from noon to 3:30 P.M. and Sundays from 2 to 4:30 P.M.

Miegunyah, on Jordan Place in Bowen Hills, is a fine example of colonial architecture, memorializing Australia's pioneer women. Furnished in the manner of the late 1800s, it holds many relics of those early days. You can view the exhibit Tuesdays from 10:30 A.M. to 3 P.M. and Saturdays and Sundays between 10:30 A.M. and 4 P.M.

Ten thousand acres of parkland

Brisbane is a city of numerous parks, each with its distinctive attractions. Near the center of the city, Victoria Park extends over 193 acres, providing playing grounds for many sports, including a municipal golf course.

The Royal National Show (Queensland's equivalent

WILLIAM JOLLY BRIDGE (upper left) is one of three spanning the Brisbane River. Pool area of TraveLodge Brisbane overlooks the river (left). Koala riding on the back of an Alsatian dog (above) delights visitors arriving at the Lone Pine Koala Sanctuary.

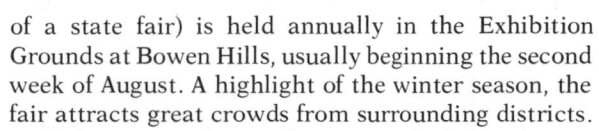

of a state fair) is held annually in the Exhibition Grounds at Bowen Hills, usually beginning the second week of August. A highlight of the winter season, the fair attracts great crowds from surrounding districts.

New Farm Park is a favorite with flower lovers. From September through November, thousands of rose bushes perfume the air; in October and November, jacaranda and bougainvillea set the park ablaze with their brilliant hues.

Another much-enjoyed spot is Oasis Aquatic Gardens at Sunnybank, 6½ acres of landscaped gardens, trimmed lawns, aviaries, swimming pools, and a garden cafe.

Bordering the river are the 50-acre Botanic Gardens, with palms, bamboos, and native flora. The gardens are open daily from sunrise to sunset.

The races, golf, and beaches

Horse racing ranks as the number one spectator sport in Brisbane. The Stradbroke Handicap and Brisbane Cup in June and the Doomben Ten Thousand and Doomben Cup in July are the chief races. Meets are held at the Queensland Turf Club at Eagle Farm, and at Doomben, Albion Park, and Bundamda.

Indooroopilly and Royal Queensland, two of the many golf courses in and around Brisbane, rate among the country's best. Brisbane River sailors test their skills in frequent yacht races along the river and across Moreton Bay. And for sun, surf, and sand, it's hard to top the beaches of the Sunshine Coast to the north and the Gold Coast to the south.

TRIPS OUT OF BRISBANE

Numerous day, half-day, and extended tours and cruises operate from Brisbane. The sampling below will give you an idea of the wide variety of possible side trips; folders and additional details are available from the Queensland Government Tourist Bureau office in Brisbane.

Moreton Bay district

After passing through the city, the Brisbane River swings northeast and empties into Moreton Bay, a huge body of water sheltered by Moreton and Stradbroke islands. The protected waters of the bay are well-known to Brisbane residents, who have camped, fished, gone crabbing, and enjoyed the bay's water sports for many years.

Moreton Island, about 20 miles east of the mouth of the Brisbane River, is 24 miles long and boasts the world's highest permanent sand dunes—Mount Tempest (914 feet elevation) and Storm Mountain (875 feet).

From Brisbane you reach Moreton Island by launch or light aircraft (Island Airways). You can visit Tangalooma, the island's main resort, on a day cruise. If you decide to stay longer, you can enjoy swimming, surfing, riding, sandhill tobogganing, tennis, fishing, skin diving, or other island activities. The resort offers comfortable accommodations (about 40 rooms).

Stradbroke Island, just south of Moreton Island, comes in two pieces—North and South Stradbroke—which stretch south for 38 miles, almost to Surfers Paradise. Accessible by launch, vehicular ferry, or light aircraft, North Stradbroke Island offers sparkling white beaches, fresh-water lakes, a wildlife sanctuary, magnificent flora (including ground orchids), and a selection of small but good resorts.

Other activity centers include Wellington Point, Cleveland, and Victoria Point, resorts along the southern mainland shores of Moreton Bay, and Bribie and Bishop islands, both popular for picnicking and camping. You can swim, surf, sunbathe, or fish at any of the numerous beaches and resorts along the Redcliffe Peninsula.

Lone Pine Koala Sanctuary

Only 7 miles west of Brisbane, this wildlife sanctuary is one of Australia's best. You can reach it by road or on a leisurely 15-mile launch ride upriver. A typical half-day tour stops first at 900-foot Mount Coot-tha for a view of the city, river, Moreton Bay, coastline, and MacPherson Range; it then proceeds to Lone Pine Koala Sanctuary, stopping for tea at the Oasis Tourist Gardens before returning.

Lone Pine shelters kangaroos, dingos, emus, and other animals and birds, but the favorites are the hundred or more tame koalas.

Toowoomba and the Darling Downs

A checkerboard of farmlands due west of Brisbane, the Darling Downs comprises 27,000 square miles of black soil plains. Here climate and topography combine with a fertile soil to make one of the country's richest agricultural districts.

The area's commercial center is Toowoomba, perched at 2,000 feet on a crest of the Great Dividing Range 80 miles west of Brisbane; the town is easily reached by rail, road, or air. Queensland's largest inland settlement, Toowoomba is famed as the state's "garden city"; its Carnival of Flowers is held annually in September.

Toowoomba's Lionel Lindsay Art Gallery, 27 Jellicoe Street, displays the works of many Australian artists of the classical tradition, and the gallery's library contains a well-rounded historical collection. At the corner of James and Water streets, the Cobb & Company Museum contains another interesting Australiana collection, including relics of horse and buggy days.

Good roads radiate from Toowoomba to a wide variety of attractions: several magnificent national parks offering spectacular scenery, abundant wildlife, and miles of graded walking tracks.

Mount Tamborine

A full-day tour south from Brisbane takes you to this popular mountain resort, through subtropical vine jungles, past waterfalls veiled in mist, and into the rich vegetation of the rain forest.

Here the trees grow tall, and their heavy top foliage provides filtered shade for creepers, palms, ferns, and lichens reminiscent of an earlier age in the earth's history. You can see thousand-year-old palm trees on the western slopes of Mount Tamborine, the strange carrabeeb trees in the rain forests, and butterflies on the wing at a butterfly farm where thousands of the colorful insects are enclosed in an open-framed building covered with mesh.

Lamington National Park

Another favorite mountain resort area, Lamington National Park lies some 70 miles south of Brisbane amid the cloudy peaks of the rugged MacPherson Range. Located about 4,000 feet above sea level, the park is a favorite of hikers, amateur naturalists, and bird watchers.

On a hike you may be able to glimpse the Rufus scrub bird, a "ventriloquist," or the magnificently plumed male Albert lyrebird.

At Moran's Falls, tons of sparkling water plunge into a deep gorge. Elsewhere on this reserve are awesome chasms, unexplored tablelands, fern-bordered creeks, forests of ancient Antarctic beech trees, and views stretching to the ocean-swept coast.

THE GOLD COAST

Australia's answer to Waikiki Beach is its Gold Coast —a 20-mile stretch of shimmering beaches and modern seaside resort towns south of Brisbane. The climate is almost perfect—average high temperature is 77°, while the average low is 59°; you can usually bask in the sun for eight days out of every ten.

The Gold Coast officially begins at Southport, about 50 miles south of Brisbane, and curves south in a series of beaches and bays—through Main Beach, Surfers Paradise, Broadbeach, Mermaid Beach, Miami, Burleigh Heads, Tallebudgera, Palm Beach, Currumbin, Tugun, Bilinga, and Kirra—to end at Coolangatta.

The Gold Coast offers something for everyone, whether you are active or lazy, a night owl or an inveterate sightseer. Water tours operate on the Nerang and Tweed rivers. You can golf at any of five courses, try out a variety of bowling greens, play tennis or squash, ride horseback, water-ski, try your skill at surf or river fishing, visit a boomerang factory (at Mudgeeraba), and above all, swim in the pounding, 70° surf. Rockhounds can take advantage of full and half-day gemstone safaris leaving from Surfers Paradise.

Accommodations and dining

Dozens of hotels and motels—and serviced apartments, as well—provide a full range of accommodations. The Coconut Grove Motel and Sea Horse Leisure Lodge in Mermaid Beach, the Hotel Currumbin and Golden Moon Motel in Currumbin, the Beachcomber Motor Lodge and Bombora Holiday Lodge in Coolangatta are among the many pleasant places to stay during your visit here.

At Surfers Paradise, the hub of this exciting region, the ultra-modern Chevron Paradise Hotel is one of the area's largest hotels, featuring a 24-lane indoor bowling center, 30 shops, and 3 acres of tropical gardens. Several good motels in the Surfers Paradise area add to the choice of accommodations.

In the Esplanade, facing Surfers Paradise Beach, Iluka Quality Motor Inn and Top of the Ten are well known for their food and wine. Other favorite restaurants include the Tiki Village, Hibiscus Room, Jolly Frog, Captain's Table, The Chateau, River Inn, La Plume De Ma Tante, the Penthouse, and McLaren's. For a panoramic view of the Gold Coast to flavor your dining, take the chairlift at Nobby's Beach to the Sky Terrace Restaurant and lookout on the top of North Nobby.

A mile and a half south of Surfers Paradise at Broadbeach stands the Broadbeach Hotel; each room has its own balcony and either a sea or mountain view. You can dine *al fresco* on meals prepared by continental chefs or for variety try a beachside barbecue. The hotel also has a large swimming pool and an open-air dance floor.

Southport—dolphins and pioneers

Clowning dolphins "sing," leap through burning hoops, and demonstrate their other skills while you watch from a 3,000-seat amphitheater at Marineland, on The Spit at Southport; you'll find a restaurant on the grounds. At Sea World, also on The Spit, daily displays of water-skiing and aquatic ballet delight visitors.

A bit of Australia's pioneer history can be seen in the Advancetown Pioneer Slab Hut (15 miles inland from Southport), a reconstruction of an early settler's cottage containing furniture, equipment, and collector's items from pioneering days.

Wildlife reserves

If the northern half of the Gold Coast is a surfer's paradise, the southern stretch is a mecca for naturalists. Fine stands of rain forest flourish on the southern slopes of Burleigh Heads National Park, a subtropical forestland of ferns, flowers, and abundant wildlife.

Fleay's Fauna Reserve, West Burleigh, shelters kangaroos, platypuses, golden possums, dingoes, Flinders Island wombats, native cats, emus, owls, anteaters, and numerous snakes.

Late every afternoon, multitudes of brilliantly colored wild parakeets and lorikeets, kookaburras, and spangled drongos fly in from the forest to feed at the Currumbin Bird Sanctuary. Visitors proffer honey-soaked bread on tin plates, a delicacy the diners relish. The birds perch on your head, arms, and shoulders.

The ubiquitous Captain Cook

The Captain Cook Memorial and Lighthouse, Point Danger, Coolangatta, commemorates Cook's discovery of the east coast of Australia and ranks among the most imposing landmarks on the Australian coast.

THE SUNSHINE COAST

Moving north along the coast from Brisbane by car, bus, or light plane, sun lovers will discover a long chain of splendid surfing beaches, appropriately named the Sunshine Coast, stretching from Caloundra to Noosa Heads and beyond.

Relatively undeveloped, this area offers quiet relaxation on uncrowded beaches, a restful complement to the honky-tonk, commercialized, playground atmosphere of the Gold Coast.

Accommodations run the gamut

Although the choice of accommodations on the Sunshine Coast is considerably more limited than on the Gold Coast, the northern resort facilities are certainly comfortable—and, in some cases, luxurious.

The seven-story Surfair International, rated as one of Australia's most elaborate resort hotels, recently opened near Maroochydore. Situated on a three-mile stretch of beach with excellent surf, the hotel's 85 rooms accommodate 170 guests. The Surfair has a rooftop restaurant and bar, a terrace dining room and poolside bar, a garden lounge under a solar dome, and three more bars inside the main tower.

More modest hotels and motels are located in Caloundra, Mooloolaba, Alexandra Headland, Buderim, Coolum, Noosa, Gympie, and Nambour. Most of these towns also have trailer parks and campgrounds.

Great fishing year round

The inland and offshore waters of the Sunshine Coast provide fishermen with first-rate sport throughout the year—whiting, bream, flathead, tailor, jew, sweetlip, cod, trevally, and dart. Around the reefs off Caloundra, Mooloolaba, and Noosa, you can fish for snapper, pearl perch, mackerel, parrot, and emperor.

The real game fish—black marlin (up to 250 lbs.), wahoo, dolphin, Spanish mackerel, kingfish, tuna, sharks, and barracuda—inhabit the deeper waters. Tackle is not usually available for rent, but shops at all the Sunshine Coast resorts can supply you with bait and boats.

In and around Noosa Heads

Sunshine Beach, at Noosa Heads, draws surfboard champions from all over the world. Noosa also has a reputation for exceptionally beautiful coastal scenery; Witches' Cauldron, Hell's Gates, Devil's Kitchen, and Paradise Caves are a few of the spots you won't want to miss. Colored Sands, just above Noosa at Teewah, is a 300-foot cliff made up of layers of sand in a variety of hues.

A ginger factory and sugar cane trains

While the Sunshine Coast hinterland does not match the grandeur of the Gold Coast's national parks, it nonetheless contains attractions worth visiting.

The striking trachyte pillars of the Glass House Mountains loom a few miles west of Caloundra. Beerwah (an Aboriginal word meaning "up in the sky") is the highest peak at 1,823 feet.

The only ginger factory in the Southern Hemisphere operates at Buderim; visitors are welcome to tour the plant, where ginger products may be purchased.

The curious "lung fish" (*Neoceratodus fosteri*), a living fossil, subsists in deep pools within Kondalilla National Park—185 acres of rain forests, palms, and other lush foliage, along with a sparkling waterfall.

Four miles south of Nambour, at Sunshine Plantation, you can ride through the tropical growth on a sugar cane train.

Queensland's biggest island

The waters of Hervey Bay are sheltered by 90-mile-long Fraser Island, the largest island off the Queensland coast. It is known for its sweeping beaches, natural flora and fauna reserves, and Aboriginal relics.

The main resort is the Polynesian-style Orchid Beach Island Village, facing the Pacific on the island's extreme northeastern tip. Air services operate to the resort from Brisbane.

All of the village buildings follow a basic Samoan *fale* (thatched hut) architectural design, featuring natural timbers and Polynesian decor.

Self-contained fales and hillside units with private bath, some air-conditioned, accommodate 79 guests. From some units you enjoy a view of bushland gardens; from others, you look across the waters of Marloo Bay.

Moonlight beach cruises on Fraser Island's beach train, beach buggy trips, and flying tours to the Great Barrier Reef's southernmost island for fossicking, barbecues, and fishing highlight village entertainment.

Although not strictly part of the Sunshine Coast, several resorts have been developed along the shores of Hervey Bay at Pialba, Scarness, Torquay, and Urangan.

PERFORMING PORPOISE leaps high at Tweed Heads on southern border of Gold Coast. You watch the outdoor program from a 3,000-seat amphitheater.

FOSSICKING on the reef (above) reveals underwater coral world. Underwater Observatory (right) on Hook Island has portholes for viewing coral and tropical fish. Cruise boat (far right) anchors off Daydream Island while passengers stroll on beach.

THE GREAT BARRIER REEF—1,250-mile watery wonderland

Most maps of the world show a dotted line off the northeast coast of Australia, running from the continent's waistline all the way north to New Guinea. Labeled the "Great Barrier Reef," it encompasses a series of detached, often isolated coral reefs, shoals, cays, and islands—the biggest agglomeration of coral in the world, 1,250 miles long and ranging in width from 10 to 150 miles. One of nature's most imposing works, the reef provides an unforgettable experience for those lucky enough to have explored even a small part of it.

Most of the vast area enclosed by the Great Barrier Reef is water. A long series of detached reefs—true coral islands (some submerged, many awash with the booming surf from huge Pacific waves, a very few topped with sand and perhaps some shrubbery and trees)—define the eastern edge or Outer Reef. Between the mainland and the Outer Reef is a north-south passage dotted with rock-and-soil islands, once part of the mainland's coast ranges. Most of these larger, high-rise islands (tops of partly submerged mountains) also have coral reefs in the waters around them.

A WATERY WONDERLAND

The unassuming architects of this "eighth wonder of the world" are coral polyps, colonies of tiny, anemone-like creatures thriving in the tropical waters off the Queensland coast. Succeeding generations secrete protective limestone shells upon the skeletons of their forebears at such an agonizingly slow rate that the creation of the Great Barrier Reef took millions of years.

Barrier Reef ecology

The staghorn, brain, and mushroom coral—to name just a few of the hundreds of colorful varieties in the Great Barrier Reef—support a huge number of animal and plant species. Goatsfoot *convolvulus* and creeping

COMING ASHORE at Lindeman Island (upper left). Resorts take guests to other islands for picnics and swimming. Underwater Skindivers' Festival on Heron Island (left) is held each November. Through portholes of the underwater observatory off Green Island (above), you watch colorful fish and see living coral.

legumes grow among the sandhills of the coral cays, where *casuarina*, *pisonia*, *tournefortias*, mangrove, and pandanus also flourish.

Above the surface, bird life is prolific. Beneath the waters live fish of every size, shape, and color; mollusks; and a host of other invertebrates, from sponges to sea cucumbers.

As in other habitats, a fierce, competitive, yet finely balanced food chain exists among the many creatures of the reef; sharks, dugongs, and turtles feed on lesser marine life; and the survivors feed on still smaller creatures, with the same pattern repeating itself.

Unfortunately, the coral polyps are not exempt. Because a recent incursion of crown-of-thorns starfish seems to have decimated entire coral communities, government authorities are investigating this threat to the reef. According to some environmentalists, the causes have been the over-hunting of the giant triton clam (a natural enemy of the starfish and prized for its shell) and pollutants carried to reef waters by Queensland rivers.

Cruising the Reef

Island resorts between the mainland and Outer Reef—as well as numerous scheduled cruises, sightseeing trips, and package tours—make it easy to enjoy the wondrous Great Barrier Reef. Most cruises sail through Whitsunday Passage on their way to the Outer Reef, stopping at several large resorts as well as at some uninhabited islands. Four and five-day cruises begin at about A$135 per person, all meals included.

Weather permitting, the ships spend a full day at the Outer Reef. The boats generally cruise into a deep-water passage between two coral banks, allowing passengers to disembark in a sheltered spot. The receding

THE ALL-YEAR RESORT on Daydream Island offers casual living with a swimming pool outside your door. Room views overlook Whitsunday Passage.

tide permits up to an hour and a half for exploring and marveling at the prolific life on the reef.

Some tour operators organize special cruises for skin divers. One such cruise is a 19-day, 500-mile trip including the services of professional dive masters, unlimited dives, and air refills. For full details on special interest cruises, contact the Queensland Government Tourist Bureau, Mary Street, Brisbane.

The best months to visit Great Barrier Reef resorts are from May through November. The reef itself puts on its best monthly show during the full or new moon, when the tide is at its lowest.

Underwater observatories

Visitors who want to see the reef's underwater life without getting their feet wet will be delighted with the $350,000 Underwater Coral Observatory adjacent to Hook Island in Whitsunday Passage.

Sunk in the midst of inner coral reefs, the steel chamber of the all-weather, air-conditioned, carpeted observatory has a viewing floor 32 feet below deck level. Through its huge glass windows, visitors experience an underwater view of a wealth of coral polyps, exotically colored tropical fish, and other sea life, all undisturbed in their natural habitat.

Another coral observatory, established several years ago, will be found on Green Island, off Cairns (see page 129).

Reef flight-seeing

Many visitors have found the most dramatic way to experience the beauty of the reef—other than swimming through its waters as a skindiver—is to skim the surface in a low-flying plane.

Between the Queensland coastal cities and the Outer Reef, passengers get a memorable sight of transparent, iridescent waters revealing the Great Barrier Reef's "stupendous mountain of coral" beneath. Thousands of islands, heaps of coral sand, and lagoon-crowned reefs sparkling like gems can be seen along the deep channel-threaded waterway. Porpoises often race launches; migrating whales, sharks, and hosts of ocean birds add to the scene.

For the overseas visitor with limited time, a number of operators conduct scenic air tours over sections of the Great Barrier Reef. These include Queensland Flying Services, Brisbane; Island Airways, Pialba; Country Air Services, Rockhampton; Pioneer Airways, Reef Air, and Lindeman Aerial Services, all at Mackay; Charter Flying Services, Townsville; Bush Pilots Airways, Cairns Air Taxis, and the Great Barrier Reef Travel Centre, all in Cairns.

Barrier Reef tours

Tour operators in Sydney have put together a comprehensive selection of Barrier Reef tours for overseas visitors. Most include a variety of transport—launch, small plane, helicopter—with connecting jet flights to international airports at Sydney and Melbourne.

Information and literature regarding the Barrier Reef and island tours are available from Australia's domestic airlines, from the Australian Tourist Commission offices overseas, and from the Queensland Government Tourist Office, Mary Street, Brisbane, which acts as booking agent for resorts and cruises.

ISLAND LIFE

On the resort islands, life revolves around the sea, the tides, the reef, and cruising. Varied activities mingle to create a fascinating vacation. You can go "fossicking" (reef exploring) or sports fishing, sailing or snorkeling, take a lazy swim or go skin diving, collect tiny sea shells or look at the giant clams growing on the Reef, climb hills clad with pine forests, or just sit on a crescent beach under coconut palms.

Evening entertainment ranges from luaus to nightclub shows and dancing. Some islands feature guided reef-walking tours and bird watching. Several resorts have six-hole golf courses, and some offer tennis and badminton courts.

Away from your hotel, you will find your island much the way nature left it—a National Parks Act protects flora and fauna, trails are well-kept and markers unobtrusive, native bush and birds are undisturbed.

Island dress is casual

The atmosphere is casual, easy, and relaxed. Visitors roam the islands in swimsuits, loose shirts or shifts, and thongs (or bare feet).

GREAT BARRIER REEF

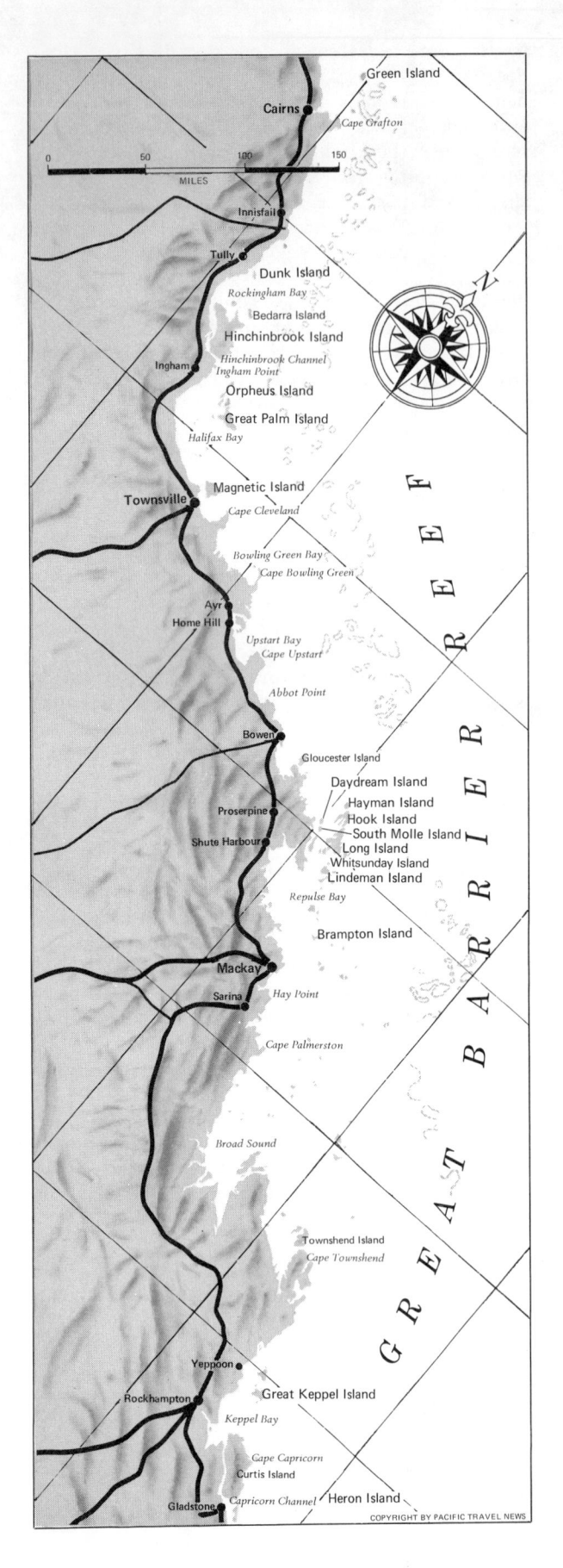

For reef exploring, wear rubber-soled sandals, tennis shoes, or hip boots—coral cuts are painful, infect easily, and heal slowly. Slacks and longsleeved shirts provide additional protection against scrapes and cuts should you slip or fall. Gloves and tongs are advisable for shell collectors, for certain kinds of conus shellfish and octopi are poisonous.

Island vacationers may also want a shade hat, sunglasses, large beach towel, a sweater for cool evenings or late launch outings, flashlight, camera, lightweight raincoat, and suntan lotion. Many islands have a shop where you may pick up miscellaneous items, in addition to coral specimens, shells, and shell jewelry.

Resorts, plain and fancy

Accommodations run the gamut from rustic to modern. Some of the smaller resorts cannot offer private baths, and a few islands are limited to saltwater showers.

Relaxed comfort rather than luxury is the keynote, with a few notable exceptions. Daily rates per person vary from about A$18 to A$38; most but not all resorts include all meals in their rates. Usually each island has only one resort, reinforcing the atmosphere of restful isolation.

Island resorts serve a full range of food, with emphasis on fish of all kinds and tropical fruit. If you like, you can collect the huge oysters, eating them raw or tossing them into a fire to steam.

During winter (April to September) the reef is the prime vacation spot for Australians, so reservations should be made well in advance. Some resorts close down from January to March; others lower their rates during the off season.

Your travel agent can be helpful in arranging your accommodations and transportation. Full schedules and booking information may be obtained from the Australian Tourist Commission.

THE GATEWAY CITIES

From Sydney you head north to the cities serving the reef—first Gladstone (immediately north of Brisbane), then Rockhampton, Mackay (usually pronounced to rhyme with *eye*), Proserpine (rhyming with *porcupine*), Townsville, and Cairns.

You can reach these departure points from Sydney via Brisbane on daily flights by Ansett Airlines and Trans-Australia Airlines. By rail from Brisbane, take the air-conditioned "Sunlander" (four days weekly). Express coach services also operate from Brisbane.

Gladstone, gateway to Heron

About 300 rail miles north of Brisbane, Gladstone lies on the shores of Port Curtis, a near-perfect natural harbor. This fast-growing town, ranking among Australia's busiest cargo ports, is also the departure point for trips to Heron Island.

Heron Island. Surrounded by 13½ miles of perhaps the best, most easily accessible coral beds of the entire reef area, this well-known, thickly wooded, low coral cay measures only 1¼ miles in circumference. Many varieties of birds nest in the island's pandanus groves and *pisonia* forest: noddy terns, herons, silver gulls, fairy terns, and the migratory mutton birds, which regularly return to the island on October 25 and leave exactly five months later.

From late October until April, giant turtles visit the island, laying their eggs in the warm coral sand. Within 10 weeks after the eggs are laid, the hatchlings emerge and head to the sea. Heron's Marine Biological Station displays many live specimens of colorful tropical fish and other marine life. The station's biologists have classified more than 1,150 varieties of fish and 200 varieties of coral in the vicinity.

Skin divers favor Heron Island—special events include an annual Divers' Rally in June and July, and the Skin Divers' Festival each November. Experienced divers provide free instruction and guide outings to Heron, Wistari, and other adjacent coral reefs.

Nondivers can test their skills at fishing aboard the 35-foot *MV Christine* or sharpen their technique at water-skiing and tennis. Other resort activities include a combined cruise and barbecue on a nearby uninhabited island, escorted walks through bird nesting areas, and reef walks at low tide.

Heron Island has modern holiday units accommodating 136 guests and additional housing for 71 in dormitory-type units.

Helicopter services from Gladstone operate on Monday, Tuesday, Wednesday, Friday, and Saturday; round-trip fare is A$72. The 2½-hour launch trip from Gladstone costs about half as much; launches run on Monday, Wednesday, and Saturday.

GAME FISHING IN THE WATERS OF THE REEF

Whether you've been game fishing for years or have yet to experience the thrill of your first strike, the Great Barrier Reef ranks among the world's best places to enjoy the sport.

In recent years game fishing enthusiasts have been drawn to the Great Barrier Reef in ever-increasing numbers, attracted by record catches of black marlin and sailfish. Reef waters offer good sport fishing—in late August and September—after the spawning season when the fish are hunting again.

The major deep-sea fishing center for Great Barrier Reef waters is Cairns, with its big new boating complex. Townsville is also well equipped for the sport, and several Barrier Reef resort islands operate game fishing launches.

From Cairns you can choose from among more than a dozen specialized, fast, fully-rigged game boats. Daily rates vary by season and passenger capacity. In the off season (January to June/July), prices for a four-passenger vessel range between A$130 to A$200. Rates peak in September, when charges for four-passenger launches climb to A$200 to A$250. Some charter boats include meals in their rates; others charge extra for "victuallying."

For more information on Great Barrier Reef game fishing boat charters, contact the Queensland Government Tourist Bureau, Mary Street, Brisbane.

More than a dozen species of game fish flourish in reef waters: barracuda, black marlin, sailfish, wahoo, giant trevally, yellowfin tuna, dogtooth tuna, cobia, rainbow runner, barramundi, threadfin, Australian salmon, small tuna, and Spanish mackerel (kingfish).

Spanish mackerel build up in coastal waters between Gladstone and Mackay from April to June, and farther north between Townsville and Cairns from July to September, when sailfish also seem to peak. Giant black marlin (1,000 to 2,000 lbs.) begin to appear at Cairns in late August and September, continuing until early December. Barracuda season starts in August and peaks in December.

TENSE MOMENT as marlin is brought alongside the boat after a long struggle in reef waters.

Rockhampton, for Keppel and cruises

Rockhampton, on the Tropic of Capricorn, lies about 400 rail miles northwest of Brisbane and is the departure point for Great Keppel Island and cruises aboard the *MV Coralita*. Country Air Services flight-seeing tours of the Great Barrier Reef are also based in Rockhampton.

Great Keppel Island. Situated 8 miles off the Queensland coast and 35 miles northeast of Rockhampton, Great Keppel attracts many overseas visitors.

The resort, located on a protected bay with an inviting white sand beach, has begun to build a reputation for fine service and good food and wine. Some accommodations are new—77 beds in motel-type units; recently renovated cabins with private showers are also available. Miles of graded walks, leading to secluded bays and beaches, traverse the island's six square miles. Along with the varied topography and vegetation that add interest, the Moreton Bay ash and other trees shading most of the resort are welcome on a hot day. The resort's glass-bottomed boat offers opportunities for unimpeded views of the coral beds, and resort guests can also go cruising, fishing, and water-skiing.

Launches to Great Keppel depart Rosslyn Bay daily. Coralair flights make the 20-minute trip from Rockhampton Airport to the island twice daily.

Mackay, base for cruises and islands

The attractive city of Mackay, with its wide, palm-shaded streets and tropical flower gardens, lies at the mouth of the Pioneer River, 709 road miles and 598 rail miles northwest of Brisbane.

Mackay is the airline destination for trips to Brampton and Lindeman islands and for Roylen and Elizabeth "E" cruises. At Mackay Aerodrome you transfer to airplanes for Lindeman and Brampton. If you plan to travel by launch or plane to Brampton Island, you must take a taxi to the outer harbor.

Brampton Island. One of the prettiest of the high-rise islands, this national park and wildlife sanctuary is also known as the "Coconut Isle." From its heights the view extends across the southern end of the Whitsunday Passage.

The island, with its white coral sand beaches, is considered a young people's resort. Daytime activities include tennis, fishing, swimming, oyster gathering, sunbathing, and hiking along scenic island paths. Cruises can be arranged to other islands and the Outer Reef.

In the evenings, you can take in a movie, go dancing, or enjoy other nighttime entertainment; the island holds a full liquor license. Friday evenings are highlighted by a smorgasbord of suckling pig, chicken, local seafood, and tropical fruits.

Set in a coconut grove facing the beach, the modern all-year resort can accommodate 182 guests. You reach Brampton Island by small plane or launch from Mackay.

Lindeman Island. Visitors to this mountainous, 2,000-acre national park can explore grassy hillsides, jungle gullies, and steep beach cliffs fringed with coral reefs. From Mount Oldfield, the highest point on the island at 695 feet, the view takes in more than 70 islands.

The reputation of the Lindeman Island resort has been built on the personalized attention guests receive from the owners, the third generation of their family to live on the island. The Australian government has entertained the British Royal family here.

Guests keep busy with a selection of island activities—bush walking to deserted bays, watching flocks of multicolored parrots sweep over the groves, free cruises, shopping at a non-profit shop, organized daily and nightly entertainment, water sports, golfing, picnics, barbecues, and coral viewing. Planes for flight-seeing and launches for special cruises or big-game fishing trips are available at extra charge.

CORAL GATHERING is popular pastime for visitors who explore along 1,250-mile coastline of Great Barrier Reef.

The 92-room resort has a large dining room, two cocktail lounges, a game room, dance floor, and swimming pool—all in a tropical setting a few minutes walk from the beach.

The Lindman Aerial Service, operating daily except Sunday, connects with flights arriving and departing Mackay. The scenic flight over more than 40 coral islands takes about 25 minutes.

Roylen cruise. This five-day cruise visits the islands in the Whitsunday group and proceeds to the Outer Reef for swimming, underwater sightseeing in glass-bottom boats, walking tours on the exposed reef, and fishing.

The Roylen fleet consists of four 112-foot vessels, each sleeping 25 guests in double and triple-berth cabins. The ships depart in a convoy and anchor each night in a protected cove. Each boat has a bar and plenty of hand lines for fishing.

The 112-foot *Petaj*, also of the Roylen fleet, carries 15 passengers and is available for charter and five-day cruises. It's a bit more luxurious—all cabins have private shower and toilet. For rates, apply to McLeans Roylen Cruises, East Mackay.

Elizabeth "E" cruise. From March to late January, this four-day cruise travels from Mackay to Lindeman Island through the Whitsunday Passage and (weather permitting) to the Outer Barrier Reef. The 112-foot *Elizabeth "E"* accommodates 24 passengers. The vessel leaves Mackay every Monday, and returns late Thursday. Stops include Lindeman, Hayman, South Molle, and Long islands.

Proserpine and its island quartet

Proserpine, about 82 road miles northwest of Mackay, is surrounded by 30,000 acres of sugar cane fields. From here you catch a bus to Shute Harbour (22 miles) for the launches transporting you to Hayman, Daydream, and South Molle Islands or to the Happy Bay Resort on Long Island. The Coral Islander helicopter service operates between Mackay, Proserpine, Hayman, Daydream, South Molle, and Happy Bay.

Hayman Island. Ranking as the largest and perhaps best-known of all Great Barrier Reef resorts, Hayman is also the closest of the resorts in the Whitsunday Group. The Royal Hayman Hotel, open the year around, provides cool, spacious accommodations in 155 rooms overlooking a lagoon.

You travel from pier to hotel via a cheery, candy-striped train. In the gardens, piped-in music serenades you at intervals during the day. An inviting pool, with underwater lights for evening swimming, shimmers in a paved terrace overlooked by the dining room.

When night comes, you can retire to the solitude of your lodge, relax in quiet, attractive lounges, or participate in the evening's entertainment. This might

AERIAL VIEW of wooded Great Keppel Island with its landing strip. Resort, with a sheltered bay and white sand beach, is only a 20-minute flight from Rockhampton.

TAKE YOUR CHOICE at Dunk Island—ocean swimming or fresh-water pool alongside beach. Planes serve island daily; you can also reach it by launch.

CANDYSTRIPED TRAIN (left) travels from Hayman Island heliport to hotel. Couple watches the arrival of Hayman's daily helicopter flight.

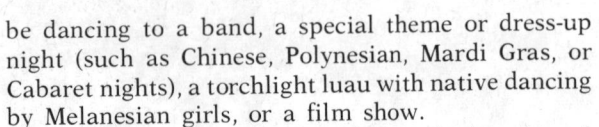

be dancing to a band, a special theme or dress-up night (such as Chinese, Polynesian, Mardi Gras, or Cabaret nights), a torchlight luau with native dancing by Melanesian girls, or a film show.

Hayman Island resort may be reached by launch from Shute Harbour daily, and daily helicopter service operates from Proserpine or Mackay.

Daydream Island. This newest resort in the Whitsunday Group can be reached by daily launch from Shute Harbor or by twin-engine, 26-passenger helicopter from Mackay or Proserpine.

With rooms for 200 guests, the buildings of the two-story hotel curve around a huge, free-form swimming pool with its own island bar in the center. Each room has a panoramic view of the Whitsunday Passage. South Sea Island decor and entertainment highlight nighttime activity. The all-year resort features a badminton court, cruises, coral viewing from a barge, and fishing and snorkeling.

South Molle. One of the most popular Reef islands, South Molle nestles in a sheltered bay amid varied scenery—mountains, valleys, tropical gardens, and a sparkling series of beaches. Known as the teenagers' favorite for its informality and gaiety, this 1,000-acre island—2½ miles long and 1¼ miles wide—has well-appointed beach cabins for 200 guests.

Visitors have easy access to bush walks among lush forests, with sparkling views of the Pacific. Free cruises and reef visits, aquaplaning, fishing, tennis, golf, and dancing are offered. Other island facilities include a modern bar and a well-stocked store, as well as an air compressor for divers.

The daily launch trip from Shute Harbour takes about an hour, or you can travel to the island by helicopter from Mackay.

Long Island. The Happy Bay Resort on Long Island fronts a magnificent swimming beach and has special appeal to all ages. Happy Bay lies only a mile from the coast. Cabins and suites with private showers and toilets accommodate 70 visitors. Launches take you on fishing and cruising trips to the other islands.

Townsville, sophisticated gateway

Townsville, Queensland's second city and one of the most sophisticated of Australia's tropical centers, is the departure point for trips to Magnetic and Orpheus islands (reached by launch), Dunk Island (reached by air or launch), and the five-day cruises of the *Beaver* and the *Kurrukajarra*.

Magnetic Island. Largest of the northern islands (20 square miles) and a national park, Magnetic rates high on the list of attractive resorts near the coast. Comfortable holiday accommodations are available at a number of resorts which nestle in secluded bays around the island.

Noted for its colorful tropical shrubs and groves of coconut palms, tamarinds, and mangoes, the island is laced with hiking paths leading to the summit of 1,682-foot Mount Cook with its far-reaching view. Cruises sail from Townsville to the Outer Barrier Reef and Palm Island Aboriginal Community.

Hinchinbrook Island. A mountainous island with beautiful palm-fringed bays and sandy beaches, Hinchinbrook is 16 miles from the mainland resort of Cardwell. It is a national park, one of the largest in the world. The Cape Richards Tourist Resort is situated on its northernmost tip. Launch service operates between Cardwell and the island on Monday, Friday, Saturday, and Sunday.

Orpheus Island. A secluded, peaceful island, Orpheus belongs to the Palm Group along the Hinchinbrook Channel (second in beauty only to the Whitsunday Passage) and lies south of huge Hinchinbrook Island near the Outer Reef. Recently renovated, the Orpheus Island Lodge accommodates 22 guests in cabins and bungalows designed especially for couples and small families. Access is by the launches *Eveley* or *Kurrukajarra*, both of which leave Townsville on Tuesdays, and by the island's own launch, *Orpheus*, which leaves from Dungeness on Sunday, Monday, Friday, and Saturday.

Dunk Island. Like so many of the area's islands, Dunk was discovered and named by Captain Cook in 1770 during his famous voyage along Australia's east coast. Covering only 6½ square miles, Dunk still retains an unspoiled tropical beauty. Penetrating the heavy jungle foliage are 12 miles of graded mountain tracks, where you see numerous species of birds and giant butterflies. The island's shell-strewn beaches make it a beachcomber's dream.

The Great Barrier Reef Hotel on Dunk has 73 units, dining room and bars, pool, tennis courts, a six-hole golf course, boats and winter sports facilities. You can reach the island by air from Townsville or Cairns or by launch from Clump Point, midway between the two towns.

Eveley cruise. On this five-day cruise, you cover a 300-mile stretch of the Great Barrier Reef waters. Departing from Townsville on Tuesday morning and returning at noon Saturday, the 85-foot Eveley *Beaver* carries 22 passengers.

You cruise through the islands of the Hinchinbrook passage, including the Outer Barrier Reef on the second day, if weather permits. You stop at Dunk Island Wednesday, at Bedarra on Thursday for swimming, and then move on to the Palm Island Group for shell collecting and a coach tour of Magnetic Island on Friday or Saturday.

Kurrukajarra cruise. This 50-foot vessel leaves Townsville on five-day cruises through the Hinchinbrook Channel, visiting the Outer Barrier Reef (weather permitting), Orpheus, Dunk, Bedarra, and Magnetic islands for coral viewing and fishing. The cruise departs Tuesday morning and returns early Saturday evening. Twelve persons can be accommodated in a four-berth and four two-berth cabins.

The busy port of Cairns

Cairns, itself a popular winter tourist resort, busy port, and commercial center, is the departure point for trips to Green, Dunk, and Bedarra islands, for some interesting trips into tropical jungle country, for day cruises, and for game fishing launches.

Green Island. Tropical plants flourish on this heavily wooded, 30-acre island that rises 10 feet above sea level. Green is one of the Reef's two true coral cays with guest facilities (Heron Island shares the distinction). Low tide exposes as much as four miles of the Reef for exploration by fossickers. Glass bottomed boats and the portholes of Green Island's famous Underwater Coral Observatory also afford firsthand views of marine world wonders.

GLASS BOTTOMED BOATS provide a favorite way for visitors to view the colorful underwater life of the reef. Boat above cruises off the shore of Green Island.

Anchored on the seabed in the midst of a living coral garden, the Observatory is a steel-and-concrete chamber with 22 large portholes. If you're not a skin diver, this is the best way to enjoy the Reef's underwater life. At Marineland you'll find a 150-foot crocodile pool, a 19-tank fish "arcade," a deep tank for large fish, and a coral grotto.

Cabins and suites of the year-round resort house 100 guests. Daily launch service gives you a choice of a one-day visit or longer stay.

Lizard Island. The most northerly resort in Queensland waters, Lizard is 53 miles northeast of Cooktown. The island is surrounded by a fringing coral reef in waters teeming with big game fish including black marlin. The only service to the island is by Bush Pilots Airways; the only accommodation is at the 10-bed Lizard Island Lodge.

Purtaboi cruises. The 60-foot cruise launch, *Purtaboi*, operates from Clump Point between Townsville and Cairns to Dunk, Bedarra, Brook, and Hinchinbrook islands. It also operates a day trip to the outer Great Barrier Reef, incorporating a visit to Dunk Island.

Land's end. You can visit historic Cape York Peninsula, Australia's northernmost point, on seven-day land and air tours from Cairns. The tours use air-conditioned four-wheel-drive vehicles and follow the tracks of Queensland's early explorers and miners, making more than 80 river crossings. Along the way, you'll get to see Aboriginal cave paintings, explore century-old gold diggings, and participate in a "sing-sing".

VISITORS WALK toward cave at base of Ayers Rock (above). Safari travelers camp (right) after a day exploring the outback southeast of Darwin. Magnetic ant hills near Darwin resemble an ancient graveyard (far right); ants build them on a north-south axis.

THE NORTHERN TERRITORY—it centers on Darwin and Alice Springs

Australia's Northern Territory is one of the world's last frontiers. Massive and empty, it stretches roughly a thousand miles north to south and 580 miles east to west, covering a sixth of Australia's land area. Its thousand-mile coastline fronting the Arafura Sea is deeply indented with bays, inlets, and tropical rivers; but Darwin is the only navigable harbor.

Only two towns of any size will be found in the territory—Darwin, the capital, on the northern coast, and Alice Springs, in the geographic center of the continent. Out of a population of approximately 85,000 in the entire territory, nearly half live in Darwin. Aborigines comprise nearly a third of the territory's population.

THE TROPICAL NORTH

The Darwin area appeals to photographers and fishermen in search of thrills and to the tourists fascinated by frontier towns, rare plants and animals, and the living vestiges of Stone Age man. All this exists near Darwin, in a setting that's lush and tropical—and hot.

Devastated by a cyclone on Christmas Day in 1974, the city was closed to tourists for more than six months. It is open once again to visitors, though complete restoration may take four or five more years.

Within easy reach of the capital, you can visit areas where wild buffalo roam or crocodiles lie at the water's edge. Where hunters once stalked, camera safaris now roam to photograph the teeming wildlife. Gigantic mining and agricultural projects attract others who want to glimpse the region's future. Historic places of interest are few, mainly remnants of early settlements but curiosities—like the big magnetic ant hills that always point north and south—are more plentiful.

Built on a peninsula on the eastern shore of Port Darwin, the city may look like a small, midwestern American town to the visitor, but it's a strategic commercial center to its 45,000 residents and those from a vast surrounding area. Commercial and residential areas are well planned, with attractive public gardens, recreation parks, and tree-lined streets. Yet within ten miles of the city center, two-thirds of the land is either swamp or water.

How to get there

International flights land in Darwin from Europe and Southeast Asia. Travelers within the country can fly to the tropical port from Brisbane, Melbourne, Sydney, Adelaide, Perth, Alice Springs, and other Australian towns.

Express coaches serve Darwin from all state capitals. From Adelaide it's a long trip up the length of the continent (2,000 miles) with a possible stopover at Alice Springs. The trip from Alice Springs to Darwin continues north on the paved Stuart Highway. Darwin can also be reached by car over two routes from Queensland and Western Australia.

Tropical climate

Darwin is a tropical city with clear blue skies and sunshine 300 days a year. The seasons are "wet" or "dry"—no spring, summer, autumn, or winter. The dry period lasts from early April through the end of October, with little rain, cloudless skies, and warm days averaging about 78°.

Getting settled in Darwin

More than a dozen hotels and motels are located in Darwin or in some of its adjacent suburbs. All of them are air-conditioned and provide dining rooms and swimming pools.

The major tourist hotels are the Territorian, the TraveLodge, and the Koala Welcome Inn. Among the numerous motels and motor lodges, visitors favor the Capricornia Motel, Darwin Motor Inn, and Don Motor Hotel.

For its size, Darwin offers a good choice of restaurants—including some reflecting the faintly Asian flavor of a town that is as near to Singapore as it is to Sydney. Here are a few restaurants to try:

• Penthouse, Capricornia Motel on East Point Road. Overlooking the sea, it offers continental cuisine in an attractive setting.
• Peppi's, at the Poinciana Hotel, offers first class cuisine in a delightful atmosphere.
• Sand Pebbles, in Lim's Hotel, has the reputation for the best Chinese meals in town.
• The Beachcomber, at the Koala Welcome Inn, offers a varied menu with good seafood.
• Top of the Don, at the Don Hotel, combines good food with a view of the city.
• Pukamani Room, at the Territorian, offers an international standard dining room set in a Territory motif.

Sightseeing in Darwin

Sightseeing in Darwin has changed dramatically since the December, 1974, cyclone hit the city. The "City Sights" tour of Darwin now includes a look at cyclone damage along with visits to the main city buildings, a few historical buildings still in use, the remains of the World War II defense installations at East Point, a small war museum, the Botanic Gardens, and the harbor. Another half or full-day tour goes to Man-

---

TAGGING ALONG WITH THE FLYING MAILMAN

The mailman makes his rounds by airplane in parts of the Northern Territory, South Australia, Western Australia, and Queensland. You can go along with him on these flights, stopping for 15 or 20 minutes at each station or mission along the way. The kangaroos scamper away as you land, and you can get out and talk to the residents (most of them will be on hand to meet the mailman).

Most of these trips—and there are many different routes on the schedule—take a full day, and most of them provide lunch along the way. They are a fascinating means of meeting and talking with people in widely scattered settlements.

For more information, contact either Ansett or TAA or the Northern Territory Government Tourist Bureau.

FLYING MAILMAN is met by Australian cowboy at Mount Wedge station in Northern Territory.

PUKAMANI POLES in Darwin's Botanic Gardens (above) are the native form of grave headstone. St. Mary's Catholic War Memorial Cathedral (right) houses relics of the war and a black Madonna with Child painting.

dorah, some six miles across the harbor by ferry. This is a pleasant spot where you can swim, fish, or sunbathe. The motel complex at Mandorah also offers an overnight package with sightseeing from Mandorah.

Tropical beaches

On Darwin's doorstep you'll find tempting silver sand beaches. Among the best beaches are Mindil, Casuarina, Dripstone, and Mica. Sports enthusiasts are in their element, drawn to swimming, skin-diving, water-skiing, sun-bathing, sailing, fishing, and beachcombing. Swimming is impossible during the wet season (December to May) because of the sea wasps (jelly fish) floating near the surface; their poisonous tentacles can be fatal.

Among seashells along the shore, beachcombers may find some estimated by geologists to be thirty million years old.

Sports around the clock

The hot climate fails to dampen the Australians' zest for recreation, with some 40 active and spectator sports available. Three codes of football, including rugby, are played throughout the year. Both men and women compete in hockey. Basketball is played at night, and during the day baseball, cricket, and softball keep sportsmen busy. Numerous golf courses, tennis courts, and squash courts are well used.

Two events that are certainly unique to the area are the N.T. Walkabout and the Beer Can Raft Regatta. The former is a walking race usually held in June; it starts 16 miles out of town and ends in the center of the city. Visitors are welcome to participate.

The regatta is held in mid-June each year at Darwin Harbour. Some 60 to 80 boats, built only of beer cans or soft-drink cans, hold a one-day regatta. Some are sailing craft, some paddle boats, some speed boats with 100 h.p. motors—all competing in different classes. Some of the boats use six to eight thousand empty cans in their construction. With Darwin such a hot and thirsty land, there's no real shortage of building material.

TRIPS FROM DARWIN

Darwin is best used as a base from which to explore the surrounding countryside. Your excursions can include geological and wildlife phenomena, Aboriginal settlement, farming and mining developments.

The outback region of the Northern Territory is a living museum, populated by animals and birds that are—in many cases—the last remaining specimens of some of the world's most unique wildlife. Along the swampy coastline and near water holes, you'll find the air thick with birds. You can watch emus running through the mulga and saltbush and kangaroos standing up to survey the land. Pelicans herd fish into the shallows of the swamps, long-legged spoonbills dab-

WEATHERED RED ROCK HILLS surround Alice Springs, a green oasis in the center of the continent. From Anzac Hill you gaze across the town's neat streets to the nearby hills. You can arrange trips into the outback from Alice Springs.

ble in the marshes, and dingoes circle camps like trained dogs. Lagoons and northern rivers abound with giant barramundi (a superb table fish), saratago, catfish, mullet, and saw fish.

Darwin tour operators arrange excursions including the best of these attractions, with travel by coach, launch, car, jeep, or light aircraft. For a full listing of trip possibilities, contact the Northern Territory Government Tourist Bureau, Smith Street, Darwin.

Close-in excursions

Several close-in attractions may be reached by a city bus or taxi. The Tourist Bureau or your Darwin hotel can provide specific directions.

Magnetic anthills can be seen at Howard and Berry springs, 15 and 40 miles south of the city. You'll see thousands of these hard mud mounds, some reaching twenty feet in height and six feet in width. White termites construct them on a north-south axis, letting the sun warm the nests.

Humpty Doo - Fogg Dam, 36 miles southeast of Darwin, is the center of an experimental rice farm. Nearby at Fogg Dam Bird Sanctuary, thousands of birds gather in and around the water lily covered reservoir, and buffaloes roam the open plains.

The War Graves Cemetery, in the town of Adelaide River, 72 miles south of Darwin, is a grim reminder that the Japanese bombed Darwin more than 60 times during World War II. It's a pleasant setting with green lawns, tropical shrubs, and trees.

Katherine Gorge is located 22 miles northeast of the town of Katherine, about 220 miles south of Darwin. Tours in flatbottomed boats take you along waterways edged by 200-foot cliffs. Canyon walls have Aboriginal paintings, trees growing at strange angles, and bird nests tucked away in small caves to which migrating swallows return each year.

Going on safari

From Darwin, safari tours travel to remote creeks and lagoons where you can watch the wildlife and make your catch with rod or camera.

Safari operators in Darwin have "re-grouped" following the cyclone, and several have developed new tours. Operated only in the dry season (approximately late April to November), the tours are by four-wheel-drive vehicle, usually on an itinerary that is tailor-made for the visitor.

Accommodations on such safaris range from simple tents, for camping out in the bush, to cabins, equipped with beds and linens and screened for protection from insects. Jim Jim, a motel accommodation about 140 miles east and south of Darwin, is a stopping place for coach passengers. Occasional water holes and small lagoons are handy for swimming and fishing.

Hunting with firearms in the Territory is strictly controlled, but your safari guide can arrange permits for hunting duck and geese the year around. Magpie geese, burdekin duck, and pygmy geese have limited seasons.

Details on these safaris and attractions may be

obtained from the Northern Territory Government Tourist Bureau, Smith Street, Darwin, N. T.

Backward in time to Arnhem Land

Arnhem Land was first described by explorers as a "god-forsaken country." Over the centuries the region hasn't changed much, and you will find it pretty much in its natural state.

This is the largest of several Aboriginal reservations in the Northern Territory—31,200 square miles of thick jungles and fertile plains, bisected by large rivers winding their way to the Arafura Sea and the Gulf of Carpentaria. Government and church settlements offer the Aborigines a chance at assimilation, but many continue to live on a Stone Age level.

Sometimes it is possible to visit mission settlements where you can meet the Aborigines and learn something of their way of life. It is interesting to see the methods used in the education of both the children and the adults. The children are particularly friendly and will give you a warm welcome. The adults are taught pottery, wood carving, silk screen design, and dress making—the products, incidentally, make very good purchases. If you happen to be especially lucky, you might happen onto a *corroboree*, a display of native dancing and music.

Flights to Mission settlements

"Mission Runs" are operated from Darwin by Connair. The planes stop at mission settlements at Croker Island, Oenpelli, Milingimbi, Elcho Island, Yirrkala, and Groote Eylandt.

These flights also give a good overview from low altitudes of the Arnhem plateau and coastal regions, including the Gulf of Carpentaria.

At some mission stores, you can purchase souvenirs of Aboriginal arts and crafts.

ALICE SPRINGS AND THE CENTER

Alice Springs lies in the center of the continent, almost exactly midway between the east and west coasts, in the true "outback," which starts at the western slopes of the Great Dividing Range in the east and extends into Western Australia—covering an area larger than Europe.

"The Alice" is a small, attractive town nestling in a bowl of ancient, weather-carved red rock hills. Its 15,000 residents live in modern structures, and buildings with shady verandas line its wide downtown streets. Comfortable bungalows, many surrounded by green lawns and beds of English flowers, border the residential streets.

Cattle trade is the mainstay of the community; as many as 40,000 head journey south on rail cars each year. That explains the saddle shops on Todd Street and the pubs where stockmen (cowboys) in muddy boots stomp out dances to popular music on Saturday night. Along the streets, you'll see stockmen and Aborigines strolling in their broad-brimmed hats, bright shirts, and high-heeled boots.

How to get there

Air services to Alice Springs operate from all state capitals, and from Darwin, Mt. Isa, and several other towns in the center.

If you prefer train travel, "The Ghan" makes the 950-mile trip from Adelaide in 39 hours. Named for the Afghan camel drivers who once delivered mail and supplies to isolated settlements by camel caravan, the railroad goes north by way of the Flinders Range, then through Marree and Oodnadatta.

Express coach services operate from Adelaide and Darwin, connecting with more distant state capitals. You will also find a selection of camping tours, four-wheel-drive safaris, and scenic bus tours operated throughout the year.

Driving from Adelaide to Alice Springs is on an unsealed road—rough, but passable enough that many of the locals drive it. Some visitors put their automobile on the train at Port Augusta (200 miles north of Adelaide) and let the train take it over the hardest sections. This can be arranged by the Tourist Bureau.

Climate—dry and warm

The tourist season for Alice Springs extends from March to November, a period of warm days (temperatures averaging about 80°), little humidity, and cool evenings—much like the winter season in Arizona. Days are clear and bright, providing about 9 hours of sunlight. During the balance of the year, temperatures soar to 100° and above.

Accommodations and restaurants

A dozen hotels and motels, most of them quite new, provide comfortable accommodations, complete with air-conditioning, swimming pools, and other amenities. Those used most frequently by visitors are the Oasis, Midland, Territory, Alice Motor Inn, and Elkira Court. You'll also find several inns, guest houses, caravan parks, and campgrounds in or near town. Your travel agent has more details, or you can contact the Northern Territory Government Tourist Bureau, Parsons Street, Alice Springs.

Restaurants in Alice Springs may not present as diverse a choice in cuisine and decor as other Australian centers, but for a town its size it boasts a surprising selection. Most of the hotels and motels have restaurants on the premises. Other restaurants have continental names and cuisine, hinting at the national origin of their owners.

- La Popote, Todd Street. Owners and chef are French, and the restaurant offers French cuisine considered locally as the best in town.
- Papa Luigi's Bistro, rear of Todd Street. Italian specialties are served in an attractive dining room with bar.
- Sylvia's, Todd Street. An American couple serves continental cuisine.
- Overlander Steak House, Hartley Street. Here you'll find the best steaks in Alice Springs.

What to see in The Alice

Alice Springs is a "two-stage" town for the tourist. The first stage concerns features of the town itself, and the second, attractions in the surrounding area.

Most half-day tours of the town include the Old Telegraph Station, built in 1872; Anzac Hill, for a panoramic view of Alice Springs; John Flynn Memorial Church, built in 1956 as a memorial to the founder of the Royal Flying Doctor Service; the Flying Doctor Base, where doctors give advice to ranchers hundreds of miles from the nearest town; School of the Air, where you listen to children at outback homesteads taking part in lessons conducted by two-way radio; and Pitchi Richi (meaning "a gap in the ranges"), a native bird and flower sanctuary, and open-air museum showing a collection of pioneer equipment.

A number of shops in Alice Springs display works of Aboriginal artists—boomerangs, wood carvings, paintings of landscapes or bark paintings of symbolic designs. The Batterbee Gallery features the work of several such artists, including Albert Namatjira, the best known of modern Aboriginal artists.

Festival time

Rousing, rollicking annual events in Alice Springs include the Bangtail Muster, held in May, and the Henley-on-Todd Regatta, presented in September.

The Bangtail Muster was named for the old practice of cutting the tails of cattle as they were counted before shipment. The program consists of a light-hearted procession and a series of sporting events and other attractions.

MYSTERIOUS PAINTINGS OF THE ABORIGINES

Among the wild red rocks and forests of the Northern Territory, Aborigines dream of times now past. Their cultural roots go back more than 30,000 years, when their ancestors began arriving from the north.

They recorded their dreamtime (beginnings of time) with paintings on cave walls and on smooth cliff sides beneath outcroppings. Here the elders instructed the young men in tribal ways, and a *corroboree* (dance festival) enacted their story in music and dance.

One of these sacred places is located on the Woolwonga Aboriginal Reserve on the South Alligator River, about 120 miles east of Darwin. Guided coach tours travel to Nourlangie Rock on the reserve, where you can view ancient paintings that are mural-size history books portraying Aboriginal myths and customs.

Created more than 5,000 years ago, the paintings were drawn with colors made by mixing pulverized rock with water—yielding white, red, brown, pink, and yellow ocher—and using fine feather or human hair brushes. They followed two styles of art: realistic drawings, and x-raylike paintings depicting both internal and external organs. The paintings chronicled great hunts, including intricate designs involving kangaroos and other marsupials. Some drawings portrayed misfortunes, which the artists blamed on a colorful array of evil spirits or on the half-human, half-animal ancestral beings they believed were the inhabitants at the beginning of time.

Tribesmen claim that many of the older single line drawings were not done by men at all but by a spirit people called Mimi. They were credited with the ability to melt into cliffs by blowing on the rocks and to leave their shadows on the wall.

For centuries, rock paintings and retouching kept alive the myths of the secret places. But with the shifting of tribes and passing of elders, many of the secrets of the Aborigines remain locked within the paintings.

ROCK PAINTINGS attract visitors to Ayers Rock, once used for Aboriginal fertility rites.

The "regatta" is held in the dry bed of the Todd River; it consists of a full program of aquatic sports without water—races of bottomless canoes, skiffs, and yachts propelled over the course by the legs of their occupants.

TRIPS OUT OF ALICE SPRINGS

Since Alice Springs is the only town for hundreds of miles in any direction, it is about the only base from which to explore the outback. Information on attractions and excursions may be obtained from the Northern Territory Government Tourist Bureau, Parsons Street, in Alice Springs. A number of tour operators offer a wide range of tours lasting 1 to 13 days. Most are air tours or combined air-coach trips. The planes fly at low altitudes, giving passengers an excellent opportunity for aerial photography.

If you want to experience daily outback life, you can make special arrangements to go on one of the regularly scheduled mail flights to cattle stations (see page 132).

MacDonnell Ranges

Stretching for 400 miles west of Alice Springs, these mountains of ancient rock known as the MacDonnell Ranges harbor palm-shaded desert oases, old gold mines, stands of white barked ghost gums, and numerous cattle stations. The best known clefts in the MacDonnell Ranges are Standley Chasm, 30 miles west of The Alice, and Ormiston Gorge and Glen Helen Gorge, both about 85 miles west.

Standley Chasm is a narrow cleft in the plain—a canyon only 18 feet wide in places but as much as 200 feet deep. The rich red glow of the rock walls under a midday sun provide a subject for spectacular photographs. During the main visiting times at the Chasm, Aborigines from nearby Jay Creek Settlement serve barbecue meals to tourists from a kiosk they set up near the canyon entrance.

Ormiston Gorge is marked by towering red and purple walls rising hundreds of feet from the bed of Ormiston Creek. And five miles away is massive Glen Helen Gorge, a slash in the ranges made by the Finke River over many thousands of years, exposing vivid red canyon walls and unusual rock formations.

Palm Valley

About 90 miles west of Alice Springs, the Finke River has carved out another huge rock canyon in which groves of prehistoric palm trees grow in an isolation that has lasted for centuries. After a rain, pools of water collect in the rocks, reflecting the rich red rock walls and the vivid green of the palms. A natural rock amphitheater in the valley is the site of many ancient Aboriginal rituals.

If you visit Palm Valley, you can combine it with a trip to Hermannsburg Aboriginal Mission, oldest in the Territory and open to visitors by special arrange-

STANDLEY CHASM (above) is a brilliantly colored cleft in plains near Alice Springs. Weathered domes of the Olgas (right) are separated by deep ravines. View overlooks spinifex plains.

SADDLING UP for a range ride near the tourist cabins at Ross River Resort (above). Ranch visitors learn to cook damper, an ash-cooked pioneer bread (right).

ment. In Alice Springs, contact the Northern Territory Government Tourist Bureau on Parsons Street, or the Welfare Department on Hartley Street for information about visiting these areas.

Ayers Rock

The most spectacular natural wonder in this region is Ayers Rock, a red mass uplifted eons ago from an ancient seabed. It rises abruptly 1,143 feet above the flat desert plain about 275 miles southwest of Alice Springs.

The visiting ritual includes a 7-mile walk around The Rock; viewing the Aboriginal wall paintings; photographing the startling color changes in the sandstone (from fiery red to delicate mauve); and a climb to the top to look across the plain and down on the red sand dunes and their cover of spinifex, mulga, eucalyptus, and desert oak.

The Olgas

From Ayers Rock you can see the blue domes of the Olgas, more than 30 smooth-faced, dome-shaped monoliths of varying size, separated by deep ravines and covering a 14-square-mile area. Mount Olga, the largest, rises 1,800 feet above the plains.

Mount Olga is much more of a challenge to climbers than Ayers Rock, but those who reach the summit say the view is worth all the effort. You can see Ayers Rock with flat-topped Mount Conner 60 miles beyond, dry Lake Amadeus to the north, and the Musgrave, Manna, and Peterman ranges to the south. Climbers also get to see simple rock carvings and paintings left by the Aborigines.

Ross River Homestead

If you find the prospect of a visit to a Central Australia dude ranch appealing, Ross River Homestead is about 98 miles east of Alice Springs. Visitors enjoy horseback riding on the range, swimming, home cooked meals, and plenty of fresh air. Accommodations are provided in twin-bedded log cabins that are air cooled and equipped with electric blankets.

The old homestead, built in the late 19th century, is still in evidence; its whitewashed mud and stone walls comprise the main house, and roaring log fires are still built in the open hearth where the settlers prepared their meals.

CALENDAR OF EVENTS—running the gamut of Australian life styles

Whether you prefer opera or rodeo, flower shows or football, you're sure to find plenty of agreeable activities on Australia's calendar of events. The major regularly scheduled events are covered below; state government tourist bureaus will be happy to provide information on upcoming activities in the areas you plan to visit.

JANUARY

New Year's Day (January 1). Public holiday observed in major cities throughout the country with surf carnivals, Scottish bagpiping, dancing, games, race meetings. The Perth Cup (horse race) is held on this day in Perth, Western Australia.

Surf carnivals. Teams of volunteer lifeguards give spectacular displays of surf and surfboat rescue, swimming, and marching (see page 45). Held each weekend and on holidays from December through early April on beaches in New South Wales, Queensland, Victoria, South and Western Australia.

Australia Day. The first Monday after January 26 is a national holiday commemorating the founding of the first settlement at Sydney in 1788. The Royal Sydney Anniversary Regatta is held in Sydney Harbor. Biggest celebration is in Sydney, but the holiday is marked by ceremonies, parades, and other special events in most of the country's major cities.

Cricket matches. Held November through March in cities and towns across the country. International matches are held in state capitals.

FEBRUARY

Royal Hobart Regatta. Big aquatic carnival, sailing, rowing, swimming events with fireworks and parades. Held on the Derwent River in early February.

Little America's Cup, Melbourne. Sailing competition (site varies year by year).

CRICKET is a popular spectator sport in Australia. International Test Matches, Australia versus England, pack the Sydney Cricket Ground grandstand.

CALENDAR OF EVENTS 139

Floral Festival. St. David's Cathedral, Hobart, Tasmania, early February.

Launceston Fiesta, Tasmania. Carnival, sports, and cultural events, parade, Mardi Gras. Usually last week in February.

Perth Festival of the Arts. Held in late February or early March, the major cultural event in Western Australia features a foreign film festival, concerts, opera, and ballet.

Moomba Festival. An annual fall celebration, held in Melbourne late February or early March (see page 71).

MARCH

Begonia Festival in Ballarat. Australia's biggest inland city, 68 miles northwest of Melbourne, where the gold rush raged.

Concerts and ballet. Season begins in Melbourne and Sydney.

Adelaide Festival of Arts. A three-week concentration of culture—with art exhibits in galleries, stores, and outdoors, plus parades and balls. Visiting international artists and noted Australian artists perform jazz, symphony concerts, drama, ballet. Held only during even-numbered years.

APRIL

Rugby football. Sydney rugby competition begins in April, runs through September.

Australian Rules football. Season begins in mid-April. Melbourne is the game's major city, but football is played in all the states.

Sydney Cup Horse Race. Easter Meeting and an important annual event at Randwick Race Course, Sydney, headquarters of Australian Jockey Club.

Anzac Day (April 25). A solemn holiday commemorating the 1915 landing of the Australian and New Zealand Army Corps (ANZAC) at Gallipoli in Turkey during World War I. War heroes of this and later conflicts are remembered with massive parades, memorial services, speeches, and sporting events. Major celebrations take place in the capital cities.

Great Eastern Steeplechase. Run at rural Oakbank in the Mt. Lofty Ranges in South Australia. Of the 10 starters who tackled the 3¼ mile course one year, eight fell at the tricky fences.

Barossa Valley Vintage Festival. Held in South Australia during late April in odd-numbered years (see page 100).

MAY and JUNE

Bangtail Muster. Horse racing, a rodeo, cattle roundup, and other "outback-style" celebrations are held in the colorful desert town of Alice Springs in early May.

Adelaide Cup. Horse race in Adelaide in mid-May.

Sydney Sheep Show. Major competition for Australia's leading breeders. Last week of May, first week of June.

Stradbroke Handicap and Brisbane Cup. Important horse racing carnival, usually held the first week of June in Brisbane.

Skiing season. Opens in June, runs through September. New South Wales, Victoria, and Tasmania snow fields.

Great Barrier Reef Islands Festival. Water sports, oyster-eating contests, other festivities; Whitsunday Passage, Queensland, June. Heron Island hosts a Skin Divers' Festival in July.

JULY and AUGUST

Doomben Ten Thousand Horse Race and Doomben Cup. First half of July in Brisbane.

North Australia Eisteddfod. Sports, singing, dancing competitions in Darwin, second week of July.

Grand National Hurdle. Melbourne, Saturdays during July.

Sydney International Trade Fair. Held mid-July to mid-August in odd-numbered years. Exhibits attract buyers of agricultural and industrial products. Educational and entertaining demonstrations are presented by experts in the fields of wool, livestock, mining, and electronics.

Grand National Steeplechase. August, at the Caulfield Race Course, Melbourne.

Brisbane Royal Show. August (see page 142).

SEPTEMBER

Rugby football. Rugby League and Rugby Union grand final competitions are held at Sydney Cricket Ground.

Australian Rules football finals. Some 100,000 spectators turn out at Melbourne Cricket Ground to watch the four final matches of this fast-moving game.

Trout season. Opens in September, runs through March. Best areas: Snowy Mountains and Tasmania.

Golf championships. Major tournaments in capital

cities, September through November.

Royal Melbourne Show. Mid-month (see page 142).

South Street competitions in Ballarat. Music, elocution, dancing, and calisthenics contests. Awards in this Eisteddfod provide a stepping stone to professional success.

Royal Adelaide Show. Usually early September.

Flower Day. This holiday in mid-to-late September launches a week-long wildflower show in Perth stores.

Spring Orchid Show. Brisbane in late September.

Perth Royal Show. Last week of September, first week of October (see page 142).

Australian Jockey Club's Derby. Important horse race of spring meetings at Randwick Race Course, Sydney, late September.

OCTOBER

Waratah Spring Festival. Sydney streets blossom with the crimson of the waratah, floral emblem of New South Wales. Parades, outdoor concerts, drama, sporting events, art exhibits, opera, ballet. The 12-day

RACING under full sail, competitors in the 650-mile Sydney-Hobart Yacht Race jockey for position in Sydney Harbour near the start of the racing classic.

AUSTRALIAN RULES football (above) attracts giant crowds to watch action-packed sport at Melbourne's Cricket Grounds in September. Moomba Festival, held in Melbourne in March, ends with fireworks display (right) casting bright reflections on the waters of the River Yarra.

CALENDAR OF EVENTS 141

festival is usually held in mid-October.

Opera. Season begins about mid-October in Melbourne.

Hobart Royal Show. Mid-October (see below).

Caulfield Cup. Major horse race, second only to Melbourne Cup. Held at Caulfield Race Course, Melbourne, late October.

Jacaranda Festival. Grafton, N.S.W. Festivities, parades, floral displays, and sporting events celebrate jacaranda blossom time. Late October, early November.

Southern Cross Cup. Sailing competition, Sydney, late October, early November.

NOVEMBER

Melbourne Cup. Australia's richest handicap race, held the first Tuesday of November, Flemington Race Course (see page 73).

Cricket matches. Held November through March in cities and towns across the country. International matches held in state capitals.

Christmas Pageant, Adelaide. Decorative floats, parade, marching animals, fairy tale characters presented by John Martin's store. Mid-November.

DECEMBER

Carols by Candlelight. Outdoor carolling in Melbourne's Myer Music Bowl, Sydney's Hyde Park, and throughout Australia, heralding the coming of Christmas, mid-December.

Boxing Day (December 26). The starting day of the 650-mile Sydney-Hobart Yacht Race, Australia's yachting classic for ocean cruisers. Spectators assemble on shorelines and in small craft to watch the "blue-water" yachts leave Sydney Harbor for the Pacific Ocean. The race ends at Derwent River, Hobart.

Pittwater Annual Regatta. Interclub yacht races held on the Pittwater, an inlet near Sydney's northern boundary in late December.

Cricket. International Test Matches between Australian and overseas teams. Held in capital cities most years, or overseas; late December to early February.

THE "ROYALS"... AUSSIE-TYPE STATE FAIRS

Australia stages more than 500 agricultural shows annually, and a visit to at least one is fascinating, particularly if you're a state fair enthusiast at home. Many of the shows are one-day events at small country centers; but the annual "Royal" shows, held in the state capitals, are world famous for outstanding livestock and agricultural exhibits, a wide variety of industrial exhibits, and many competitive events.

More than 4½ million people visit the "Royals" each year. The shows are larger than most American state and county fairs, and they also boast several uniquely Australian attractions: sheep dog trials, wood chopping contests, and camp drafts.

In the sheep dog trials, owners command their animals by voice or whistle as the dogs round up and maneuver small flocks of sheep around obstacles and into pens in the central arena.

In the wood-chopping and the tree-felling contests, huge "chips" fly in all directions as burly contestants with their razor-sharp axes cut through Australian hardwood logs in a matter of seconds.

For the camp draft, a peculiarly Australian rodeo event, cattle are driven over an involved course in a supreme test of both horse and rider.

Here's the schedule of "Royals":

Royal Easter Show. The most popular of the country's Royal shows, held at Sydney's 71-acre show grounds early to mid-April.

Brisbane Royal Show. Noted for its unusual display of tropical plants and flowers from all over the huge state of Queensland. August.

Royal Melbourne Show, Royal Adelaide Show, Perth Royal Show. September.

Hobart Royal Show. Mid-October.

COMPETITORS of all sizes enter riding events and parade before crowd at the "Royals."

142 CALENDAR OF EVENTS

Index

Aborigines, 10, 17, 90, 101, 108, 110, 131, 135, 137, 138
Abrolhos Islands, 110
Accommodations, 10
  (see also under cities)
Adelaide, 95-99
  (see also South Australia)
Air services, 9, 12, 13, 15, 132, 135
  (see also under cities)
Alice Springs, 135-137
  Climate, 135
  Festivals, 136
  How to get there, 135
  Restaurants, 135–136
  What to see, 136
Andamooka, 99
Angaston, 100
Animals, 21, 22
Arkaroola, 103
Arnhem Land, 135
Australian Alps, 83, 100
Australian Capital Territory (ACT), 7, 8, 56-63
Australian Consulates-General, 14
Australian Embassy, 14
Australian Tourist Commission, 11, 15
Australian Trader, 86
Ayers Rock, 138

Ballarat, 78
Barmah State Forest, 81
Barossa Valley, 12, 18, 95, 100
Bateman's Bay, 55
Bathurst, 49
Beaches, 43, 44, 73, 75-78, 80, 92, 98, 107, 117, 118, 119, 124, 126-129, 133
Beechworth, 79
Beerwah, 119
Belair National Park, 100
Bellarine Peninsula, 79, 80
Bendigo, 79
Beverages, 12
Bicheno, 92
Big game fishing, 93, 119, 125
Birds, 23, 24
Bligh, Captain, 88
Blue Mountains, 47
Boat services, 13, 14
  (see also cruises and ferries)
Bowling, lawn, 28
Brampton Island, 126
Brisbane, 113-116
  (see also Queensland)
Brisbane River, 113, 116
British influence, 7
Burleigh Heads National Park, 118
Burnie, 93
Bus services, 13, 59, 67, 87, 114, 132, 135
Bush meetings, 29

Cairns, 129
Calendar of events, 139-142
Camper-vans, 12
Canberra, 7, 56-63

Canberra (cont.)
  Capital Hill, 60
  Cruises, 60
  Getting around, 59
  Hotels, 59
  Lake Burley Griffin, 60
  Restaurants, 59
Carlton, 70
Carnarvon, 110
Carpentaria, Gulf of, 30
Castlemaine, 79
Cataract Gorge, 91
Cave country, 109, 110
Circular Quay, 35
Clare District, 19
Climate, 8
  (see also under cities)
Clothes, 16
Coles Bay, 92
Como House, 73
Coober Pedy, 99
Cook, Captain James, 7, 118
Coolgardie, 109
Coonawarra, 19
Coral polyps, 121, 122
Corroboree, 17, 135
Cradle Mountain-Lake St. Clair National Park, 92, 93
Cricket, 28, 29
Cruises, 15, 42, 43, 50, 51, 60, 79, 82, 93, 100, 102, 108, 111, 119, 122-129, 132
  (see also under cities)
Currency, 14
Currimbin, 118
Currimbin Bird Sanctuary, 20, 118
Customs regulations, 14
Cygnet, 88

Dampier, 110
Dandenong Ranges, 65, 75
Darling Downs, 113, 117
Darling Ranges, 131
Darwin, 130-134
  Accommodations, 132
  Arnhem Land, 135
  Beaches, 133
  Climate, 132
  How to get there, 132
  Mission flights, 135
  Restaurants, 132
  Safaris, 134
  Sightseeing, 132
  Sports, 133
Daydream Island, 128
Derwent River, 87
Devonport, 92
Didgeridoo, 17, 135
Driving, 9, 12
Dubbo, 51
Dunk Island, 127

Eaglehawk Neck, 30, 89
Echidna, 22
Echuca, 81
Ecology, Barrier Reef, 121
Electrical appliances, 16
Empress of Australia, 86
Emu, 23
Emu Bottom, 81
Encounter Bay, 100
Entertainment, 35, 68, 87, 96, 137
Entry requirements, 14

Eucalyptus, 25
Exmouth, 110
Eyre Peninsula, 103

Falls Creek, 83
Fannie Bay, 132
Ferries, 86, 101
Festivals, 98, 100, 139–142
Fishing, 30, 77, 93, 119, 125
Fleahy's Fauna Reserve, 118
Flinders Ranges, 102, 103
Flying mailman, 132
Food, 11, 15 (see also restaurants under cities)
Football, 28
Fortesque River, 111
Fraser Island, 119
Fremantle, 105, 109

Geelong, 80
Geography, 8
Geraldton, 110
Ghan, the, 135
  (see rail travel)
Gibson Desert, 105
Gippsland Lakes, 78
Gladstone Island, 124, 125
Gold, 78, 109
Gold Coast, 117, 118
Golf, 29, 30
Goolwa, 100
Goulburn, 81
Government, 7
Grampians, 81
Granite Island, 101
Great Australian Bight, 103
Great Barrier Reef, 120-129
  Climate, 123
  Coral polyps, 121, 122
  Cruises, 122-129
  Ecology, 121
  Fishing, 125
  Lifestyle, 123
  Observatories, underwater, 123, 129
  Resorts, 124
  Skin diving, 125
  Tours, 123
  (see also islands listed by name)
Great Dividing Range, 113
Great Keppel Island, 126
Great Lake, 92
Great Ocean Road, 80
Great Sandy Desert, 105
Great Victoria Desert, 105
Great Western District, 19
Green Island, 31, 129
Griffin, Walter Burley, 57, 58

Hamersley Ranges, 110, 111
Hawkesbury River, 50
Hayman Island, 127
Health conditions, 15, 16
Heron Island, 31, 125
Hervey Bay, 119
History, 7
Hobart, 87, 88
  (see also Tasmania)
Horse racing, 27, 28, 29
Hostels, 11, 87
Hotels, 10, 11 (see also under cities)

Hunter Valley, 19, 52
Hunting, 30, 135 (see also safaris)
Huon Valley, 88

Illawarra Coast, 54
Indian Ocean, 105
Inoculations, 14

Jamison Valley, 47
Jenolan Caves, 48
Jim Jim, 135

Kalgoorlie, 109
Kangaroo Island, 99, 100
Kangaroo paw, 24, 25
Kangaroo Valley, 55
Kangaroos, 21
Katherine Gorge, 134, 135
Katoomba, 47
Kiama, 54
Kimberley Plateau, 111
Kinglake National Park, 76
King's Domain, 67, 71, 72
Koalas, 21, 22
Kookaburra, 25
Kosciusko National Park, 63
Kununurra, 111
Ku-ring-gai Chase National Park, 51

Lake Alexander, 100
Lake Macquarie, 52
Lake Pedder, 89
Lamington National Park, 117
Langhorne Creek, 19
Language, 17
Launceston, 91, 93
Lawn bowling, 28
Light, Colonel William, 96
Lindeman Island, 126
Liquor, 11, 12
London Court, 106
Lone Pine Koala Sanctuary, 117
Longford, 90
Long Island, 128
Lyrebird, 23, 76

MacDonnell Range, 137
Mackay, 126
MacPherson Range, 117
Macquarie Valley, 51
Magnetic Island, 128
Maldon, 79
Marsupials, 21
Melbourne, 64-73
  Climate, 67
  Dining, 67
  Getting around, 67
  Hotels, 67
  Night life, 68
  Shopping, 68
  Sightseeing, 69-73
  Sports, 73
Melbourne Cricket Ground, 70
Melbourne Cup, 27, 73
Mildura, 82
Mission flights, 135
Molonglo River, 57, 58
Moreton Bay, 116, 117
Moreton Island, 117
Mornington Peninsula, 77
Motels, 10-11
Mt. Ainslie, 59

Mt. Buffalo National Park, 24, 83
Mt. Buller, 83
Mt. Coot-tha, 117
Mt. Dandenong, 76
Mt. Field National Park, 89, 93
Mt. Gambier, 102, 103
Mt. Hotham, 83
Mt. Kosciusko, 63
Mt. Lofty Ranges, 95, 100
Mt. Tamborine, 117
Mt. Wellington, 87
Murella Park, 135
Murray River, 8, 19, 76, 81
Myer, Sidney Music Bowl, 69, 73

Nambour, 119
Naringal, 81
Newcastle, 52
New England, 53
New England National Park, 54
New South Wales, 32-55
Ninety Mile Beach, 77
Noosa Heads, 119
North Coast, 52
Northern Territory, 7, 130-137
Nourlangie, 135
Nowra, 55
Nullarbor Plain, 106, 109
Nuriootpa, 100

Oatlands, 90
Observatories, underwater, 123, 129
Olgas, 8, 138
Onslow, 110
Opals, 37, 68, 69, 97, 99
Opera House, Sydney, 33, 38
Ord River, 111
Ormiston Gorge, 138
Orpheus Island, 128
Outback, 133, 134, 135, 137

Paddington, 40
Palm Valley, 137
Parkville, 70
Parramatta, 48, 49
Passenger-car ferries, 86
Passports and visas, 14
Patonga, 135
Penguins, 82
Perth, 105-107 (see also Western Australia)
Phillip, Captain Arthur, 7

Phillip Island, 77, 82
Platypus, 22
Port Albert, 78
Port Arthur, 89
Port Campbell National Park, 80
Port Hedland, 110
Port Lincoln, 30, 103
Port Phillip Bay, 65, 76
Proserpine, 127

Queensland, 112-119
　Accommodations, 114, 118
　Brisbane, 113-116
　Climate, 114
　Fishing, 119
　Gold Coast, 117, 118
　How to get there, 114
　Sightseeing, 115
　Sports, 116
　Sunshine Coast, 118, 119
　Toowoomba, 117
Queenstown, 93

Rail travel, 13, 47, 52, 106, 114, 135
Rent-a-car, 9, 12, 87
Richmond, 49
Riverina District, 19
Rockhampton, 126
Roebourne, 110
Ross, 90
Ross River, 138
Rottnest Island, 108
Royal National Park, 54
Rugby football, 28
Russell Falls, 89
Rutherglen, 19

Safaris, 30, 135
St. Helen's, 92
St. Vincent Gulf, 95
Seafood, 11
Sea wasps, 133
Sharks, 44, 45
Sheep, 51, 81
Sherbrooke Forest, 76
Shopping, 14, 15, 16; tax-free, 15 (see also under cities)
Skiing, 30, 31, 83 (see sports)
Skin diving, 31, 125
Snowy Mountains, 55, 63, 83
Soccer, 28
South Australia, 94-103
　Adelaide, 95
　Beaches, 98
　Dining, 96

South Australia (cont.)
　Festivals, 98, 99 (see Calendar of events)
　Sightseeing, 96-103
South Coast Road, 102
South Molle Island, 128
Southern Vales District, 19
Southport, 118
Sovereign Hill, 78
Spencer Gulf, 103
Sports, 27-31 (see also under cities)
Standley Chasm, 137, 138
Steamship companies, 9
Stradbroke Island, 117
Strahan, 93
Sunshine Coast, 118, 119
Surf carnivals, 45
Surfers Paradise, 118
Surfing, 31
Swan Hill, 11, 82
Swan River, 105, 107
Sydney, 4, 32-45
　Beaches, 43, 44
　Climate, 35
　Dining, 35
　Ferries, 42, 43
　Getting around, 35
　Harbor, 38
　Historic buildings, 41
　Hotels and motels, 35
　Night life, 35
　Shopping, 37
　Sightseeing, 37-41
　Sports, 44, 45
　Sydney Town, 52

Tanunda, 100
Taronga Zoo, 22, 41
Tasman, Abel, 85
Tasman Peninsula, 88
Tasmania, 84-93
　Getting there, 86
　Hobart, 87, 88
　Hotels, 87
　Huon Valley, 88
　Launceston, 91
　Midlands, 90
　Night life, 87
　Port Arthur, 89
　Sightseeing, 86-93
　Sports, 93
　Weather, 86
Tax-free stores, 15
Taxis, 35, 59, 67
Tennis, 29
Tidbinbilla Nature Reserve, 63
Time zones, 15

Timor Sea, 105
Tipping, 16, 17
Tom Price, 111
Toowoomba, 117
Torrens River, 95
Townsville, 128
Trailer hire, 13
Transportation, 8, 9, 12, 13
Triabunna, 92
Trout fishing, 30, 77, 93

United States Consulates, 14
United States Embassy, 14

Victor Harbour, 100
Victoria, 64-73
Victoria Park, 115
Visas, 14

Wakefield, Edward Gibbon, 95
Waratah, red-flowered, 25
Warrnambool, 81
Water-skiing, 118
Western Australia, 104-111
　Beaches, 107
　Caves, 109, 110
　Climate, 106
　Coolgardie, 109
　Darling Ranges, 105, 108
　Fremantle, 105, 109
　Hamersley Ranges, 111
　Hotels and motels, 106
　How to get there, 106
　Kalgoorlie, 109
　Kimberley Plateau, 111
　Perth, 105-107
　Restaurants, 106
　Rottnest Island, 108
　Sightseeing, 106-111
　Sports, 107
　Wildflowers, 24, 25, 108, 109
　Yanchep Park, 108
Western Port Bay, 77
Whim Creek, 110
Wildflowers, 24, 25, 81, 108, 109
Wildlife sanctuaries, 25, 75, 76
Wilson's Promontory, 77
Windsor, 49
Wines, 12, 18-19
Wittenoom, 111
Wyndham, 111

Yanchep Park, 108
Yarra River, 65
Youth hostels, 11, 87

PHOTOGRAPHERS

American Airlines: 22. **Australia News & Information Bureau:** 76. **Australia Tourist Commission:** 4, 8, 9, 10, 11, 12, 13, 15, 16, 18, 20 bottom, 21, 23 bottom, 24 top left and right, bottom left, 26 bottom, 27, 28, 29, 31, 32 top, 33, 36 bottom right and top, 38, 39, 41 right, 43 bottom, 44, 45, 47, 48, 49, 53 top left and right, 55 right, 56 bottom, 61, 64, 65, 70, 71, 72 top right and bottom left, 74, 75, 77, 79, 80, 82, 83, 84 bottom, 86 top right and bottom, 87, 88 left, 89 bottom, 91 top, 92, 94 bottom, 95, 97 bottom, 101, 102, 103, 104 top, 108, 111, 112 bottom, 116, 120, 121, 122 bottom left, 123, 125, 126, 127, 129, 130, 131, 132, 134, 136, 137, 138, 139, 141, 142. **Werner Bartel:** 41 left. **Jeff Carter:** 55 left, 119. **Michael Cheshire:** 72 top left. **Frances Coleberd:** 51, 62, 90. **John Crowther:** 56 top. **Gordon F. de'Lisle:** 20 top, 133 right. **Shirley Fockler:** 122 top left. **James C. Gebbie:** 32 bottom, 42 top, 43 right, 46 bottom, 54, 122 top right, 128. **Eastman Kodak:** 13 right. **New South Wales Government Tourist Bureau:** 48 right. **Northern Territory Government Tourist Bureau:** 133 left. **Christine Osborne:** 46 top, 53 bottom left and right. **Pacific Area Travel Association:** 26 top, 69, 85, 105, 115. **Jeff Phillips:** 5, 49, 50. **Polkinghorne & Stevens Pty. Ltd:** 36 bottom left. **Qantasw;** 112 top. **Queensland Government Tourist Bureau:** 113. **Edward R. Rotherham:** 24 bottom right. **L. H. Smith:** 23 top. **Don Stephens:** 84 top, 86 top left, 88 right, 89 top, 91 bottom left and right, 93. **Snowy Mountains Authority:** 57. **South Australia Government Tourist Bureau:** 94 top, 97 top, 98, 99. **Western Australia Government Tourist Bureau:** 104 bottom. **Richard Woldendorp:** 107.